Consuelo
Byrd

Número Uno

Oct. 2003

OMT

John Brennan

CÓMO ENTENDER LOS #*¿?*© GRINGOS

(Modismos estadounidenses traducidos al español)

grijalbo

COMO ENTENDER LOS #*¿?*@ GRINGOS

© 1998, by EDITORIAL GRIJALBO S.A.
　　Grupo Grijalbo - Mondadori
　　Almirante Barroso 27, Santiago de Chile
　　Teléfonos: 6723027 - 6962689

© John Brennan
Inscripción en el registro de propiedad intelectual N° 103178
ISBN N° 956-258-073-3
Primera edición, octubre de 1998

Reservados todos los derechos. Queda rigurosamente prohibida sin la autorización escrita de los titulares del copyright, bajo las sanciones establecidas en las leyes, la reproducción total o parcial de esta obra por cualquier medio o procedimiento, comprendidos la reprografía y el tratamiento informático, y la distribución de ella mediante alquiler o préstamo público.

Diseño de portada: Claroscuro Diseño
Diagramación y composición: Claroscuro Diseño
Ilustraciones: Luis Saavedra

Impreso por: Publicaciones Almendral
Impreso en Chile/Printed in Chile

Prefacio

La idea de hacer este libro surgió luego de haber vivido algunos años en Chile, donde debí luchar a diario para tratar de entender la jerga chilena que constituye casi un nuevo y propio idioma. Cada día se presentaban ante mí nuevos desafíos lingüísticos. Por ejemplo, un ladrón no es solamente aquella persona que termina en la cárcel, además es un alargador electrónico con varios enchufes. Si me daba dolor de cabeza, me decían, "Ah, te duele el mate", y una vez cuando pregunté a un amigo acerca de una compañera de trabajo, me dijo, "Bueno, ella tiene bonita letra", y con esta respuesta debí entender que era una mujer con poca personalidad, sin gracia. Era lo mejor que pudo decir de ella.

Un día, "pateé la perra" = "vented some steam" = di expresión a mi frustraciones ante la dificultad de entender a los chilenos (finalmente tuve que escribir un libro de los modismos chilenos traducidos al inglés, que se llama "How to Survive in the Chilean Jungle"). Ante esto, un amigo me dijo, "¿Y nosotros, John? ¿No crees que los gringos tienen cualquier cantidad de modismos también?"

Entonces me puse a pensar en su observación. Recordé las experiencias de amigos extranjeros que venían a verme a Nueva York y sufrían tratando de entender las conversaciones entre mis amigos y yo. Después de discutir la idea de este libro que ahora se encuentra en sus manos con varios amigos bilingües, terminé por convencerme de su utilidad cuando hablé con Pablo Valenzuela.

El pobre Pablo que estudió en un colegio inglés y tenía un buen manejo del idioma, tomó un avión de Santiago de Chile a San Francisco,

California, donde iba a vivir. En el viaje, hizo escala en Los Ángeles. Allá, tuvo que pasar por la aduana con las maletas, y después, cuando se dirigía al vuelo a San Francisco, un portero se le acercó para llevar sus maletas al avión. El diálogo entre ellos fue algo así:

Portero: (habla muy rápido) "Goina Frisco?"
Pablo: (un poco nervioso) "What?"
Portero: (impaciente) "Goina Frisco?"
Pablo: (ahora, muy nervioso) "What? I do not understand."
Portero: (ahora, habla despacio) "Are you going to San Francisco?"
Pablo: (muy contento y con sonrisa) "Oh yes, yes I am!"

Conversando de sus experiencias en los Estados Unidos, me dijo que le hubiera sido muy útil un léxico de los modismos estadounidenses traducidos al español... Por Pablo y los demás, ¡aquí está!

Antes de agradecer a quienes contribuyeron en este libro, quiero reflexionar un poco sobre la relación entre la jerga y la cultura de un país. Creo que el lenguaje es una guía que nos indica algunos de los intereses, obsesiones y hasta las neurosis de un país, especialmente cuando ponemos atención a la cantidad de sinónimos con que se puede nombrar algunas ideas o cosas - y no me estoy refiriendo a los sinónimos de *fiesta*, o al hecho de tomar alcohol o drogas o a las partes pudendas de nuestra anatomía, donde la sinonimia es abundante en todas partes. Aquí encontrará doce sinónimos para *engañar a alguien*, catorce para *dinero* (aparte de esos catorce, hay muchas expresiones que relacionan el dinero con tiempo o el valor del dinero, como "nickel and dime"; "on someone's dime"; "time is money"; "no such thing as a free lunch", etc.). Quince sinónimos para *matar a alguien*, diecisie-

te para *golpear a alguien*, y TREINTA sinónimos para referirse a una *persona loca*. Y lo que más me sorprendió, ¡tenemos doce formas para decir *vomitar* (vea "chuck up" si no me cree)!

¿Qué está pasando en Estados Unidos? ¿Estamos tan obsesionados por el dinero, preocupados de que alguien pueda estafarnos, locos de ansiedad y estresados ante la posibilidad de que quieran golpearnos o matarnos y entonces, para olvidar, nos emborrachamos hasta vomitar? ¿Los países en desarrollo están seguros de que quieren seguir el modelo norteamericano?

Últimos tres puntos, lo prometo. Primero, debe ser consciente de que casi todos los modismos registrados aquí son expresiones que se encuentran en los diccionarios, pero que en el uso, en la calle, adquieren significados no contemplados en las definiciones oficiales. Segundo, hay ejemplos de cómo usar casi todos los modismos y, muchas veces, incluyo otros en las frases para que el lector pueda seguir aprendiendo. Entonces, si no sabe una palabra, búsquela dentro del léxico. Si no la encuentra ahí, es porque no es un modismo. Finalmente, "Cómo Entender los #*¿?*@ Gringos" no pretende ser el léxico definitivo de los modismos estadounidenses. Tal libro sería muy grande y quiero que usted pueda llevar mi libro dondequiera que vaya y necesite apoyo para comunicarse en un lenguaje común y corriente. Ojalá le guste y sea un aporte para acercarnos en un mundo que cada día nos hace más interdependientes.

AGRADECIMIENTOS:

A mi mamá por su insistencia en que la educación es lo más importante en la vida.

A Lucila Recart, cuyo aporte en el libro ha sido inolvidable. No hubiera podido hacerlo sin ella, y sin su espíritu de supervivencia.

A Kit Cody, José Miguel Barros, Lia Lloyd Clarke, Andrea Winkler, Víctor Henríquez, María Teresa Parada e Isabel M. Buzeta que ayudaron en las correcciones e hicieron valiosas sugerencias para el mejoramiento del libro.

A mi esposa Mercedes. El amor de mi vida y el faro en el mar turbulento de mi cerebro, mientras trataba de definir aun más modismos. Su risa es la joya de mi alegría.

Y, finalmente, a mi hijo Cole de ocho meses, que nació en Chile. Él es el futuro: un puente entre dos culturas que se van acercando.

Abreviaciones

[Vul.]	vulgar
abr.	abreviación/abbreviation
s.	sustantivo/noun
s.pl.	sustantivo plural/ plural noun
v.	verbo/verb
adj.	adjetivo/adjective
adv.	adverbio/adverb
exp.	dicho/expression
exp-v.	expresión verbal/ verbal expression
exp-vi.	dicho con verbo irregular/irregular verb expression
int.	interjección/interjection
Ej.	Ejemplo/Example
(sin.)	sinónimo/synonym
(Ing.)	Inglaterra/England
(Desp.)	Despectivo/Derogatory
(nota de ed.)	nota de editor/editor's note
gen.	generalmente/usually
esp.	especialmente/especially
etim.	etimología/etymology

Cómo Usar Este Léxico

Al buscar una expresión, primero trate de ubicar la expresión completa. Por ejemplo, la expresión *dead duck* se localiza por *dead*. Si se trata de una expresión con verbo, primero trate de ubicar el verbo. En los casos en que se usan varias palabras – por ejemplo, *catch some shut eye* — se puede ubicar la expresión por más de una palabra, como este caso que se encuentra por *catch* y *eye*. Otro ejemplo — *I mean business* — se puede ubicar por *I* y *business*.

****Muy Importante Saber que en inglés, ONE se usa para referirse al que habla o actúa. Al referirnos al número, pusimos entre paréntesis el número uno (1)****

Ejemplos:

Caso #1 Presentación

SMOKING: (A) *adj.* (B) Excelente, increíble. (C) *Ej.* "We had a smokin' good time last night."

    (A) **SMOKING** es un adjetivo.

    (B) Excelente, increíble es la definición.

    (C) Ejemplo de como usarlo.

Caso #2 Los Sinónimos

Hemos intentado encontrar sinónimos para que el lector pueda ver los demás sinónimos a partir de un caso. No obstante, un modismo puede tener varios significados, en esos casos, habrá una estrella (*) después del sinónimo. Para no repetir la lista de los sinónimos,

elegimos el modismo más común e incluimos todos los demás sinónimos. Al tratarse de un sinónimo de menos uso, pusimos el aviso Ver ...

Ejemplos:

CIG: (sin. cancer stick, butt*, smoke*) s. Cigarrillo. *Ej.* "Hey Franky, pass me a cig."

SMOKE: 1) *v.* Avanzar o actuar con gran velocidad y brillo. *Ej.* "He was smoking in the race and won easily." 2) *v.* Actuar bien, tener éxito. *Ej.* "I think I smoked that test." 3) *s.* Cigarrillo. *Ej.* "Who's got a smoke?" Ver cig.

También se puede ver que en el caso de **SMOKE**, la primera y segunda definiciones no tienen sinónimos.

En los casos en que un modismo con más de una definición también tenga un sinónimo, tal sinónimo está puesto antes de 1).

Ejemplo:

SPENT: (sin. played) *adj.* 1) Algo que se ha usado hasta agotar sus reservas. *Ej.* "The keg is spent, man. Someone needs to make a beer run." 2) Persona sin energía, gen. como consecuencia de agotamiento. *Ej.* "We were spent after a long day of football."

Caso #3 Los símbolos: /.../ y (...)

/.../ Hay muchos modismos que siempre se usan con su artículo. Para facilitar su localización, el artículo sigue al modismo de esta forma: ticket /the/ o thing or two /a/. En estos casos, las expresiones son *the ticket* y *a thing or two*, pero creemos que es más fácil ubicarlos sin

el artículo. Si no lleva /.../, significa que se puede usar en varias formas.

(...) Sucede frecuentemente que se puede usar una expresión con o sin todas las palabras de la expresión, y en esos casos, pusimos paréntesis en la palabra que se usa o no. Por ejemplo, unload (on) se puede usar con o sin on, sin cambiar el sentido. Otro ejemplo es give someone (some) lip. Así, se puede usar como *"He gave me some lip"* o *"Give me lip and you'll be sorry!"*

A TO Z

A TO Z /FROM/: *exp.* Completo, desde el principio hasta el fin. *Ej.* "It's all wrong! We're going to have to go over it from a to z."

AC/DC: *s.* Bisexual. *Ej.* "So I hear Mary is A.C./D.C. and she's dating both Ted and Sarah." Ver *double gated*.

ACE: *v.* Irle a uno muy bien en una prueba. *Ej.* "I can't believe it. I thought I aced the exam, but I failed it!"

ACE IN THE HOLE: (sin. ace up one's sleeve) *exp.* Algo desconocido que se guarda para un momento crítico para lograr triunfar en una situación dada. *Ej.* "The deal looks good, but wait and see if he doesn't have an ace in the hole."

ACE UP ONE'S SLEEVE: VER *ace in the hole*.

ACID: *s.* L.S.D., una droga alucinógena. *Ej.* "You can go crazy droppin' acid."

ACIDHEAD: *s.* Consumidor habitual de LSD. *Ej.* "He must be some kind of acidhead the way he acts so weird all the time."

ACT UP: *exp-v.* 1) Portarse mal, hacer travesuras. *Ej.* "You kids better stop acting up or else!" 2) Echarse a perder, estropearse. *Ej.* "The damn TV is acting up, the picture is all fuzzy."

ACTION: *s.* Actividad excitante, gen. sexual o prohibida. *Ej.* "If you're out to get some action, you'd better bring some protection."

AFTER SOMEONE /BE/: *exp-vi.* Presionar a alguien, o constantemente pedirle algo a alguien. *Ej.* "He's been after me to go out with him, but I'm not interested." Or "I've been after my daughter to clean up her room for a week!"

AH SNAP: *int.* Algo realmente bueno. *Ej.* "Ah snap, you won first prize!"

AIR HEAD: *s.* Una persona tonta, poco inteligente. *Ej.* "She acts like an air head, but it's just a put-on."

ALKY: *s.* Alcohólico. *Ej.* "If you're drinking a bottle of booze a day, I'd say you're an alky."

ALL FLUFF, NO SUBSTANCE: *exp.* Se dice de algo que parece ser valioso pero no lo es. Se dice del hablar o de un objeto. *Ej.* "Tell them to forget it. What they're offering you is all fluff, no substance."

ALL OVER ONE/IT: *exp.* 1) Muy en-

ALL rIGHt

tusiasta con respecto a una expectativa. *Ej.* "There's a party this weekend Hal." "Cool, I'm all over it." 2) Toqueteo o caricia sexual. *Ej.* "Some Neanderthal was all over me at the party." 3) Estar disponible para hacer algo. *Ej.* "Would you make dinner?" "Sure, I'm all over it." 4) Darle excesiva atención a alguien para obtener un favor. *Ej.* "She's all over me to give her the promotion instead of Sarah. It's really annoying."

ALL RIGHT: *int.* Expresa vibraciones positivas, una reacción favorable hacia una idea, afirmación o relación. *Ej.* "You got me concert tickets? All right!" Or "All right, I'm super psyched on your plan!"

ALL ROADS LEAD TO ROME: *exp.* Un proverbio que significa que muchos caminos conducen a la misma meta. *Ej.* "Your way or my way, it's the same difference. All roads lead to Rome."

ALL TALK, NO ACTION: *exp.* Describe a una persona que siempre habla de hacer algo, pero nunca lo hace. *Ej.* "George may try to scare you, but he's all talk, no action."

ALL THAT GLITTERS IS NOT GOLD: *exp.* Un proverbio que dice que muchas cosas que son atractivas y seductoras no tienen valor. *Ej.* "It looks appealing, but remember, all that glitters isn't gold."

ALRIGHT: VER *all right*.

AMBIENT: *s.* Música ambiental a un volumen bajo y agradable de escuchar. *Ej.* "I like this club because they play ambient."

AMBULANCE CHASER: *exp.* Abogado inescrupuloso, esp. aquél que espera en salas de emergencia de hospitales o llama a las víctimas de accidentes para instarlos a demandar, quedándose con hasta 50% de un ajuste. A este tipo se debe en parte que Shakespeare haya escrito, ¡Abogados, mátenlos a todos! *Ej.* "These damn ambulance chasers are driving up insurance premiums like mad with their stupid lawsuits."

AMPED: (sin. *fired up**) *adj.* Sumamente entusiasmado. *Ej.* "Everyone is amped for the graduation party."

ANAL: *adj.* 1) Excesivamente exigente, esp. en cuanto a limpieza.

ASS

Ej. "He's so anal, he cleans the john with a tooth brush." 2) Nervioso, poco relajado. *Ej.* "Lighten up, dude, you're so anal, you're like a perfectionist or something!"

ANAL RETENTIVE: *exp.* Poco relajado/a, demasiado exigente. *Ej.* "She's so anal retentive, she throws a conniption fit if you forget to put the cap back on the toothpaste."

ANGLE: *s.* Motivo personal o secreto esp. si esconde una estrategia para ganancia personal. *Ej.* "How does he think he is going to make money? What's his angle?"

ANTS IN ONE'S PANTS: *exp.* Impaciencia y/o inquietud extrema. *Ej.* "What's going on? You're acting like you've got ants in your pants."

ANTSY: *adj.* Intranquilo, impaciente, inquieto. *Ej.* "I get antsy waiting for the bus."

A-NUMBER ONE (1): *exp.* Lo mejor, de primera clase. *Ej.* "The boss wants the a-number one guy for the job."

APPLE OF ONE'S EYE: *exp.* El objeto de atención o de amor profundo. *Ej.* "He's so in love with her that he tells everyone she's the apple of his eye."

ARM: VER *charge an arm and a leg; shot in the arm; twist someone's arm.*

ARMPIT OF /THE/: *exp.* El peor lugar existente o imaginable. *Ej.* "They say New Jersey is the armpit of the United States, but there are a lot of nice places there."

AROUND THE BLOCK /BEEN/: *exp.* Alguien que ha tenido muchas experiencias y, como resultado, ha adquirido gran sabiduría. También se refiere a una persona que ha tenido muchas relaciones sexuales. *Ej.* "If you need advice, ask your grandfather. He's been around the block a few times."

ARROW: VER *straight arrow.*

ASS: [Vul.] *s.* 1) Trasero. *Ej.* "He sure does have a nice ass." 2) Mujer, cuando se ve únicamente como objeto sexual. (Desp.) *Ej.* "Hey, that's a nice piece of ass walkin' by." 3) Acto sexual. *Ej.* "I hope I get some ass tonight!" 4) *one's ass:* Uno mismo. *Ej.* "Get your ass over here!" 5) *be one's ass:* Recibir castigo o tener que responder por

ASSBACKWARDS

consecuencias. Ej. "Yeah, you don't care, but if we don't finish this job it's my ass they're gonna chew off!" VER TAMBIEN bad-ass; candy ass; clap someone's ass; get off one's ass; hard-ass; haul ass; kick (some) ass; kick someone's ass; kiss ass; kiss-ass; kiss my ass; out on one's ass; pain in the ass; piece of ass; smart-ass; up to one's ass in; work one's ass off; worth a rat's ass.

ASSBACKWARDS: [Vul.] adj. Retrocediendo, al revés, generalmente en forma confusa o desordenadamente. Ej. "My mechanic is horrible, he does everything assbackwards."

ASSHOLE: [Vul.] s. Imbécil; Una manera muy insultante de llamar a alguien estúpido o de expresar la baja opinión que de el se tiene. Ej. "Don't be upset by anything he says, he's a total asshole." Or "Hey, asshole, get your car out of my way!"

ATTITUDE: s. Mala actitud, gen. hostil o intransigente. Ej. "My husband gets such an attitude when I disagree with him."

AUSSIE: s. Australiano. Ej. "Those Aussies do a lot of travelling. They're all over the world."

AVOID SOMEONE/SOMETHING LIKE THE PLAGUE: exp-v. Evitar a toda costa. Ej. "That gal is pure trouble, I'd avoid her like the plague!"

AWESOME: (sin. cherry, fab, fresh, gnarly, killer, money, stoked, sweet, bitching, unreal) adj. Óptimo, genial, excelente, fantástico, buenísimo. Jerga de jóvenes para describir una variedad de situaciones. Para una fiesta, una película, una persona, una acción, etc. Ej. "I went to an awesome party last weekend. There was killer music and food. Man, was I stoked!"

B.

J.: abr. Blow job = Felonía.

B.S.: Abreviatura de bullshit. 1) s. Hablar necio e insolente, a menudo mentiras o cuentos exagerados. Ej. "If you believe that B.S. you'd believe anything!" 2) s. Trato malo o irrespetuoso. Ej. "I cannot believe the B.S. I have to put up with at work!" 3) v. Pasar el rato en conversación ociosa. Ej. "What did you do last night?" "Oh I just

BACK-SEAT DRIVER

sat around B.S'ing with a friend. 4) *v.* Intentar engañar o despistar hablando disparates. *Ej.* "I'm not going to buy your old car, so stop trying to B.S. me." 5) *inter.* Se usa para expresar gran disgusto o molestia. *Ej.* "B.S.! There's no way you ever dated Sharon Stone."

B.S.ER: *s.* Abreviación de *bullshitter*. Persona que miente, exagera o cuenta mentiras, y/o farsante. *Ej.* "That B.S.er would even lie to the Pope."

B.Y.O.B: *abr.* Bring your own booze/bottle/beer = Trae tu propio licor. *Ej.* "Is the party B.Y.O.B.?"

BABE: (sin. *tomato, knockout, hot number*) *s.* Una mujer muy 'sexy'. *Ej.* "Check out that babe!"

BABE IN THE WOODS: (sin. *wet behind the ears*) *s.* Persona inocente o inexperta. *Ej.* "He's twenty-one, but still a babe in the woods."

BABY: *s.* 1) Un objeto de especial interés para una persona. *Ej.* "This boat is my baby." 2) Una manera cariñosa de llamar uno/a amigo/a o pareja. *Ej.* "Hey baby, let's go get some food." VER TAMBIEN *throw out the baby with the bath water.*

BACH IT: *v.* Vivir solo, vivir como soltero. *Ej.* "Girlfriends are great, but I prefer to bach it and have my own space."

BACK: VER *break one's back; greenback; kick back; kickback; laid-back; lay back; monkey on one's back; nothing but the shirt on one's back; off someone's back; quarterback; straw that broke the camel's back; throw back; tip back; watch someone's back; wetback.*

BACK BURNER /ON THE/: *exp.* Una posición de relativamente baja prioridad o poca importancia. *Ej.* "It's a good idea, but let's put it on the back burner until we finish this project."

BACK-SEAT DRIVER: *s.* Pasajero de un auto, camión, etc. que da instrucciones al chofer, provocán-

BACK-STABBER

dole molestia. *Ej.* "If you don't stop being a back-seat driver, you can get out and walk!"

BACK-STABBER: *s.* Traicionero, desleal, alguien que negaría ayuda a un supuesto amigo, especialmente a aquél que se la había prestado. *Ej.* "I don't even want to see John. I got him a job in my firm and then he turns around and gets me fired. The bastard's a back-stabber!"

BACON: VER *bring home the bacon; save someone's bacon.*

BAD: 1) *adv.* Mucho. *Ej.* "I want it so bad!" 2) *adj.* Estupendo, fantástico. *Ej.* "Oh man, that's one bad shiner he gave you!"

BAD APPLE: *s.* Persona conflictiva, no confiable. *Ej.* "That guy is a bad apple. Stay away from him."

BAD GUYS: *s.* Gente mala. Ojo con esta gente que son los ladrones, asesinos potenciales y malhechores del mundo. ¡Algunos hasta han sido elegidos! *Ej.* "Don't mess with them, they're the bad guys in town."

BAD HAIR DAY: *exp.* Un día difícil atribuido en broma al hecho de tener un peinado feo o ridículo. *Ej.* "Leave me alone, I'm having a bad hair day."

BAD MOUTH: *exp-v.* Criticar o desacreditar, a menudo maliciosamente o injustamente. *Ej.* "She gets off on bad mouthing other people."

BAD NEWS: *exp.* Alguien a quien nadie quiere o que hay que eludir, gen. porque es desagradable o causa problemas. *Ej.* "That girl is always

BAD HAIR DAY

BAG oF BONeS

getting into trouble. She's bad news."

BAD RAP: *exp.* Crítica o mala fama a menudo injusta. *Ej.* "She got a bad rap after dating some big mouth."

BAD SCENE: *exp.* Situación o acontecimiento malo, desagradable. *Ej.* "It was a bad scene at the disco last night. A guy got shot."

BAD TASTE: *exp.* 1) (sin. tacky) De mal gusto. *Ej.* "Even though he's filthy rich, his bad taste in clothes and flashy jewelry make him look like a real schmo." 2) Decir o hacer algo desatinado. *Ej.* "It was in very bad taste for Joe to come to the funeral in a clown's costume."

BAD TRIP: *s.* Una mala experiencia o situación desagradable, esp. una mala experiencia con drogas. *Ej.* "I had a bad trip the first time I took acid."

BAD-ASS: *s.* 1) Lanzado. Aquella persona, gen. un hombre, que no le teme a una situación que requiere osadía y audacia. Posiblemente una persona peligrosa. *Ej.* "That guy's a real bad-ass; he just drove over a car on his motorcycle and didn't even fall!" 2) Un objeto extraordinario, notable o impresionante. *Ej.* "He bought himself a bad-ass car – a Ferrari!"

BADDER: *adj.* Mejor, muy impresionante. Un ejemplo de lógica al revés o en sentido figurado. *Ej.* "You think you're bad, but I'm badder than you'll ever be!"

BADDEST: *adj.* El mejor, el más impresionante de todos. *Ej.* "Yo, that's the baddest car I've ever seen!"

BAG: 1) *v.* Adquirir, obtener, asegurar. *Ej.* "I'm gonna bag this job if it kills me!" 2) *s.* Una mujer considerada fea o desaseada. *Ej.* "You look like a bag in those rags." 3) *one's bag: s.* Un área de interés o destreza. *Ej.* "I like cooking, but washing the dishes afterwards just isn't my bag."

BAG IT: *int.* Terminar con la discusión de un tema. *Ej.* "Just bag it, I don't want to hear any more whining about going on vacation with your girlfriend."

BAG OF BONES: *exp.* Un ser sumamente flaco. *Ej.* "You need to eat more, you're a bag of bones."

BAG PEOPLE

BAG PEOPLE: *exp.* Personas sin hogar, se dice porque a menudo llevan todas sus pertenencias en bolsas. *Ej.* "It breaks my heart to see all these bag people on the streets."

BAIL: *v.* Desertar; abandonar un lugar antes de los demás o no cumplir un plan convenido, esp. a último minuto. *Ej.* "How can you bail on us after we've made all these plans?"

BAIL (SOMEONE) OUT: *exp-v.* Ayudar a alguien en un momento difícil. *Ej.* "I was really behind in my work until Sarah bailed me out."

BALL: *v.* Tener relaciones sexuales. *Ej.* "I balled the broad in the backseat of my car." VER TAMBIEN *behind the eight ball; goof ball; have a ball; have someone by the balls; on the ball; play ball; screw ball; slimeball; that's the way the ball bounces.*

BALL AND CHAIN: *exp.* Una manera poco halagadora de describir a una novia o novio. *Ej.* "I can't go fishing. The ball and chain won't let me."

BALL OF WAX: *exp.* Un conjunto no especificado de puntos o circunstancias, referidas a la totalidad, generalmente dicho *the whole ball of wax*. *Ej.* "I don't just want a job, I want the whole ball of wax: perks, vacation time and a chance to become a partner in the firm."

BALL-BUSTER: *s.* 1) Tarea, trabajo, faena muy difícil, esp. una que requiere gran esfuerzo. *Ej.* "It's been a ball-buster restoring this antique car." 2) Mujer percibida como castradora. *Ej.* "His new girlfriend is such a ball-buster that she won't allow him to hang with his friends."

BALLPARK FIGURE: *exp.* Cálculo aproximado, gen. de cantidad o precio. *Ej.* "Just give me a ballpark figure of how much we're talking about."

BALLPARK: *exp.* Un margen aproximado de cantidad o números. *Ej.* "Those numbers are in the ballpark."

BALLS: [Vul.] 1) *s.* Testículos. *Ej.* "He got hit right in the balls." 2) *s.* Coraje, valor, valentía. *Ej.* "It takes balls to stand up for your rights."

BARF

3) *int.* Expresión de gran desaprobación. *Ej.* "Oh balls! You're full of it!" (Ing.)

BALLSY: *adj.* Muy fuerte y atrevido, a menudo en forma arriesgada o presumida. *Ej.* "That was a ballsy move climbing the tower."

BALONEY: *s.* Un disparate, esp. un cuento falso o exagerado. (etim. de una carne de fiambrería de cuya composición es imposible cerciorarse.) *Ej.* "Don't give me that baloney, just tell me the truth."

BANANA: VER *make like a banana and split; second banana; top banana.*

BANANAS: 1) *adj.* Loco. *Ej.* "Alice must be bananas to dress in her father's clothes all the time." Ver *bats*. 2) *go bananas*: Entusiasmarse o agitarse por algo. *Ej.* "The kids will go bananas when we tell them we're taking them to Disneyland."

BANDIT: VER *make out like a bandit.*

BANG FOR ONE'S BUCK: *exp.* El valor percibido del dinero gastado en algo. *Ej.* "You get a good bang for your buck in this restaurant."

BANG: [Vul.] *v.* Tener relaciones sexuales. *Ej.* "So, is it true he banged her?"

BANG-UP: 1) *adj.* Muy bien hecho, interpretado en forma sobresaliente. *Ej.* "You did a bang-up job on your presentation." 2) *v.* Quedar golpeado, herido físicamente. *Ej.* "Stan was badly banged-up in the accident."

BANK: *s.* 1) Dinero. *Ej.* "I hear she's making bank making music videos." 2) Una cosa segura o alguien en quien se puede confiar. *Ej.* "Down the stretch, Jordan is bank." VER TAMBIEN *make bank*.

BANK ON: *exp-v.* Confiar en, contar con, estar seguro de, tener certeza de. *Ej.* "You can bank on Tony to get the job done." Or "I'm so sure they'll win that you can bank on it."

BARBIE: *s.* Parrillada al aire libre. (etim. Australia, de barbecue.) *Ej.* "We're gonna have a barbie at my place."

BARF: 1) (sin. puke*) *s.* Vómito. *Ej.* "You got barf on my new shoes!" 2) *v.* Vomitar. *Ej.* "I feel like I'm going to barf." Ver *chuck up*.

BARF BAG

BARF BAG: s. Bolsa desechable plástica o de papel que se le entrega al pasajero de una línea aérea para su uso en caso de mareo. Ej. "His mom always carries a barf bag in case he gets sick."

BARFLY: s. Persona que visita establecimientos de expendio de bebidas alcohólicas con demasiada frecuencia. Ej. "Every time I come to this place, that barfly is here."

BARGAIN BASEMENT PRICE: exp. Precio muy barato. Ej. "A hundred bucks is my bargain basement price. I won't go any lower."

BARHOP: v. Frecuentar una serie de bares durante una noche, gen. resultando en un consumo excesivo de alcohol y la inevitable resaca. Ej. "We went out barhopping last night. We must've been in six different places."

BARK IS WORSE THAN ONE'S BITE /ONE'S/: (sin. barking dogs seldom bite) exp. Aquellas personas que amenazan o fanfarronean generalmente no actúan de acuerdo a lo dicho. Ej. "Don't worry about my dad, he may seem threatening, but his bark is worse than his bite."

BARK UP THE WRONG TREE: exp-v. Estar desorientado o equivocado en una acusación, una investigación o un raciocinio. Ej. "You're barking up the wrong tree if you think that goody two-shoes Tom is involved in any illegalities."

BARKING DOGS SELDOM BITE: VER one's bark is worse than one's bite.

BARREL: adj. 1) Un montón. Ej. "We had a barrel of fun last night." 2) Avanzar rápidamente, a menudo imprudentemente, en un vehículo motorizado. Ej. "He was barreling down the highway at 100 miles per hour." VER TAMBIEN bottom of the barrel; pork barrel; over the barrel.

BASE: VER first base; second base; third base; touch base.

BASH: 1) (sin. shindig) s. Fiesta o celebración. Ej. "We're gonna have a bash down at the lake." 2) v. Golpear fuerte. Ej. "I bashed my head against the window frame."

BASKET CASE: exp. Alguien cuya condición no tiene remedio, o alguien abatido por un conflicto emocional. Ej. "He's been a basket

B-DAy

case ever since they gave him electric shock therapy." Or "Virginia was a basket case for a week after her dog died."

BASTARD: [Vul.] s. Una persona, esp. a quien se considera miserable o desagradable. *Ej.* "I cannot believe that bastard lied to you again."

BAT A THOUSAND: *exp-v.* Lograr mucho éxito, no equivocarse. También se usan números inferiores para indicar éxito menor, ej. bat five hundred. *Ej.* "I was a batting a thousand on my sales trip until I lost a client."

BATS: (sin. screwy, wacky, bananas, batty, bonkers, cuckoo, gaga, loony, loopy, nuts*, nutty*) *adj.* Loco, demente. *Ej.* "Don't mind Old Al playing with himself. He's bats, but harmless."

BATTLE-AX: s. Una mujer considerada hostil o dictatorial. (etim. Hacha de armas; un hacha usado durante la Edad Media como arma de batalla). *Ej.* "Oh no! I've got the old battle-ax for my chemistry class!"

BATTY: *adj.* Loco, demente. *Ej.* "He must be batty to give a blind man the keys to his car!" VER bats.

BAWL SOMEONE OUT: *exp-v.* Retar a alguien, gen. en tonos fuertes. *Ej.* "John's mom bawled him out last night for coming home at dawn."

BAZILLION: (sin. gazillion) s. Número grande inventado, mucho de, muchas veces. *Ej.* "If I've told you once, I've told you a bazillion times. Shut the damn door!"

BAZOOM: (sin. boob*) s. Seno de mujer. *Ej.* "He only dates girls with big bazooms."

B-DAY: *abr.* Birthday = Cumpleaños. *Ej.* "When's your b-day?"

BASKET CASE

BE ALL EARS

BE ALL EARS: *exp-vi.* Estar atento, estar escuchando o estar dispuesto a escuchar. *Ej.* "I'm all ears. What did you want to speak with me about?"

BEAK: (sin. schnoz, honker) *s.* Nariz. *Ej.* "He needs plastic surgery on that beak."

BEAN: 1) *s.* Cabeza de una persona, gen. en referencia al cerebro. *Ej.* "Try using the old bean next time." 2) *v.* Pegarle a alguien en la cabeza con un proyectil, especialmente una pelota de béisbol. *Ej.* "He got beaned with a fastball." 3) beans: *adj.* Poco, de muy poco valor o mérito. A menudo utilizado con una connotación negativa. *Ej.* "If you don't know beans about investing, you should ask a broker." Or "She's a secretary, but she can't type worth beans." VER TAMBIEN hill of beans; full of beans; spill the beans; string bean.

BEAN TOWN: *s.* Boston, Massachusetts. *Ej.* "I hear there are a lot of preppies in Bean Town."

BEANER: *s.* Mexicano. (Desp.) *Ej.* "Farmers need the beaners to harvest their crops."

BEAR: *s.* Algo difícil o desagradable. *Ej.* "Final exam week at the University is a real bear."

BEAST: *s.* 1) Persona que le falta el último gen que separa a los seres humanos de los animales. Entonces, una persona tonta, poco refinada y culta. *Ej.* "You don't want to mess with him, he's a beast." 2) Vehículo poderoso. *Ej.* "Watch what this beast can do on the highway."

BEAT: (sin. spent, bushed) *adj.* Muy cansado/a. *Ej.* "I'm beat; I'm going to bed." VER TAMBIEN dead beat.

BEAT AROUND THE BUSH: *exp-vi.* Aproximarse en forma indirecta a una situación. No expresarse en forma directa y clara. *Ej.* "Just tell me what you want and stop beating around the bush."

BEAT IT: (sin. scram) *vi.* Escapar, huir, arrancar de algo o alguien. *Ej.* "Hey kid, beat it before I do a number on you!"

BEAT OFF: [Vul.] 1) (sin. jerk off, jack off, whack off) *vi.* Masturbarse. 2) Malgastar o perder el tiempo. *Ej.* "Stop beating off and get

BEEf

back to work!"

BEAT SOMEONE UP: (sin. tear apart*, take apart*, work someone over, break someone's face*, clean someone's clock, clobber*, cream*, kick someone's ass*, lick*, massacre*, mess (someone) up, shellac*, slaughter*) *exp-vi.* Pegarle fuerte a alguien, golpear en forma sostenida a una persona. *Ej.* "They beat him up so badly that he's in the hospital."

BEAT THE BAND: *exp-vi.* Actuar con gran energía y pompa. *Ej.* "It was a smashing performance. She was singing just to beat the band."

BEAT THE RAP: *exp-vi.* Ser declarado no culpable de un cargo o ser absuelto de un cargo, esp. cuando en verdad se es culpable. *Ej.* "Everyone knew O.J. was guilty. I don't know how he beat the rap."

BEAT THE SHIT OUT OF: [Vul.] *exp-vi.* Darle una paliza muy fuerte a alguien. *Ej.* "Hey, touch my girlfriend and I'll beat the shit out of you."

BEAUCOUP: *adj.* Harto, mucho. (etim. Francés) *Ej.* "He's makin' beaucoup money selling tires."

BEAUT: *s.* Algo extradorinario o notable. *Ej.* "Sarah doesn't goof up often, but when she does, it's a beaut!"

BEAVER: (sin. bush) *s.* Vello pubiano de mujer y/o vagina. *Ej.* "He swears he saw her beaver."

BED: VER *wake up on the wrong side of the bed*.

BED HEAD: *exp.* Persona despeinada, gen. después de tomar una siesta o después de un acto sexual. *Ej.* "You're gonna need a hair stylist to get rid of that bed head."

BEDSIDE MANNER: *s.* Una actitud solícita, servicial, hacia otros. Gen. se refiere a alguien de la profesión médica o aquella persona en ese papel. *Ej.* "When you're feeling lousy, there's nothing like being nursed by someone with a good bedside manner."

BEEF: 1) *s.* Queja, pleito. *Ej.* "You got a beef with me?" 2) *v.* Quejarse. *Ej.* "Why do you have to beef about every small problem?" 3) Acusación criminal. *Ej.* "They brought him in on a robbery beef." VER TAMBIEN *hot beef injection*.

BEEMER

BEEMER: s. Vehículo BMW. Ej. "Her daddy gave her a Beemer for her 18th birthday."

BEGIN A NEW CHAPTER: exp-vi. Experimentar un cambio radical de vida, negocios, relación, etc. Ej. "Okay, let's just begin a new chapter and forget all our past disputes."

BEHIND THE EIGHT BALL: exp. En posición desfavorable o incómoda, esp. de la cual no pareciera haber salida segura. Ej. "We're really behind the eight ball now that our computers are shut down. I don't know how we'll get the work finished in time."

BEJESUS: s. Se usa para enfatizar. Ej. "She scared the bejesus out of him when she jumped out of the closet."

BELL-BOTTOMS: s. Pantalones marineros, que se ensanchan hacia abajo. Ej. "I guess the 70's are in style again if models are wearing platform shoes and bell bottoms."

BELLS AND WHISTLES: exp. Puntos adicionales, extras especiales. Ej. "This car comes with all the bells and whistles. It practically drives itself!"

BELLY UP TO: exp-v. Avanzar hacia o acercarse, esp. cuando se busca satisfacción propia o un favor. Ej. "Watch Joe belly up to the bar for another scotch!"

BELLYACHE: v. Quejarse, esp. como niño, de un deseo no satisfecho. Ej. "Stop your bellyaching and just clean up the mess you made."

BELLYBUTTON: s. Ombligo. Ej. "Look at her funny bellybutton!"

BELT: 1) s. Un golpe fuerte, gen. con el puño. Ej. "That was some belt he took from Tyson." 2) s. Una fuerte reacción emocional. Ej. "It was a belt to see my aspirations smashed against the shores of fate." 3) s. Un trago de licor fuerte. Ej. "One last belt for the road?" 4) v. Golpear con fuerza, dar un puñete. Ej. "He belted him in the face three times." 5) v. Cantar con voz fuerte y vigorosa. Ej. "I love to belt out songs in the shower." VER TAMBIEN *tighten the belt a notch*.

BELT DOWN: exp-v. Beber de una vez, tragar algo al seco, esp. alcohol. Ej. "Give me a sec to belt down

BIBLE-THUMPER

my beer."

BENDER: s. Tomatera, juerga, borrachera; una noche de tomar en exceso. Ej. "My kidneys are hurting after yesterday's bender."

BENNY: s. 1) Una tableta de anfetamina que se toma como estimulante. Ej. "He took a benny to stay awake for the overnight car trip." 2) Un beneficio que se recibe como parte de un puesto o situación. Ej. "I took the job for the great bennies."

BENT OUT OF SHAPE: exp. Haber experimentado alguna agitación emocional o gran trastorno. Ej. "She got so bent out of shape when her soap opera ended."

BEST OF BOTH WORLDS: exp. Los mejores aspectos de cosas o situaciones diferentes. Ej. "She has a wonderful family and fantastic friends. It's really the best of both worlds."

BETCHA /YOU/ : int. Por supuesto, de todas maneras. Ej. "Do I want tickets for the World Series? You betcha!"

BETTER A BIRD IN THE HAND THAN TWO IN THE BUSH: (sin. bird in the hand is worth two in the bush /a/) exp. Mejor una sola cosa segura que dos o más inseguras. Ej. "I wouldn't recommend leaving your job to try and find a better one. Hey, better a bird in the hand than two in the bush."

BETTER SAFE THAN SORRY: exp. Hacer las cosas sin riesgos y de manera segura. Ej. "Don't take the shortcut, go the way you know. Hey, better safe than sorry."

BETWEEN A ROCK AND A HARD PLACE: exp. Estar en una situación extremadamente difícil que no tiene una salida fácil. Ej. "You're my friend, Ted, but you've also been owing me $10,000 for a year now. You're putting me between a rock and a hard place."

BEYOND REPAIR /BE/: exp-vi. Algo que se considera sin remedio o imposible de mejorar. Ej. "Forget it Joey. Our relationship is beyond repair."

BI: s. Bisexual. Ej. "So, she's bi, huh?" VER double gated.

BIBLE-THUMPER: s. Fundamentalista protestante. Ej. "Tell that bible-thumper to stop his

BIG APPLE

hollering and leave us alone."

BIG APPLE /THE/: s. La gran manzana; Nueva York. Ej. "If you want to make it big time, you've got to go to the Big Apple."

BIG AS A HOUSE: exp. Algo enorme. Ej. "Don't talk to me about credit card debt, mine is as big as a house."

BIG BOYS /THE/: exp. Hombres poderosos o que ejercen gran autoridad/influencia. Ej. "You better know what you're doing before you play with the big boys."

BIG C /THE/: s. Cáncer. Ej. "He got the big C from smoking three packs of cigs a day for over twenty years."

BIG CHEESE /THE/: (sin. big wig, big shot, big deal*) s. Persona influyente o importante. Ej. "The big cheese is coming to oversee operations today, so everyone better look sharp."

BIG DEAL: s. Persona influyente o importante. Ej. "Perhaps you are a big deal in the company, but in this house, you're still expected to help out."

BIG GUN: s. Persona poderosa o influyente, esp. una que controla acontecimientos. Ej. "Hank is the big gun of our firm."

BIG HOUSE: s. La cárcel. Ej. "Lou got sent up to the big house." VER clink /the/.

BIG LEAGUES: (sin. Major League) exp. Muy grande, afortunado o importante. (etim. Liga de atletas profesionales, por lo tanto prestigioso y de alta remuneración.) Ej. "You're in the Big Leagues now, you've got to start handling serious responsibilites."

BIG MOUTH: s. Una persona chismosa o aquella que habla demasiado, o hace comentarios poco apropiados. Ej. "Don't tell that big mouth, she'll have the news all over school by lunch time."

BIG SHOT: (sin. big wig, big cheese) s. Persona importante o influyente. Ej. "Stop acting like a big shot and help me do the dishes."

BIG WIG: (sin. big cheese, big shot) s. Persona importante o influyente. Ej. "She's the big wig in the firm."

BIGGIE: s. 1) Persona muy importante. Ej. "He's Mr. Biggie around

BIRDBRAIN

BIG WIG

here." 2) Algo considerado grande o importante. *Ej.* "My movie is gonna be a biggie!"

BILL: *s.* Dólar. *Ej.* "Can you lend me a few bills?" VER *buck*.

BIMBO: *s.* Una mujer, esp. aquella percibida como hueca o que tiene un interés exagerado en lo sexual. *Ej.* "Why did he marry that bimbo?"

BIRD: *s.* 1) Cohete, satélite o avión. *Ej.* "Look at that bird fly!" 2) Una persona, esp. aquella que es rara o sobresaliente. *Ej.* "You could say he's a different kind of bird or you could say he's just plain off his rocker. It's a matter of opinion." 3) Una mujer joven. *Ej.* "Look at the legs on that bird!" (Ing.) 4) *bird /the/:* (sin. *finger /the/*) *s.* El dedo índice extendido hacia arriba, cuando la mano esta hecha un puño. La expresión física de *fuck you*. (nota del editor: Son malos modales dar esta señal, pero si estás contando un cuento o historia en el cual es necesario describir esta acción, lo correcto es decir *the bird* o *the finger* en vez de realmente hacer el gesto.) *Ej.* "I gave the guy the bird when he didn't stop to help us."

BIRD IN THE HAND IS WORTH TWO IN THE BUSH /A/: VER *better a bird in the hand than two in the bush*.

BIRDBRAIN: *s.* Una persona considerada tonta o estúpida. *Ej.* "Tony's a birdbrain. What does he

BIRDS AND THE BEES

know about philosophy?"

BIRDS AND THE BEES /THE/: *exp.* Lecciones iniciales de educación sexual básica. *Ej.* "Son, you're 15. It's time we talked about the birds and the bees."

BIRDS OF A FEATHER FLOCK TOGETHER: *exp.* Juntarse o formar amistades con personas similares a uno, especialmente en lo que se refiere a gustos u opiniones. *Ej.* "He's a criminal, she's a criminal. Hey, birds of a feather flock together."

BIRTHDAY SUIT: (sin. butt naked) *exp.* Desnudo, estado de desnudez. *Ej.* "I have this dream where I walk into my office and there's my secretary, wearing nothing but her birthday suit."

BITCH: [Vul.] 1) *s.* Hembra exigente y desagradable. *Ej.* "I can't stand that bitch!" 2) Algo muy difícil de hacer. *Ej.* "It was a bitch climbing the mountain." 3) Algo desagradable. *Ej.* "It's been a bitch of a day." 4) *s.* Queja. *Ej.* "Jack always has some bitch about my cooking." 5) *v.* Quejarse. *Ej.* "The guy is never content, he's always bitchin' about something." VER TAMBIEN *son of a bitch.*

BITCH SOMEONE OUT: (sin. curse someone out) *exp-v.* Gritarle a alguien de manera amenazante. *Ej.* "She bitched me out for flirting with her old man."

BITCHING: *adj.* Estupendo, fantástico. *Ej.* "We had a

THE BIRDS AND THE BEES

BLIND DRUNK

bitchin' time over the summer." VER awesome.

BITCHY: *adj.* Antipático, desagradable, gen. usado para referirse a una mujer o a un homosexual. *Ej.* "Well, you sure are in a bitchy mood today."

BITE: *vi.* Estar/ser muy malo, estar/ser de mala calidad. *Ej.* "This place bites the big one, let's go." Or "The food bit!" VER TAMBIEN bark is worse than one's bite; put the bite on.

BITE OFF MORE THAN ONE CAN CHEW: *exp-vi.* Intentar más de lo que se es capaz. *Ej.* "You want a high paying job, you want to do volunteer work, and you want to raise a family. I think you're biting off more than you can chew."

BITE ONE'S LIP: *exp-vi.* Mantener silencio con respecto a un tema que se conoce o sobre el cual se tiene una opinión. *Ej.* "You'd better bite your lip! If you repeat what I told you, I'll never forgive you."

BITE THE BULLET: *exp-vi.* Aceptar la necesidad de tener que hacer algo desagradable. *Ej.* "It's time to bite the bullet; I have to meet my in-laws this weekend."

BITE THE DUST: *exp-vi.* 1) Ser derrotado. *Ej.* "The team bit the dust on Sunday." 2) Dejar de existir, llegar al fin, morir. *Ej.* "You're gonna bite the dust if you don't give me back my toy!"

BIZ: *s.* Negocios. *Ej.* "Let's have your people talk with my people and see if we can do some biz together."

BLACKED OUT: *exp.* Perder la conciencia gen. por exceso de alcohol o drogas (no sencillamente quedarse dormido). *Ej.* "I drank so much tequila I blacked out."

BLANKITY-BLANK: *exp.* Término que reemplaza cualquier garabato o grosería. *Ej.* "I'd like to beat the blankity-blank out of him!"

BLANKS: VER shoot blanks.

BLAST: *s.* Una ocasión muy entretenida. *Ej.* "How was the party?" "Oh it was a blast!"

BLIMP: *s.* Persona muy gorda. *Ej.* "It was such a drag. I had to sit next to this blimp on the airplane."

BLIND DRUNK: *exp.* Tan borracho que necesitará ayuda médica en la mañana. *Ej.* "He must have been blind drunk to call the boss a filthy-no-good-two-timing-pig." VER plastered.

BLINK: VER on the blink.

BLITZED: adj. Sumamente ebrio, listo para la clínica. Ej. "She got blitzed drinking shots of whiskey."

BLOCK: s. La cabeza de una persona. Ej. "I'll knock your block off if you mess with me!" VER TAMBIEN around the block /been/; chip off the old block /be a/; mental block.

BLOKE: s. Un hombre. Ej. "Who's the bloke she's with?" (Ing.)

BLOOD: s. Amigo íntimo, gen. usado entre afroamericanos. Ej. "Yo blood, how's it hanging?" VER TAMBIEN scream bloody murder; sweat blood.

BLOODY: adj. Extremadamente bueno o malo. Ej. "Bloody good job Susan!" Or "You made a bloody mess of this painting." (Ing.)

BLOOMING: adj. Molesto, irritante, despreciable. Ej. "I cannot stand his bloomin' attitude any longer!" (Ing.)

BLOTTO: adj. Totalmente borracho. Ej. "I got so blotto I don't remember half the night." VER plastered.

BLOW: 1) vi. Gastar dinero en forma desenfrenada y descuidada. Ej. "This big shot came into the store and blew a few grand on two suits." 2) vi. Desperdiciar o perder algo por ineptitud propia. Ej. "I blew a golden opportunity by showing up late." 3) vi. Partir apresuradamente, esp. debido a peligro. Ej. "We'd better blow before the fuzz shows up." 4) s. Cocaína. Ej. "Do you want to do some blow tonight?" 5) vi. Desilusionar, no cumplir. Ej. "You blow! Once again you've broken a promise."

BLOW A FUSE: (sin. blow one's stack, blow one's top, blow a gasket) exp-vi. Perder la compostura, la calma, la paciencia, y enojarse mucho. Ej. "Don't tell Dad about the car or he'll blow a fuse."

BLOW A GASKET: VER blow a fuse.

BLOW AWAY: exp-vi. 1) Quedar emocionalmente abatido por algo, gen. una mala noticia, pero también un libro, una película, etc. de tal manera que uno queda sin habla. Ej. "That movie blew me away." Or "I was blown away by the news

BLOW OUT

of my uncle's death." 2) Matar a tiros. *Ej.* "They blew him away as he walked out of the restaurant." VER *waste*.

BLOW CHUNKS: *exp-vi.* Vomitar. *Ej.* "You're going to blow chunks if you drink that whole bottle of gin." VER *chuck up*.

BLOW HOT AND COLD: *exp-vi.* Vacilar, cambiar frecuentemente de opinión sobre un tema. *Ej.* "I blow hot and cold on the idea of moving to Nebraska."

BLOW IN(TO): *exp-vi.* Llegar, aparecer, presentarse, esp. de manera sorpresiva. *Ej.* "Wow, look who blew into town!"

BLOW IT: *vi.* Desperdiciar una oportunidad o dinero. *Ej.* "I had everything going for me, then I started with coke and blew it all away."

BLOW JOB: [Vul.] (sin. smoker) *s.* Felonía. *Ej.* "Is it true he got a blow job in the elevator?"

BLOW OFF STEAM: *exp-vi.* Dar rienda suelta a las frustraciones. *Ej.* "I need to blow off steam before I totally stress out."

BLOW OFF: 1) *exp-vi.* No hacer algo que se debe hacer. *Ej.* "I blew off class today." 2) *s.* Persona que continuamente deja tareas sin cumplir o abandona sus responsabilidades. *Ej.* "I'd never hire her, she's a blow off."

BLOW ONE'S COOL: *exp-vi.* Perder la calma, esp. enojarse. *Ej.* "I blew my cool when he said he preferred McDonalds to my cooking."

BLOW ONE'S MIND: *exp-vi.* Animarse con gran emoción, esp. estar asombrado, maravillado, o conmovido. *Ej.* "The concert blew my mind. It was so heavy!"

BLOW ONE'S STACK: VER *blow a fuse*.

BLOW ONE'S TOP: *exp-vi.* Perder la compostura, enojarse y expresarlo, gen. gritando. *Ej.* "When she blows her top it's like she's about to do a Lizzy Borden on you."

BLOW OUT: 1) *s.* Fiesta loca, gen. con mucho sexo y drogas. *Ej.* "Dude, you missed a killer party. It was a total blow out." 2) *s.* El neumático de un auto que pierde todo su aire de golpe, casi como una explosión. *Ej.* "The accident occurred when a car had a blow out

BLOW SMOKE

going 100 miles per hour." 3) s. Resultado muy desigual. *Ej.* "The election was a blow out. The incumbent won by a landslide." 4) *vi.* Ser derrotado decisivamente. *Ej.* "Once again the team was blown out, losing by 30 points."

BLOW SMOKE: *exp-vi.* Crear un pretexto para engañar. *Ej.* "They're just blowing smoke when they talk about a take-over because I know they don't have the necessary capital."

BLOW THE WHISTLE ON: *exp-vi.* Informar sobre alguien. *Ej.* "It's about time someone blew the whistle on that company. They've been dumping chemicals in the river for years now."

BLOW WITH THE WIND: *exp-vi.* Para describir a una persona que cambia de opinión, afiliación, etc. ya sea para mantenerse dentro de la facción popular o por conveniencia. *Ej.* "There are some Presidents who think their job is to blow with the wind of popular opinion."

BLOW-HARD: *s.* Un farsante: alguien que pretende saber todo, gen. un tanto ofensivo para hacerlo realmente detestable. *Ej.* "He's such a blow-hard. He goes on and on about any subject under the sun."

BLUE: *adj.* Deprimido. *Ej.* "I feel blue today. I need some Prozac." VER TAMBIEN *out of the blue.*

BLUE IN THE FACE: *exp.* Sentir o parecer que se está a punto de estellar por hablar tanto. Se usa figurativamente. *Ej.* "I warned you and warned you until I was blue in the face, but you didn't listen."

BO: *abr.* Body odor = Cuerpo maloliente. *Ej.* "Take a bath man, you've got a nasty case of BO."

BOAT: VER *float one's boat; miss the boat; rock the boat.*

BOD: (sin. frame) *s.* Cuerpo humano. (etim. Abreviación de body) *Ej.* "Check out the bod on that guy!"

BODY: VER *over my dead body; busy body.*

BOGEY MAN: *s.* Personaje maligno que atemoriza a los niños chicos. *Ej.* "If you're not a good boy, the bogey man will get you."

BOGUS: *adj.* Malo, desagradable. *Ej.* "That's a bogus answer." Or "It was bogus for him not to help you."

BOINK: *v.* Tener relaciones sexuales. *Ej.* "If she's on the pill, than I assume she's boinking someone."

BOMB: 1) *s.* Un fiasco, desastre, fracaso. *Ej.* "The play was a bomb." 2) *v.* Fracasar totalmente o resultar muy mal. *Ej.* "I was so nervous during the interview that I bombed it." 3) *v.* Pintar un grafito. *Ej.* "Let's go down to the train yards and bomb the trains."

BOMBSHELL: *s.* 1) Una mujer muy atractiva y sexy. *Ej.* "There's always a few bombshells in a James Bond movie." 2) Una gran sorpresa. *Ej.* "My promotion was a bombshell."

BOND: *v.* Formar un lazo de amistad con alguien, esp. descubrir características mutuamente compatibles con otro persona. *Ej.* "I met this guy I really bonded with. We're so similar."

BONE SOMEONE: [Vul.] *exp-v.* Tener una relación sexual casual con alguien. *Ej.* "I boned her in the back seat of my car."

BONE TO PICK: *exp.* Un punto que causa argumento o desacuerdo. *Ej.* "I've got a bone to pick with you son. When you're told to do something, like clean up your room, you get to it no questions asked!"

BONEHEAD: *s.* Limitado, poco astuto, tonto, además, a menudo aburrido. *Ej.* "What kind of a bonehead would leave his kid in a car with the windows all rolled up?"

BONER: *s.* 1) Un pene erecto. VER woody. 2) Una equivocación, un error. *Ej.* "Anymore boners and you're outta here!"

BONES: VER bag of bones; jump someone's bones; lazy bones; make no bones about it; need to put some meat on one's bones

BONK: 1) *v.* Golpear o pegar. *Ej.* "I bonked him on the head." 2) *s.* Un golpe. *Ej.* "That was some bonk she took."

BONKERS: *adj.* 1) Loco, demente. *Ej.* "That guy is so bonkers he should be locked up." VER bats. 2) Exageradamente o locamente entusiasmado. *Ej.* "I'm bonkers over basketball."

BONUS: (sin. sweet) *adj.* Excelente, fantástico. *Ej.* "Bonus dude! I can't believe the school is going to give you twenty grand while you're

B○0b

studying for a Ph.d. That's sweet!"

BOOB: s. 1) (sin. bazoom) Seno de mujer. Ej. "He actually said to me, 'Can I touch your boobs?' Unbelievable!" 2) Una persona demasiado tonta. Ej. "Most people mature as they age, but you're still a boob."

BOOB TUBE: (sin. tube /the/, idiot box) s. Televisión. Ej. "Stop watching the boob tube!"

BOOGER: (sin. snot*) s. Moco nasal seco. Ej. "Gross, you have a booger on your shirt!"

BOOGIE: v. Bailar. Ej. "Let's go boogie!"

BOOK: v. Detener, arrestar. Ej. "Book him for indecent exposure in a public place, and then get that pervert in the cooler!" VER TAMBIEN cook the books; hit the books; throw the book at.

BOOK WORM: s. Persona muy estudiosa. Ej. "I'm glad my daughter is a book worm, that way she's not interested in boys."

BOOKIE: s. Corredor de apuestas ilegal. Ej. "My bookie is a nice guy. He gives you a week to pay up before he sends his thugs after you."

BOOM BOX: s. Un sistema de sonido portátil muy poderoso. Ej. "That boom box makes a lot of noise."

BOONDOCKS: s. pl. Un área, zona rural alejada de la civilización. Ej. "She lives in the boondocks. There's not even a store near her house."

BOOST: v. Hurtar, robar. Ej. "No one's looking, let's boost the TV." VER swipe.

BOOT: 1) (sin. heave-ho) s. Un despido sin gloria de un trabajo o una destitución abrupta de un lugar. Ej. "Yeah it sucked, I got the boot for coming in late again." 2) v. Despedir. Ej. "He's such a slacker, it's high time we booted him." 3) v. Vomitar. Ej. "He got loaded on whiskey and then booted on the carpet." VER chuck up. 4) boot / to/: exp. Además, también. Ej. "Buy the big screen TV and I'll give you the VCR to boot."

BOOZE: (sin. drink, sauce) s. Bebida alcohólica, licor. Ej. "Should we get some booze for the camping trip?"

BOOZE IT UP: exp-v. Beber alcohol

BOUNCER

en exceso. *Ej.* "That guy looks like Rudolph the Red Nosed reindeer. Boy, he must really booze it up."

BOP ON DOWN/UP TO: *exp-v.* Ir a. *Ej.* "I'm gonna bop on down to the corner and buy a soda." Or "Let's bop on up to Tim's place."

BORED STIFF: *exp.* Estar muy aburrido, tan aburrido que uno casi queda tieso por inacción. *Ej.* "I was bored stiff at the opera."

BORN WITH A SILVER SPOON IN ONE'S MOUTH: *exp.* Alguien que ha nacido en una familia rica. *Ej.* "He'll never have to work a day in his life. He was born with a silver spoon in his mouth."

BOTTOM: *s.pl.* Gluteus maximus, las nalgas. *Ej.* "How did your bottom get all wet?" VER *bum*.

BOTTOM OF THE BARREL: *exp.* Borra, escoria. *Ej.* "I knew we should have arrived on time to the barbie. There's nothing left but the bottom of the barrel."

BOUNCE: *v.* Huir, abandonar un lugar inmediatamente. *Ej.* "Yo man, let's bounce. This place sucks."

BOUNCE SOMETHING OFF SOMEONE: *exp-v.* Contarle a alguien una idea o pensamiento para ver su reacción y escuchar sugerencias. *Ej.* "Let me bounce this idea off you — you fund my decorative food business and I'll give you half the profits."

BOUNCED CHECK: VER *rubber check*.

BOUNCER: *s.* Matón. Persona empleada para echar a elementos conflictivos de un lugar público, especialmente un bar. *Ej.* "The bouncer broke up the fight

BORN WITH A SILVER SPOON IN ONE'S MOUTH

# BOXERS

and then threw the two guys out of the bar."

BOXERS: s. Calzoncillos hasta medio muslo. Ej. "The only problem with boxers is that you can't really wear them with jeans."

BOZO: s. Un idiota, un estúpido. Ej. "Get that bozo off the machine before he hurts himself."

BRACELETS: s. Esposas. Ej. "Sargent, put the bracelets on him."

BRAINER: VER no brainer /a/.

BRAINS /THE/: s. Líder intelectual. Ej. "We need to arrest the brains of the operation and then the organization will fall apart."

BREAD: s. Dinero. Ej. "Can you lend me some bread?" VER dough.

BREADBASKET /THE/: s. El estómago. Ej. "He hit me right in the breadbasket."

BREAK: Ver get the breaks; take a break; give me a break.

BREAK DOWN: exp-vi. 1) Cuando el auto, moto, etc. no funciona. Ej. "Sorry I'm late, my car broke down." 2) Sufrir una crisis emocional hasta tal punto de perder el control de las emociones. Ej. "I guess it was too much stress, because suddenly she broke down in the middle of a meeting and started screaming like a banshee."

BREAK ONE'S BACK: exp-v. Trabajar hasta quedar exhausto, o hacer un gran esfuerzo en nombre de otra persona. Ej. "I broke my back getting the house ready for the wedding."

BREAK SOMEONE'S FACE: exp-vi. Reventarle la cara (a alguien), golpear a alguien, esp. en la cara. Ej. "I'm gonna break your face if you don't get out of here!" VER beat someone up.

BREAK THE ICE: exp-vi. "romper el hielo" 1) Comenzar, partir con algo. Ej. "I need some help breaking the ice with our new clients." 2) Para relajar la tensión o formalidad en una situación profesional o social. Ej. "A joke is always a good way to break the ice."

BREAK WIND: (sin. cut one) vi. Expulsar gases intestinales. Ej. "It was very embarrassing. I broke wind during the lecture."

BREAKNECK SPEED: exp. Hacer algo a toda velocidad (ej. manejar

BROWN NOSE

un auto, hacer diligencias, etc.). *Ej.* "I was running around at breakneck speed trying to get everything ready."

BREAK-UP WITH: (sin. dump) *exp-vi.* Terminar una relación romántica, separarse. *Ej.* "I just had to break-up with him. I couldn't stand his laugh any longer."

BREEZE IN: (sin. waltz) *v.* Llegar como una fresca brisa primaveral - sin cuidado y despreocupado. *Ej.* "He knows he's late, but he still breezes in like nothing is wrong."

BREW: (sin. cold one, brewsky, frosty, pint) *s.* Cerveza, ojalá helada. *Ej.* "I could do with a brew on a hot day like this."

BREWSKY: *s.* Cerveza. VER brew.

BRICK: VER shit a brick.

BRILLIANT: *adj.* Excelente. *Ej.* "Thank you, I had a brilliant time last night!" (Ing.)

BRING HOME THE BACON: *exp-vi.* Ganar dinero para los gastos diarios, esp. dinero para mantener a una familia. *Ej.* "It's not the most interesting job, but at least it brings home the bacon."

BRING IT TO SOMEONE: *exp-vi.* Incitar a alguien a pelear. *Ej.* "Bring it to him man, you can cream that pussy!"

BRING YOUR OWN BOOZE/ BOTTLE/BEER: *exp.* Reunión informal en que todos aportan su bebida. Gen. se dice BYOB. *Ej.* "I'm providing the space for the party, but everyone has to BYOB."

BRING YOUR OWN: *exp.* Reunión informal en que todos aportan algo (gen. comida o bebida). También se dice BYO. *Ej.* "Hey is the party BYO or are they providing everything?"

BRO: (sin. daddy-o) *s.* Amigo. *Ej.* "Hey bro, how's it going?"

BROAD: *s.* Una mujer o chiquilla. *Ej.* "The broads are getting together for another hen party." VER gal.

BRONX CHEER: *exp.* Sonido de desprecio producido por la vibración de la lengua entre los labios. *Ej.* "The actor was so bad the crowd gave him a Bronx cheer."

BROWN NOSE: 1) *exp-v.* Congraciarse con alguien por motivos ulteriores, interesados. Gen. el jefe. *Ej.* "Talk about brown nosing, the guy

BUBBLY

brings home-made cookies to his boss." 2) s. Persona que se congracia con otros. Ej. "That brown nose always gets the easiest job."

BUBBLY: s. Champaña. Ej. "We need some bubbly to celebrate our engagement."

BUCK: (sin. smackeroo, smacker, clam, bill, greenback) s. Dólar. Ej. "It'll cost you ten bucks." VER TAMBIEN bang for one's buck; fast buck; pass the buck.

BUCK STOPS HERE /THE/: exp. La responsabilidad final se encuentra aquí. Ej. "Yes, I do get paid more, but that's because whenever there's a problem, the buck stops here."

BUCKLE DOWN: exp-v. Enfrentar una tarea o trabajo difícil o desagradable para lograr una meta. Ej. "There's no easy way to get this done, you just have to buckle down and do it." Or "He buckled down and asked her to marry him."

BUDDAH: s. Marihuana

BUDDY: s. 1) (sin. pal, sport) Amigo. Ej. "I ley buddy, how you been?" 2) Modo de dirigirse a un desconocido para caerle bien. Ej. "Buddy, you got a smoke?".

BUDDY-BUDDY: adj. Demostrando gran cariño, frecuentemente usado en forma peyorativa para indicar desconfianza de la aparente intimidad entre dos personas. Ej. "Something is fishy here. Those two hated each other last week and now they're all buddy-buddy."

BUFFED: adj. Un muy buen estado físico y/o musculoso del cuerpo. Ej. "He's looking buffed after working out with weights for a year."

BUG: v. Molestar o enojar a alguien. Ej. "If you don't stop bugging me, I'm going to scream!"

BUG OFF: int. ¡Ándate! o ¡Lárgate! Ej. "Bug off! I don't want to speak with you ever again."

BUG OUT: exp-v. 1) De repente comenzar a comportarse de manera rara o irracional como si se hubiera enloquecido. Ej. "Take it easy Frank, you're bugging out over nothing. She said she'd be back in a few days." 2) Repentinamente dejar un lugar, a menudo ignominiosamente. Ej. "The enemy is coming. It's time to bug out."

BUMMER

BUGGER: (sin. snot*) s. Moco nasal seco. Ej. "Get a Kleenex, you've got a bugger hanging out."

BUGGING: (sin. freaking out) adj. Actuando de manera irracional o descontrolada. Ej. "Yo man, you're buggin'. Take it easy."

BULL: s. 1) Habla sin fundamento o pretencioso, a menudo una mentira o gran exageración. Ej. "That's a lot of bull about you dating Sylvester Stallone." 2) Trato malo o faltando el respeto. Ej. "I cannot believe the bull I have to put up with at work!" 3) Tareas irritantes o aburridas. Ej. "I hate having to do all this bull." VER TAMBIEN *hit the bull's eye; shoot the bull; take the bull by the horns.*

BULL DYKE: (sin. butch) s. Una lesbiana, esp. una lesbiana con características muy masculinas. (Desp.) Ej. "Wow, is that a man or a bull dyke?"

BULL IN A CHINA SHOP: s. Una persona muy torpe que causa daño. Ej. "He's so klutzy he's like a bull in a china shop."

BULLET: VER *bite the bullet; sweat bullets.*

BULLSHIT: VER *B.S.*

BULLSHITTER: VER *B.S.er.*

BUM: (sin. bottom, duff, tush, heinie) s. Gluteus maximus, las nalgas. Ej. "She has a nice bum."

BUM OUT: exp-v. Defraudar o sentirse defraudado. Ej. "You bum me out when you make such negative comments." Or "I'll be bummed out if I can't go to the beach this weekend."

BUM RAP: s. Castigo o acusación injusto/a. Ej. "I know he's innocent. He just got a bum rap."

BUM STEER: s. Consejo o información engañoso/a que a menudo conduce a gran desilusión o fracaso. Ej. "It was a bum steer telling me to invest in that company. They went belly up."

BUMMED: adj. Estar desganado, sin energía, deprimido. Ej. "Mary's bummed she didn't get invited to our wedding." Or "I've been really bummed since I stopped taking lithium."

BUMMER: (sin. drag*) s. Algo o alguien desagradable y/o aburrido y/o cansador. Ej. "What a bummer that your friends didn't invite you."

41

# BUMP OFF

Or "He's such a bummer to be around, he's like a ready-made mortician."

BUMP OFF: *exp-v.* Asesinar, matar. *Ej.* "They bumped him off on a deserted road." VER *waste*.

BUN IN THE OVEN /HAVE A/: (sin. be in the family way) *exp-vi.* Estar embarazada. *Ej.* "Either she's really fat or she has a bun in the oven."

BUNDLE: *s.* 1) Mucho, gran cantidad de algo. *Ej.* "You shouldn't drink so much coffee. You're a bundle of nerves." 2) Una gran cantidad de dinero. *Ej.* "I made a bundle on the market last year."

BURN: 1) *v.* Engañar o estafar, esp. causarle desengaño y/o trastorno a otro. *Ej.* "I got burned buying a used car from him." 2) *s.* Un acción que hace uno en lo que daña, se atormenta, o persigue a otra, y que se vuelve a uno. *Ej.* "It's a burn on you for always teasing younger kids that older kids tease you now." VER TAMBIEN *crash and burn; there still burns a spark*.

BURN BRIDGES: *exp.* Evitar romper una relación, por orgullo, o para no perder una posibilidad o un contacto con una persona o lugar. *Ej.* "You're quitting, but don't say anything you might regret. There's no need to burn bridges."

BURN THE CANDLE AT BOTH ENDS: *exp-vi.* Trabajar y divertirse excesivamente, esp. durante muchas horas. *Ej.* "You work all day and party all night. You need to

HAVE A BUN IN THE OVEN

stop burning the candle at both ends before you burn out."

BURY THE HATCHET: *exp-v.* Poner fin a una desavenencia y hacer las paces. *Ej.* "We've been fighting too long, it's time we buried the hatchet."

BUSH: (sin. beaver) *s.* Vello pubiano de mujer y/o vagina. *Ej.* "You liar, you didn't see her bush and you know it!"

BUSHED: (sin. spent, beat) *adj.* Muy cansado/a. *Ej.* "Are you too bushed for a game of tennis?"

BUSINESS: VER *I mean business; like nobody's business; monkey business; mind one's own business.*

BUST: 1) *v.* Detener. *Ej.* "Let's bust him before he skips town." 2) *v.* Allanar, entrar con la intención de poner fin a una actividad ilegal. *Ej.* "They busted the illegal casino." 3) *s.* Una detención. *Ej.* "He added another bust to a long list of convictions." 4) *s.* Un allanamiento. *Ej.* "Okay, everyone freeze! This is a bust!"

BUST A MOVE: *exp-v.* Actuar decididamente, tomar una acción definitiva. *Ej.* "Yo man, if you want to get ahead in this rat race you've got to bust a move."

BUST ONE'S CHOPS: *exp-v.* Trabajar fuerte, esforzarse mucho, gen. para lograr un objetivo. *Ej.* "I busted my chops building this house."

BUSY BODY: *s.* Una persona que habla de o se mete en los asuntos de otros, esp. sus vidas privadas. *Ej.* "Why do you want to know what he's doing all the time? Stop being a busy body."

BUTCH: 1) (sin. bull dyke) *s.* Una lesbiana, esp. una lesbiana de rasgos muy masculinos. (Desp.) *Ej.* "It's hard not to take it personally when your girlfriend goes butch on you." 2) De apariencia masculina, esp. en el caso de una mujer que se ve masculina. (Desp.) *Ej.* "You're looking awfully butch these days."

BUTT: *s.* 1) Gluteus maximus, las nalgas. *Ej.* "You've got something on your butt." 2) (sin. cig) Cigarrillo. *Ej.* "Anyone want a butt?" 3) *one's butt:* Uno mismo, a menudo usado en forma peyorativa. *Ej.* "I need to get off my butt and get serious about life."

43

BUTT IN TO: *exp-v.* Interrumpir una conversación o inmiscuirse en asuntos ajenos. *Ej.* "We weren't talking to you, so don't butt in to our conversation."

BUTT LOAD: [Vul.] *adj.* Un montón de (ej. gente, libros, etc.) *Ej.* "What a butt load of bills to pay!" Or "I've got a butt load of work to do."

BUTT NAKED: (sin. birthday suit) *exp.* Desnudo. *Ej.* "I'm telling you, he was butt naked when I walked into his room."

BUTT OUT: *exp.* No intervenir, no entrometerse en algo, gen. dicho como orden. *Ej.* "Hey, butt out, this is none of your business!"

BUTTER SOMEONE UP: (sin. butter up to someone) *exp-v.* Adular servilmente para lograr un propósito o halagar a alguien con fines interesados, gen. para aprovecharse de esa persona. *Ej.* "He's trying to butter you up so you'll lend him the car for the weekend."

BUTTER UP TO SOMEONE: VER butter someone up.

BUTTER WOULD NOT MELT IN ONE'S MOUTH: *exp.* Se dice de una persona santurrona. *Ej.* "He's such a goody-goody, butter wouldn't melt in his mouth."

BUTTERFLIES: *s.* Una sensación de nervios o hasta nauseas gen. causada al anticipar ansiosamente una ocasión. *Ej.* "I always get the butterflies before speaking in public."

BUTTON ONE'S LIP: (sin. lips sealed) *exp-v.* Mantener silencio con respecto a cierta información. Esp. callarse por temor a las consecuencias de repetir la información. *Ej.* "You'd better button your lip and pay attention!"

BUTTON PUSHER: *s.* Persona que intencionalmente toca temas delicados para incomodar a alguien. *Ej.* "She's a button pusher who'll make you sorry for any weakness she knows of."

BUTTON UP: *exp-v.* Mantener silencio, no hablar, esp. no emitir una opinión. *Ej.* "He got so angry when I disagreed with him that I decided it was better to button up and discuss it later."

BUTTONS TO PUSH: *exp.* Tocar temas delicados para incomodar a alguien. *Ej.* "He knows what

CAKe wAlk

buttons to push to make me cry."

BUTTONS: VER *push (someone's) buttons*.

BUUNY: VER *do bunny*.

BUY: *vi.* 1) Aceptar la verdad o una posibilidad. *Ej.* "Cops never buy my excuses for speeding, but at least they laugh." 2) Sobornar. *Ej.* "You won't be able to buy her vote, she's a straight shooter."

BUY IT: *exp-vi.* Morir o matarse. *Ej.* "He bought it when he tried to be like Superman and leap from tall buildings." VER *waste*.

BUY OFF: *exp-vi.* Sobornar para obtener trato especial o preferencia o para evadir intromisión o enjuiciamiento en las actividades de uno. *Ej.* "He was arrested for trying to buy off a public official."

BUY THE FARM: *exp-vi.* Morirse. *Ej.* "Poor guy bought the farm right after he retired." VER *kick the bucket*.

BUZZ: 1) *s.* Leve y agradable intoxicación, de alcohol o de drogas. *Ej.* "I got a buzz from one beer." 2) *v.* Llamar por teléfono. *Ej.* "I should buzz my folks to tell them I arrived safely." 3) *s.* Una llamada telefónica. *Ej.* "I need to give my old lady a buzz."

BUZZ OFF: *int.* ¡Córrete! *Ej.* "Buzz off you snot-nosed loser!"

BY A HAIR: (sin. *close-call*) *exp.* Salvarse, escaparse por poco. *Ej.* "We escaped that accident by a hair".

BY THE SKIN OF ONE'S TEETH: *exp.* Escapar del peligro o lograr algo dentro de un pequeño margen. *Ej.* "I escaped getting caught by the skin of my teeth."

C

CADDY: *abr.* Cadillac; vehículo norteamericano grande y lujoso. *Ej.* "Hey, did you hear Joey bought a Caddy?"

CADET: VER *space cadet*.

CAIN: VER *rasie Cain*.

CAKE: VER *cut oneself a bigger piece of the cake; eat one's cake and have it too; icing on the cake; piece of cake*.

CAKE WALK: *s.* Algo sumamente fácil de hacer, esp. algo que trae un gran y/o deseable premio. *Ej.* "No, it was a cake walk getting it all done. I went to one place and

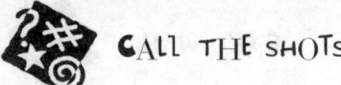
CALL THE SHOTS

they had everything." Or "Her life was a cake walk after winning the multi-million dollar lottery."

CALL THE SHOTS: *exp-v.* Tomar el mando o controlar una situación o grupo. *Ej.* "Listen pal, there's only one person who calls the shots here, and that's me."

CALLING CARD: *s.* La marca típica o de identificación, seña o característica por la cual se identifica a alguien. *Ej.* "Yeah, the velvet glove is our robber's calling card."

CAMEL: VER *straw that broke the camel's back.*

CAN: *v.* 1) (sin. fire) Despedir del trabajo o del colegio. *Ej.* "They canned me at work today." Or "Stan got canned for mouthing off to the boss." 2) Dejar de hacer algo. Gen. se usa en el imperativo. *Ej.* "I told you to be quiet, so can it!" 3) Gluteus maximus, las nalgas. 4) can /the/: *s.* Excusado. VER *throne /the/.*

CAN OF WORMS: *s.* Una fuente de imprevistos complejos y problemáticos. *Ej.* "Getting this book published has been a real can of worms."

CANCER STICK: *s.* Cigarrillo. *Ej.* "You're gonna kill yourself with those cancer sticks."

CANDY ASS: [Vul.] *s.* Una persona tímida, poco atrevida. *Ej.* "He's such a candy ass he doesn't even jaywalk."

CANNOT STAND SOMEONE: *exp-v.* Tenerle una aversión o gran antipatía a alguien. *Ej.* "I can't stand him. He's got such a dirty mind it gives me the creeps."

CAP: *v.* Matar a tiros. *Ej.* "You're gonna get your ass capped if you mess with the Chinese mob."

CARD: *v.* VERificar la identificación de alguien, esp. para comprobar su edad legal para admitirlo a un bar, un club, etc. *Ej.* "I'm 30, and they still card me at the pub." VER TAMBIEN *calling card; keep one's cards close to one's chest; play one's cards right.*

CARRY ON: *exp-v.* 1) Comportarse mal. *Ej.* "The students carried on throughout the class, making life a living hell for the substitute teacher." 2) Hablar demasiado. *Ej.* "He's such a boor. He carried on about his new car throughout the

CATCH HELL

meal."

CARRYING: *adj.* 1) Portar un arma oculta. *Ej.* "Frisk him to see if he's carrying." 2) Traer consigo drogas ilegales. *Ej.* "He was carrying when he crossed the border."

CASE: VER basket case; nut case; off someone's case; on someone's case.

CASE THE JOINT: *exp-v.* Investigar un lugar examinándolo cuidadosamente con el fin de determinar su contenido y/o rutina. Gen. lo dicen criminales que investigan un lugar escogido como blanco para robar. *Ej.* "It looks like the thieves cased the joint pretty good. They knew the guard's schedule and the exact location of the jewels."

CASH COW: *s.* Un negocio de alta rentabilidad, a menudo empleado por la compañía matriz para financiar otros negocios menos rentables. *Ej.* "This business is a cash cow that I use to fund my developmental projects."

CASH IN ONE'S CHIPS: *exp-v.* "Soltar la maleta"; Forma sarcástica de referirse a la muerte. Morirse. *Ej.* "Well, Paul finally cashed in his chips after 85 years." VER *kick the bucket*.

CAT: *s.* Una persona, esp. un hombre. *Ej.* "Tell that cat to get a move on, we're late." VER TAMBIEN *look what the cat dragged in; scardy cat; let the cat out of the bag; get the cat by the tail; fat cat*.

CAT CALLS: *s.* Comentarios groseros generalmente de naturaleza sexual, típicos de los maestros de la construcción, dirigidos a peatones, gen. femeninos. *Ej.* "I think my husband's loosing it. Now he makes cat calls when I get out of the shower."

CAT NAP: VER *catch a few winks*.

CAT'S MEOW /THE/: *exp.* Persona o cosa excelente, superior o sumamente deseable. *Ej.* "Getting a back massage is the cat's meow."

CATCH A FEW WINKS: (sin. catch a little shuteye) *exp-vi.* Dormir un rato. *Ej.* "I'm really beat, I need to catch a few winks if I'm going to go out tonight."

CATCH A LITTLE SHUTEYE: VER *catch a few winks*.

CATCH HELL: *exp-vi.* Recibir, o ser

CATCH ONE'S EYE

objeto de críticas o injurias fuertes y mordaces. Ej. "Susan caught hell for smashing her mom's car."

CATCH ONE'S EYE: *exp-vi.* Parecerle muy atractivo a alguien en un momento dado. Ej. "I was walking down the street when she caught my eye."

CATCH SHIT FROM: [Vul.] *exp-vi.* Que le griten o critiquen severamente a uno. Ej. "Boy did I catch shit from my wife for coming home drunk and smelling of perfume. She's so over-sensitive!"

CATCH SOMEONE RED HANDED: (sin. catch someone with one's hands in the cookie jar/till) *exp-vi.* Pillar a alguien en el acto de hacer algo ilegal o prohibido. Ej. "I caught her red handed as she was taking money from my purse."

CATCH SOMEONE WITH ONE'S HANDS IN THE COOKIE JAR: VER catch someone red handed.

CATCH SOMEONE WITH ONE'S HANDS IN THE TILL: VER catch someone red handed.

CATCH SOMEONE WITH ONE'S PANTS DOWN: *exp-vi.* Encontrar a alguien en una situación vergonzosa o comprometedora. Ej. "The senator got caught with his pants down when a photographer took pictures of him receiving a bribe from a lobbyist."

CATCH UP WITH (SOME)ONE: *exp-vi.* 1) Final e inevitablemente tener problemas originados en una acción del pasado. Ej. "You keep on

CATCH SOMEONE WITH ONE'S PANTS DOWN

CHEAT ON

smoking and eventually it's going to catch up with you." 2) Ponerse al día con noticias de otro. Ej. "I want to catch up with Julie; I haven't talked to her in weeks."

CATCH-22: *exp.* Un problema sin solución. Una situación en que todas las alternativas llevan a consecuencias negativas o indeseables. Ej. "If I don't tell him, he'll be mad he heard it from someone else, but if I do tell him, he'll resent me for having told him. What a catch-22!"

CATHOLIC: VER *is the Pope Catholic?*

CATHOUSE: *s.* Un burdel. Ej. "They found the sailor at a cathouse."

CAUSE: *abr.* Because = Porque. Ej. "I can't go 'cause I got work to do."

CENT: VER *red cent; two cents in.*

CHAIN: VER *ball and chain; pull someone's chain.*

CHAIR: *s.* La silla eléctrica, usada para ejecuciones. Ej. "If you don't tell us who did it, it's gonna be the chair for you, Sam." VER TAMBIEN *take the chair out from underneath one.*

CHANGE /THE/: *exp.* Pubertad. Ej. "It must be the change. He's put his toys away and is interested in girls. I guess it's time I explain the birds and the bees."

CHANGE ONE'S STRIPES: *exp-v.* Cambiar la afiliación y/o asociación para ser popular. Ej. "Show some backbone! Don't go changing your stripes every time popular opinion changes."

CHANNEL SURF: *exp.* Cambiar constantemente el canal de televisión o radio con control remoto. Ej. "Are you just gonna sit around and channel surf all day?"

CHARGE AN ARM AND A LEG: *exp-v.* Cobrar demasiado dinero por algo. Ej. "Ten smackeroos for a soda! This places charges an arm and a leg."

CHARM: VER *third time's the charm /the/.*

CHASE SKIRTS: *exp-v.* Perseguir mujeres, ser mujeriego. Ej. "The guy is 60 years old, ugly as sin and still chasing skirts. When will he ever stop?"

CHEAPSKATE: VER *tight fisted.*

CHEAT ON: *exp-v.* Serle infiel a la esposa, marido o amante. Ej. "He

49

CHECK IN

left her after he found out that she'd been cheating on him with her dentist."

CHECK IN: *exp-v.* Llamar por teléfono al novio/a o al marido/mujer ya sea para decir que uno esta bien, o dónde uno esta. También puede ser una manera de controlar las acciones del otro. *Ej.* "Excuse me guys, I've got to check in with the old lady."

CHECK OUT: *exp-v.* 1) Examinar, inspeccionar, investigar. *Ej.* "There's something suspicious about that place. Let's check it out." 2) Morirse. *Ej.* "You pay us back or you're gonna check out a lot sooner than you'd like."

CHECKERED PAST: *exp.* Un pasado poco halagador, o sea, manchado de hechos inmorales o ilegales. *Ej.* "I don't know how the Senator got elected with his checkered past."

CHEEK: *s.* 1) Cualquiera de las nalgas. *Ej.* "Your cheek is red." 2) Impertinencia insolente o una comentario atrevido. *Ej.* "You give me any cheek and you'll be washing dishes for the next week." VER TAMBIEN *tongue in cheek*.

CHEEKY: *adj.* Atrevido. *Ej.* "Fifteen years old and already getting cheeky with his father. That's not a good sign." (Ing.)

CHEESE: VER *cut the cheese; big cheese /the/*.

CHEESY: *adj.* Sin gusto, de baja clase, esp. imitación cursi de estilo elegante. *Ej.* "He gave his wife such a cheesy gift for her b'day - a vacuum cleaner."

CHERRY: 1) *adj.* Excelente, fantástico, esp. algo en una condición perfecta. *Ej.* "The waves were cherry today." VER *awesome.* 2) *s.* El himen. Gen. se usa como *pop someone's cherry. Ej.* "So, is it true he popped her cherry?"

CHEW OUT: *exp-v.* Retar, regañar severamente. *Ej.* "My mom chewed me out for coming home late."

CHEW THE CUD: *exp-v.* Reflexionar, meditar (nota de ed: Piense en una vaca tranquilamente rumiando, viendo pasar el mundo sin ninguna preocupación; ¡ahora comprende la etim. y el significado de la expresión!) *Ej.* "I was chewing the cud over whether I'd plant carrots or broccoli this season."

CHEW THE FAT: *exp-v.* Conversar de manera amistosa, relajada y extendida. Ej. "I love having time to chew the fat with a good friend."

CHICK: *s.* Mujer, tipa. Ej. "That's a cute chick over there." VER *gal*.

CHICKEN FEED: *s.* Una cantidad insignificante de dinero. Ej. "100 dollars a week in wages, that's chicken feed!"

CHICKEN: 1) *s.* Un cobarde. Ej. "You're a chicken if you don't come with us." VER *yellow-belly*. 2) *s.* Una competencia realmente estúpida en que los concursantes hacen cosas muy peligrosas (típicamente dos autos se enfrentan) hasta que uno de ellos se arrepiente y cambia su curso o se detiene. Ej. "They're gonna play chicken with cars? What idiots!" 3) *adj.* Miedoso, asustado, cobarde. Ej. "Are you feeling too chicken to jump in the water?" VER TAMBIEN *count one's chickens before they've hatched /don't/; spring chicken*.

CHICKEN OUT: *exp-v.* Dejar o abandonar un plan debido a miedo. Ej. "Where's Bob?" "He chickened out and refused to come."

CHICKEN-SHIT: [Vul.] *exp.* 1) Disparate insignificante, despreciable y trivial. Ej. "Don't give me these chicken-shit excuses." 2) Cobarde, miedoso. Ej. "Don't even bother to invite him, he's too chicken-shit to go out at night."

CHILL: 1) *v.* Relajarse, tranquilizarse. Ej. "Chill man, you're so uptight you're making me nervous." 2) *adj.* Bueno, divertido, entretenido. Ej. "We had a chill time at the party. There were some sweet babes and plenty of brew." 3) *chilling*: *int.* Se dice respondiendo a un *how are you?*, significando bien: ni demasiado bien ni mal. Ej. "How's it going bro?" "I'm chillin'."

CHILL OUT: *int.* Un pedido a alguien para que desista en una actividad. Ej. "Chill out dude, you're going to get us in trouble if you don't be quiet."

CHIMNEY: VER *smoke like a chimney*.

CHIN: Ver *keep one's chin up*; *take it on the chin*.

CHINK

CHINK: s. Chino. (Desp.) Ej. "Let's go get some chink food."

CHIP OFF THE OLD BLOCK /BE A/: exp-vi. Se dice de un hijo que demuestra alguna característica de un padre. Ej. "He's going into the shoe business just like his old man. He's a chip off the old block."

CHIP ON ONE'S SHOULDER: exp. Un actitud de resentimiento en una persona que lo lleva a tener un aire desagradable, frecuentemente acompañado de comentarios o referencias al respecto Ej. "He still has a chip on his shoulder about having been unfairly dismissed."

CHISEL: (sin. burn*, cross, do someone dirty, gyp*, hustle*, scam*, screw*, skin*, snooker, stick, suck in) v. Engañar o estafar. Ej. "Don't try to chisel me out of my money."

CHISELER: s. Tramposo o estafador. Ej. "I don't want to deal with that guy, he's a chiseler."

CHOMPING AT THE BIT: exp-v. Estar impaciente por actuar. Ej. "He's chomping at the bit to get going on the project."

CHOP SHOP: exp. Un lugar donde se desarman los autos robados para vender sus piezas. Ej. "They stole his car and took it to a chop shop."

CHOP-CHOP: (on the double) adv. Hacer algo en forma muy rápida y/o inmediata. Ej. "Chop-chop, let's go!"

CHOPPER: 1) s. Una motocicleta, esp. una en que hay una gran distancia entre la rueda delantera y el asiento. Ej. "What a cool looking chopper!" 2) Helicóptero. Ej. "Talk about style, the guy takes a chopper to work every day." 3) choppers: s.pl. Dientes, a menudo una dentadura. Ej. "The old man left his choppers at the restaurant."

CHOPS /THE/: s. Mandíbula o área alrededor de la boca. Ej. "He got hit right in the chops."

CHOW: 1) s. Comida. Ej. "I'm ready for some chow." 2) v. Comer. Ej. "It's time to chow." Or "We chowed at Bill's house."

CHOW DOWN: exp. Comer, especialmente gran cantidad. Ej. "I'm starving! I can't wait to chow down!"

CHRONIC: s. Marihuana de bueno

CLASS ACT

calidad y muy potente. *Ej.* "We got wasted smoking the chronic."

CHUCK UP: (sin. lose one's lunch, upchuck, toss one's cookies, pray to the porcelain goddess, blow chunks, hurl, boot*, ralph, yuke, barf*, puke*) *v.* Vomitar. *Ej.* "The little twerp chucked up all over the carpet."

CHUG: *v.* Beber con grandes tragos. *Ej.* "I was so thirsty I chugged a whole bottle of water."

CHUGALUG: *v.* Tragar de una vez, gen. refiriéndose a una cerveza. *Ej.* "He's awesome! He can chugalug a whole beer!"

CHUTZPA: *adj.* Audacia, osadía, gen. usado en sentido positivo. *Ej.* "He might be a pain in the butt, but you have to admire his chutzpa."

CIG: (sin. cancer stick, butt*, smoke*) *s.* Cigarrillo. *Ej.* "Hey Franky, pass me a cig."

CINCH: 1) *s.* Algo muy fácil de hacer o lograr. *Ej.* "It's a cinch climbing the hill." 2) *s.* Certeza de ganar o ser victorioso. *Ej.* "They're a cinch to win the championship." 3) *v.* Asegurar el triunfo de. *Ej.* "He cinched the victory with 3 goals."

CIRCULAR FILE: *s.* Un basurero. *Ej.* "Put all of that junk mail in the circular file."

CITY: *adj.* Una situación, experiencia, lugar o cosa que implica mucho de algo. *Ej.* "What a party! This is fun city!"

CLAM: *s.* Dólar. *Ej.* "Ellen has a few clams in the bank." VER *buck*.

CLAM UP: *exp-v.* Negarse a hablar, esp. a dar información. *Ej.* "He clammed up as soon as we arrested him."

CLAMBAKE: *s.* Gran fiesta o celebración, gen. con mariscos (a menudo almejas y otros mariscos preparados en la playa en la arena) y bebida. *Ej.* "We're going to have a clambake this Saturday."

CLAP: [Vul.] *s.* Gonorrea. *Ej.* "He got the clap from some hoe."

CLAP SOMEONE'S ASS: [Vul.] *exp-v.* Matar a alguien. *Ej.* "After what he's done to my family I ought to clap his ass!" VER *waste*.

CLASS ACT: *s.* 1) Persona de calidad superior y distinción, esp. de gran integridad. *Ej.* "That guy is a real class act. He buys presents

53

CLEAN

for all his employees and gives six months of maternity leave." 2) Acción o comportamiento digno de elogios. *Ej.* "Helping those old ladies was a class act."

CLEAN: *adj.* 1) Sin llevar armas o drogas ocultas. *Ej.* "Yo cops, I'm clean, I ain't got no weapons!" 2) Libre de un enviciamiento a narcóticos. *Ej.* "I've been clean for six months now." 3) Inocente de un crimen sospechado. *Ej.* "He's clean. We established his alibi at the time of the crime." 4) *come clean*: Confesar, contar la verdad. *Ej.* "Come clean Hank and it'll be easier for you with the judge."

CLEAN AS A WHISTLE: *exp.* Muy limpio. *Ej.* "You're not leaving here till this place is clean as a whistle."

CLEAN HOUSE: *exp-v.* Deshacerse de aquello que es indeseable. *Ej.* "The police precinct had better clean house before another scandal erupts."

CLEAN ONE'S CLOCK: *exp-v.* Golpear a alguien, gen. muy severamente. *Ej.* "He cleaned his clock with a few left hooks." VER beat someone up.

CLEAN OUT: *exp-v.* Sacar o perder todo el dinero o riqueza material. *Ej.* "I got cleaned out at the casino."

CLEAN UP: *exp-v.* Generar grandes ganancias, a menudo dentro de poco tiempo. *Ej.* "I cleaned up in the stock market this month."

CLEANERS: VER take to the cleaners.

CLICK: *v.* 1) Tener gran éxito. *Ej.* "Our business really clicked after the publicity campaign." 2) Avenirse muy bien, esp. formar una amistad instantánea con un desconocido. *Ej.* "I met this guy I really clicked with last night." 3) Aclarar, entender; finalmente percibir o comprender. *Ej.* "It took a while to understand the concept of postmodernism, but then suddenly it all clicked."

CLIMB THE WALLS: *exp-v.* 1) Estar sumamente aburrido, casi desesperadamente. *Ej.* "My plane was delayed five hours. I was so bored I was ready to start climbing the walls!" 2) Estar demasiado ansioso o nervioso. *Ej.* "Waiting for the medical results, I was practically climbing the walls."

COCKAMAMIE

CLINK /THE/: (sin. tank, lock up, big house /the/, joint /the/, slammer, cooler, pen) s. Prisión, cárcel. Ej. "What did you get sent to the clink for?"

CLIP: v. 1) Robar. Ej. "The bastard clipped my radio." VER swipe. 2) Cobrar demasiado, estafar. Ej. "Don't buy from that store, they always clip you."

CLIT: [Vul.] s. El clítoris.

CLOBBER: v. 1) Golpear en forma violenta y repetida. Ej. "You'll get clobbered fighting him." VER beat someone up. 2) Derrotar en forma decisiva. Ej. "The team got clobbered." VER smear. 3) Criticar duramente. Ej. "The teacher clobbered my paper."

BE ON CLOUD NINE

CLOCK CLEANED /ONE'S/: exp. Recibir golpes severos. Ej. "He got his clock cleaned fighting a bigger guy." VER TAMBIEN clean one's clock.

CLOSE CALL: (sin. by a hair) exp. Salvarse, escaparse por poco. Ej. "That was a close call, you arrived just a minute before mom got home."

CLOSET: VER out of the closet; skeletons in the closet.

CLOUD NINE /BE ON/: exp-vi. Sensación de levedad debido a la felicidad. gen. al estar enamorado. Ej. "I was on cloud nine when she said she'd marry me."

CLUELESS: adj. El no entender o seguir los códigos sociales. Ej. "Joe must be clueless to be flirting with the boss's wife."

C-NOTE: s. Billete de cien dólares. Ej. "Can you spot me a c-note till Friday?"

COALS: VER rake someone over the coals.

COCK: [Vul.] s. El pene.

COCKAMAMIE: adj. Ridículo, ab-

COCKSUCKER

surdo. *Ej. "Recycle condoms? Now, that's a cockamamie idea."*

COCKSUCKER: [Vul.] s. 1) Persona o cosa molestosa. *Ej. "I can't get this cocksucker to work properly!"* 2) Persona muy mala, despreciable. *Ej. "That cocksucker better not show his face around here or I'll give him some free plastic surgery!"* 3) Alguien que realiza felonía.

COCKTEASE: [Vul.] s. Mujer que coquetea para excitar sexualmente a un hombre pero no realiza el acto sexual. *Ej. "She's a cocktease. You're never going to get any action from her."*

COFFEE: VER *wake up and smell the coffee.*

COIN: VER *other side of the coin.*

COKE: (sin. blow*, flake*, snow) s. Cocaína.

COLD FEET /GET/: *exp-vi.* Echarse para atrás; arrepentirse de comprometerse a algo. *Ej. "Henry's not going with us. He got cold feet yesterday after talking it over with his wife."*

COLD FEET /HAVE/: *exp-vi.* Tener miedo o arrepentirse de hacer algo, por temor a que no resulte. *Ej. "The guy's a chicken. He has cold feet about leaving his job to work in a start-up computer company."*

COLD ONE: s. Cerveza. VER *brew.*

COLLAR: 1) s. Una detención, como en el caso de un criminal. *Ej. "It was a big collar, worthy of a promotion."* 2) v. Capturar, detener o arrestar. *Ej. "Collar him before he skips town."*

COLORS: VER *show one's true colors.*

COME: [Vul.] vi. Tener un orgasmo. *Ej. "I saw stars when I came."*

COME ACROSS: *exp-vi.* 1) Pagar dinero exigido. *Ej. "You come across with the dough or else!"* 2) Dar una impresión. *Ej. "He comes across as a smart guy."*

COME DOWN ON: *exp-vi.* Castigar o regañar severamente y a menudo con fuerza. *Ej. "My mom came down on me like a ton of bricks for failing math."*

COME DOWN: *exp-vi.* Perder la sensación de alegría, esp. perder el efecto de una droga o estimulante. *Ej. "He came down hard after snorting coke all night."*

COME HELL OR HIGH WATER: *exp-vi.* Suceder u ocurrir sin importar las circunstancias. *Ej.* "I'll be at the wedding come hell or high water."

COME HOME: *exp-vi.* Volver a penar a uno. *Ej.* "You mess with guns and it will come home to you."

COME OFF IT: *exp.* Dejar de actuar tontamente o exageradamente, o dejar de hablar en forma pretenciosa o tonta. A menudo se usa en el imperativo. *Ej.* "Come off it, who do you think you are, the king?"

COME ON: *int.* No puedes hablar en serio. *Ej.* "Come on, there's no way you're going to be an astronaut, you have problems just adding two numbers together." VER TAMBIEN *come-on*.

COME ON TO: *exp-vi.* Coquetear con alguien, demostrar un interés sexual. *Ej.* "I'm married. Don't try to come on to me."

COME UNGLUED: *exp-vi.* Perder la compostura o control emocional. *Ej.* "I came unglued when I found out Princess Diana had died."

COME-ON: *s.* Un acercamiento o propuesta romántico/a o sexual. *Ej.* "What kind of loser uses the come-on, 'what sign are you?'" VER TAMBIEN *come on*.

CON: 1) *v.* Estafar a alguien después de ganar su confianza. *Ej.* "Don't try to con me, I know your game." 2) *s.* Una estafa. *Ej.* "It's a simple rule in life. Anytime someone tells you that you'll make fast money with your investment, you can be damn sure that it's a con." 3) *adj.* Relacionado a o implicando una estafa o fraude. *Ej.* Con job, con artist, con game, etc. 4) *s.* Un presidiario, un convicto. *Ej.* "Nobody wants to hire an ex-con for a job."

CON MAN: (sin. *rip-off artist*) *s.* Persona que intenta quitarle dinero a otros por medios ilegales como estafas financieras. *Ej.* "She married a con man and lost a fortune."

CONK: 1) *s.* Un golpe, frecuentemente a la cabeza. *Ej.* "That looks like more than a conk on the head. It might be a concussion." 2) *v.* Golpear o pegar, a menudo en la cabeza. *Ej.* "I conked myself on the head when I went to look out the window."

CONk OUT

CONK OUT: *v.* 1) Dejar de funcionar. *Ej.* "My motor conked out. I need to take it to a mechanic." 2) Quedarse dormido, a menudo inesperada y repentinamente. *Ej.* "I was so tired I conked out on the bus."

CONNECTION: (sin. an in) *s.* Un contacto que le permite a uno recibir un trato especial o ciertos privilegios. *Ej.* "The game is sold out? No problem, I've got a great connection for getting tickets."

contract: VER *put a contract out on.*

cook: *v.* 1) Adelantar o avanzar muy bien. *Ej.* "I was cooking on my novel." 2) *cooking:* Ocurriendo, sucediendo. *Ej.* "What's cooking tonight? Any parties?"

cook the books: *exp-v.* Falsificar registros financieros con fines ilegales. *Ej.* "They cooked the books to hide the loses from investors."

COOK UP: *exp-v.* Contar un cuento. Inventar una historia falsa. *Ej.* "She must have cooked up some tale to not get in trouble after being caught red handed."

COOKIE: *s.* 1) Persona de carácter bien definido. *Ej.* "He's a tough cookie. You don't want to mess with him." 2) Mensaje electrónico de la red/internet mandado de un sitio/home page a un usuario. *Ej.* "It's so annoying. Some porno company keeps sending me cookies." VER TAMBIEN *catch someone with one's hands in the cookie jar; that's the way the cookie crumbles; toss one's cookies; tough cookie.*

COOL: (sin. neat) *adj.* 1) Expresión que refleja satisfacción con un objeto, persona o idea. Describe aprobación de película, música, etc. *Ej.* "The professor is a cool guy." Or "The movie was so cool!" 2) Un objeto o idea que esta muy de moda o del cual se tiene una alta opinión. *Ej.* "It's cool to like disco again." Or "I think it's cool that he wants to be a ballerina." VER TAMBIEN *blow one's cool; keep one's cool; lose one's cool; play it cool; uncool.*

COOL IT: *int.* 1) ¡Cálmate!, ¡relájate! *Ej.* "You need to cool it with your work or you'll die an early death." 2) Dejar de hacer o decir algo, generalmente desagradable. A menudo se usa en el imperativo. *Ej.* "I

COTTON PICKING

don't want to hear any more back talk, so just cool it!"

COOL ONE'S HEELS: *exp-v.* Esperar o que lo dejen a uno esperando. *Ej.* "I know you're impatient, but you just have to cool your heels and wait."

COOL OUT: *exp-v.* Calmarse, relajarse, esp. permitir que pase la ira de uno. A menudo usado en el imperativo. *Ej.* "You had better cool out before you talk to her." Or "Cool out dude, we'll be there soon."

COOLER: *s.* La cárcel. *Ej.* "You're gonna have a lot of time to think about your mistake in the cooler." Ver *clink /the/*.

COON: *s.* Un afroamericano, una persona negra. (Desp.) Ver *darky*.

COOTIES: *s.pl.* Literalmente piojos del curepo, pero se usa en lenguaje infantil para describir un catagio imaginario. *Ej.* "Stay away from her, she's got cooties!"

COP: 1) (sin. *fuzz /the/, heat /the/*) *s.* Policía. (Desp.) *Ej.* "Some damn cop pulled me over for speeding!" 2) *v.* Adquirir, obtener algo, de menudo sin comprarlo. *Ej.* "I want to cop some dope for the weekend." Or "He copped a buzz."

COP A FEEL: *exp-v.* Acariciar sin permiso y de una forma mal intencionada, o tocar las partes pudendas, o partes naturales de una persona. *Ej.* "She slapped him for copping a feel."

COP A PLEA: *exp-v.* Declararse culpable por un cargo menor para evitar un juicio por un cargo mayor. *Ej.* "Here's the deal; you cop a plea and we reduce the charge to manslaughter. Otherwise you're looking at the chair."

COP OUT: 1) *v.* No cumplir o evadir responsabilidades o un compromiso. *Ej.* "Don't cop out, you said you were going to do it." 2) *s.* Una persona que hace esto. *Ej.* "You can't trust him, he's a cop out."

COPE: *v.* Aguantar, soportar, manejar una situación. *Ej.* "There's a lot of pressure, are you sure you can cope?"

CORK: VER *put a cork in it*.

COTTON PICKING: *exp.* Se usa para denotar la característica extrema, intensa de algo. *Ej.* "He's a cotton picking fool!" Or "Get your cotton picking hands off me!"

COUCH POTATO

COUCH POTATO: (sin. lazy bones) exp. Persona muy perezosa o desganada. Ej. "My son may not be a rocket scientist, but at least he's not a couch potato."

COUGH UP: exp-v. Soltar información o algo, esp. dinero, que no se quiere entregar. Ej. "All right Al, cough up the dough before we beat it out of you." Or "I know you took my book, so cough it up."

COUNT ONE'S CHICKENS BEFORE THEY'VE HATCHED /DON'T/: exp-v. Recomendación para esperar un resultado positivo antes de planificar el paso siguiente, esp. si se trata de gastar dinero. Ej. "I think I'm going to get the job, but I'm not going to buy anything until I do. I just don't want to count my chickens before they've hatched."

COW: VER cash cow; have a cow; holy cow.

COYOTE: s. Contrabandista de inmigrantes a los Estados Unidos desde México. Ej. "The border patrol caught a coyote bringing ten people across the border."

CRABBY: adj. De mal humor, descontento. Ej. "Why are you so crabby today? Did you have a bad night's sleep?"

CRABS: s.pl. Piojos del pubis. Ej. "He says he got the crabs from a public toilet…yeah right!"

CRACK: 1) s. Cocaína que se fuma. Ej. "They were smoking crack in the basement." 2) s. Una observación, un comentario. Ej. "No more cracks about my hair cut." 3) v. Contar, decir. Ej. "He cracks too many jokes."

CRACK UP: exp-v. 1) Perder la estabilidad mental y tener un colapso mental y/o físico. Ej. "One day he was fine and the next he cracked up." 2) Reírse con ganas, experimentar o provocar hilaridad. Ej. "Steve Martin makes me crack up." 3) Chocar, destruir. Ej. "The bastard cracked up my car."

CRACKER: s. Persona blanca pobre de zona rural, esp. el sudeste de los EE.UU. (Desp.) Ej. "The crackers in that town still give black folk a whole lot of trouble."

CRACKERJACK: s. Un experto, una persona que desempeña su trabajo con pericia. Gen. se usa antes del nombre de tal actividad. Ej.

"You'll need a crackerjack mechanic to fix that car."

CRADLE: VER *rob the cradle.*

CRAP: [Vul.] 1) s. Excremento. *Ej.* "There was dog crap on her shoe." 2) s. Una mentira, una distorción de la verdad. *Ej.* "That's a load of crap! You know that's not true." 3) Tareas o exigencias fastidiosas o aburridas. *Ej.* "I have a lot of crap to do at work." 4) s. Cosas, posesiones, esp. las de uno. *Ej.* "I have to clean up my crap before my girlfriend arrives." 5) s. Trato malo o injusto. *Ej.* "I quit because my boss treated me like crap." 6) *int.* Expresión de molestia, frustración y/o enojo. *Ej.* "Crap! My in-laws are coming over." VER TAMBIEN *give a crap.*

CRAP OUT: [Vul.] *exp-v.* Retirarse de una actividad o plan, gen. por perder entusiasmo o asustarse. *Ej.* "We can ask him to come along, but I'm sure he'll crap out."

CRAP SHOOT: *exp.* Un acto arriesgado. (etim. de un juego de azar con dados). *Ej.* "Falling in love with him, a notorious philanderer, was a crap shoot."

CRAPPER: [Vul.] (sin. *shitter*) s. Excusado. *Ej.* "You got any reading material in the crapper?"

CRAPPY: [Vul.] *adj.* 1) Malo, inferior, de baja calidad. *Ej.* "What a crappy movie! My kid sister could've done a better job." 2) Horrible, despreciable. *Ej.* "He's a crappy teacher. He's so boring we all fall asleep during his lectures." 3) Indispuesto, con mala salud o sintiéndose mal. *Ej.* "I feel crappy. I think I have the flu."

CRACK UP

CRASH

CRASH: 1) (sin. come down) *s.* Experimentar un período de depresión como resultado del término de los efectos narcóticos de las drogas. *Ej.* "I need some more junk, man, I'm starting to crash." 2) *v.* Encontrar alojamiento o refugio provisional gratis, gen. por una noche. *Ej.* "Can I crash at your place tonight?" 3) *v.* Dormirse. *Ej.* "I'm so tired I have to crash." 4) *v.* Entrar sin invitación, gen. a una fiesta. *Ej.* "Let's go crash that black tie party." 5) *s.* Se caracteriza por un esfuerzo intensivo para producir o lograr algo. *Ej.* "I need to take a crash course in basic Algebra if I'm going to pass the test." 6) *s.* Una falla seria de computadora que resulta en la pérdida de memoria o peor. *Ej.* "I lost a year's work when my computer crashed".

CRASH AND BURN: *exp-v.* Fracasar miserablemente y totalmente. *Ej.* "Not only did he not pass the test, he crashed and burned on it!"

CRASH PAD: *s.* Un lugar gratis pero provisional para quedarse y alojar. *Ej.* "Everyone seems to think my house is a crash pad."

CRAZY: 1) *adj.* Maravilloso, estupendo, fantástico. *Ej.* "He's one crazy fine man!" 2) *like crazy:* En grado sumo. *Ej.* "I'm working like crazy on this damn book!"

CREAM: *v.* 1) Derrotar abrumadoramente. *Ej.* "The Knicks creamed the Bulls last night." VER *smear.* 2) Golpear severamente. *Ej.* "The bully creamed the nerd in a fight." VER *beat someone up.* 3) [Vul.] Eyacular. *Ej.* "I got so excited I nearly creamed in my pants."

CREEK: VER *up a creek without a paddle /be/; up shit creek without a paddle /be/.*

CREEP: *s.* 1) Persona repulsiva o sumamente desagradable. *Ej.* "I don't like her. I think she's a creep." 2) *creeps /the/:* Sensación de miedo o repugnancia como si cientos de insectos caminarán sobre la piel. *Ej.* "This house gives me the creeps. It's so old and abandoned there are probably ghosts here."

CRIB: (sin. pad) *s.* El departamento, dormitorio, habitacion de uno. *Ej.* "Steve only likes to hang in his crib."

CRIB SHEET: s. Un papel que contiene información que se usa para hacer trampa en una prueba o examen. *Ej.* "I'll never pass the test unless I bring a crib sheet."

CROAK: v. Morirse. *Ej.* "You'll croak if you drink that poison."

CROCK: s. Discurso absurdo, esp. cuento falso o exagerado. *Ej.* "That's a load of crock! I know you've never been to Africa."

CROCK OF SHIT: [Vul.] *exp.* Habla absurda, esp. cuento falso o exagerado. *Ej.* "His story is a crock of shit."

CROSS: v. Engañar o estafar. *Ej.* "He crossed his friend just to make a few bucks."

CRUD: 1) s. Mugre, suciedad o basura, gen. seco y/o incrustado. *Ej.* "Grody! There's some crud on my plate." 2) s. Algo o alguien detestable, despreciable, y/o sin valor. *Ej.* "She's a real crud to rat on her own brother." 3) s. Cosa, objeto, esp. las cosas de uno. *Ej.* "Look at all this crud I have to pick up!" 4) *int.* Expresión de molestia, frustración y/o enojo. *Ej.* "Oh crud! I have to go back to the store."

CRUDDY: *adj.* Repugnante o detestable. *Ej.* "She's a cruddy friend for hitting you with a bat."

CRUISE: v. 1) Buscar una pareja sexual. *Ej.* "It looks like everyone's out cruising for some action tonight." 2) Andar en auto para divertirse, esp. para buscar aventura romántica o sexual. *Ej.* "The kids are so bored in this town their only fun is cruising around all night." 3) Ir a alguna parte para encontrar algo entretenido que hacer. *Ej.* "I'm bored. Let's cruise over to Ted's house and see what's happening there."

CRUISING FOR A BRUISING: *exp.* Actuando de una manera que provoca castigo. Gen. se dice en tono jocoso y se dirige a los niños. *Ej.* "You're cruising for a bruising if you keep giving me lip."

CRUMB: s. 1) Persona despreciable, indigna de confianza o repugnante. *Ej.* "She's a real crumb for telling the teacher who pulled the prank." 2) crumbs: Los restos insignificantes de algo valioso. *Ej.* "He gets the real money and leaves me the crumbs."

CRUMMY

CRUMMY: *adj.* 1) Afligido, desdichado, infeliz. *Ej.* "He's in a crummy mood because he lost the finals of the French Open." 2) Malo o de baja calidad. *Ej.* "This is a crummy room for $50 a night."

CRUNCHY: VER *granola*.

CRUSH: *s.* Una inocente atracción (sexual o emocional) por alguien. *Ej.* "I have a crush on a girl in my math class. She's really cute!"

CRUSTIE: *s.* Hippie de hace 30 años que sigue siendo hippie. (¡Y que Dios lo bendiga por eso!) *Ej.* "They're having a crustie gathering to pray for world peace."

CRY ONE'S EYES OUT: *exp-v.* Llorar mucho durante largo rato. *Ej.* "Her story was so sad I cried my eyes out."

CRY OVER SPILLED MILK: *exp-v.* Expresar molestia frente a lo que ya no tiene remedio. *Ej.* "Alright, we've made a mistake and the damage is done, but there's no use crying over spilled milk."

CRY WOLF: *exp-v.* Dar la alarma precipitadamente y frecuentemente sin fundamento. *Ej.* "If you cry wolf all the time you're going to lose your credibility."

CUCKOO: 1) *s.* Una persona tonta o loca. *Ej.* "She's a cuckoo to live on the streets by choice." 2) *adj.* Loco, demente. *Ej.* "Don't mind him, he's a little cuckoo." VER *bats*.

CUFF: VER *off the cuff*.

CUM: [Vul.] *s.* Esperma, semen. *Ej.* "How gross! There's cum on the sheets!"

CUNT: [Vul.] *s.* 1) Vagina. VER *poontang*. 2) Mujer muy despreciada. *Ej.* "I wouldn't trust that cunt in a million years."

CUP OF TEA: *exp.* Preferencia, gusto. *Ej.* "Going for a long walk in the rain is not my cup of tea."

CURSE SOMEONE OUT: VER *bitch someone out*.

CURTAINS: *s.* El término o fin de algo (ej. trabajo, relación, vida, etc.) *Ej.* "It's curtains for you Bugsy, curtains!"

CUSHY: *adj.* Poco exigente, fácil, cómodo. *Ej.* "I've got a cushy job. It pays well and I only have to work a few hours."

CUT: 1) *vi.* Poder manejar, o llevar con éxito. *Ej.* "Can he cut it working two jobs?" 2) *not cut it*:

CUT THE CHEESE

exp. Actuar de una manera no aceptable. Ej. "Sorry pal, that attitude just doesn't cut it around here."

CUT A RUG: *exp-vi.* Bailar entusiastmente. Ej. "You should see my dad on the dance floor. He can really cut a rug."

CUT CLASS: *exp-vi.* No ir a clases. Ej. "Let's cut class, I hate geometry."

CUT IT OUT: *int.* Orden para desistir. Ej. "Cut it out! Any more fooling around and you'll get spanked."

CUT LOOSE: *exp-vi.* 1) Hablar o actuar desenfrenadamente, esp. en forma agresiva. Ej. "It was so strange. He was silent all class until he suddenly cut loose a string of curses not to be believed!" 2) Hacer algo inusitado o que normalmente no corresponde a la edad que se tiene. Ej. "Ted appears quite conservative, but he cuts loose every now and then."

CUT ONE (1): (sin. break wind) *exp-vi.* Expulsar gases intestinales. Ej. "He cut one right as he was leaving the room."

CUT ONE'S TEETH ON: *exp-vi.* Aprender o actuar como principiante o al comienzo de la carrera. Ej. "I cut my teeth on little construction jobs before moving on to large projects."

CUT ONESELF A BIGGER PIECE OF THE CAKE: *exp-vi.* Se refiere a una persona que está a cargo de algo (ej. un negocio, cortar una torta, etc.) y su derecho exigido de sacar una porción un poco más grande de algo que debería repartirse en forma equitativa. Ej. "If you leave the dividing of the profits up to George, you can be certain he'll cut himself a bigger piece of the cake than he deserves."

CUT OUT: (sin. split, take off*) *exp-vi.* Irse, partir, esp. apresuradamente. Ej. "Let's cut out before the teacher arrives."

CUT SOMEONE SOME SLACK: *exp-vi.* Permitir un margen de movimiento para que sea posible divergir de una norma estricta de conducta; ser indulgente. Ej. "Why don't you get off his back and cut him some slack?"

CUT THE CHEESE: *exp-v.* Forma

CUT tHE MusTArd

jocosa para decir peer = tirarse un pedo. *Ej.* "What's that smell? All right, who cut the cheese?"

CUT THE MUSTARD: *exp-vi.* Alcanzar un nivel exigido, esp. un nivel de excelencia. *Ej.* "With his terrible work ethic, he'll never cut the mustard in college."

CUT TO THE CHASE: *exp-v.* Hablar sin preámbulo. *Ej.* "Forget the unimportant details Henry, let's cut to the chase."

CYBERPUNK: *s.* Fanático de la tecnología, esp. referente a la más avanzada tecnología en computadoras. *Ej.* "I hear some cyberpunks invented computer sex."

DADDY'S GIRL: *s.* Mujer de buenos modales, aparentemente bien cuidada y muy querida por su padre. *Ej.* "She's such a daddy's girl that she won't even go out with anyone until her father gives his approval."

DADDY-O: (sin. bro) *s.* Buen amigo o sencillamente amigo. *Ej.* "Yo daddy-o, how's it going?"

DAGO: *s.* Italo-americano, italiano. (Desp.) *Ej.* "Is he a dago, or does he just have an Italian accent?"

DAISY: VER *pushing up daisies.*

DAME: *s.* Mujer. *Ej.* "So, who's the dame?" VER *gal.*

DAMN STRAIGHT: *int.* Absolutamente correcto, esp. cuando lo que se pregunta es obvio. *Ej.* "Damn straight I'm going to the prom. Who isn't?"

DARK: VER *shot in the dark /a/.*

DARKY: (sin. spade, spook, coon, nigger) *s.* Un afroamericano, una persona negra. (Desp.) *Ej.* "There's them that say that whitey's got a plan to get darky."

DARN TOOTING: *exp.* Absolutamente, sin lugar a dudas, de todas formas. *Ej.* "You're darn tooting I'm the father. Who else would it be?"

DAYLIGHTS: VER *scare the living daylights out of.*

DAYS ARE NUMBERED /ONE'S/: *exp.* Anuncio que los días que quedan a uno para vivir o quedarse en un lugar son finitos (es decir, luego se acabarán). *Ej.* "You'd better start packing your bags because your days are numbered here."

DEAD: VER *drop dead; drop-dead;*

DEEP SHIT

knock someone dead; over my dead body.

DEAD BEAT: s. Alguien que no paga o no puede pagar sus deudas. Ej. "Another dead beat leaving us hanging with his debt."

DEAD DUCK: s. Alguien condenado a muerte o a una gran tragedia, pero gen. se dice en forma jocosa. Ej. "You're a dead duck if you touch my sister!"

DEAD MEAT: s. Un muerto, gen. refiriéndose a alguien vivo. Ej. "If you don't give me back my book, you're dead meat."

DEAD RINGER: s. Persona que tiene un gran parecido con otra. Ej. "I swear, you're a dead ringer for my sister."

DEAL: 1) s. A menudo se usa en una pregunta sobre el carácter de una persona o la naturaleza de un lugar, evento, acción, etc. Ej. "What's the deal with this place?" Or "What's his deal? What does he do for a living?" 2) vi. Vender drogas ilegales. Ej. "The cops busted him dealing crack."

DEAR JOHN LETTER: s. Carta escrita por una mujer para terminar una relación. Ej. "Why do all my girlfriends send me Dear John letters? Why don't they end it in person?"

DEATH: VER *tickled to death*.

DECK: v. Dar un puñetazo o golpear, gen. hasta derribar a la víctima. Ej. "He decked him with a hard right."

DEEP /IN/: exp. Muy implicado, esp. peligrosamente implicado en algo. Ej. "Once you get in deep with the mob, you're history."

DEEP SHIT /IN/: [Vul.] exp. Con serios problemas, esp. con problemas peligrosos. Ej. "You're in deep shit with mom for coming home

late."

DEEP-SIX: 1) *v.* Deshacerse de o rechazar algo. *Ej.* "The boss deep-sixed my idea. He thought it sucked." 2) *s.* Sepultura en el mar. *Ej.* "The captain'll deep six anyone who mutinies."

DERRIERE: *s.* 1) Las asentaderas; Gluteus maximus, las nalgas. *Ej.* "You've got something on your derriere." 2) Uno mismo. *Ej.* "You had better get your derriere going or you'll be late again."

DESK JOCKEY: (sin. pencil pusher) *s.* Oficinista, esp. aquel que pasa el día entero en su escritorio. *Ej.* "I'm getting hemorrhoids from being a desk jockey."

DEVIL: VER speak of the devil.

DIAL ONE IN: *exp-v.* Informar a alguien sobre algo. *Ej.* "Dial us in, man. Tell us what's up."

DIALED IN: *adj.* Bien informado; muy al tanto de lo que está de moda o lugares populares. *Ej.* "Ask Alan, he's always dialed in to all the happening places in the city."

DIAMOND IN THE ROUGH: *exp.* Algo o alguien excepcional que resalta en un montón o grupo de poco valor. *Ej.* "Talk about finding a diamond in the rough, I was going through my grandfather's junk when I came across a Van Gogh print!"

DIBS: *s.* Derecho de ir primero o tomar algo primero. *Ej.* "I've got dibs on the last burger."

DICE /NO/: *exp.* No hay acuerdo, no pasa nada. *Ej.* "No dice on getting my dad's car for the weekend."

DICEY: *adj.* Resultado incierto y arriesgado, gen. implica cierto peligro. *Ej.* "That was a dicey move climbing the building."

DICK: *s.* 1) [Vul.] Pene. *Ej.* "The difference is that you have a dick and she doesn't." 2) Un detective. *Ej.* "After reading Raymond Chandler, I decided to become a dick."

DICK AROUND WITH: [Vul.] *exp-v.* 1) Tener relaciones sexuales con alguien, esp. relaciones muy informales. *Ej.* "Is she my girlfriend? No, we're just dicking around with each other." 2) Manejar con descuido, tratar sin respeto. *Ej.* "Don't dick around with my stuff."

DIMWIT

DICK AROUND: [Vul.] *exp-v.* Hacer algo sin entusiasmo, perder el tiempo. *Ej.* "When are you going to get serious about life and stop dicking around?"

DICK HEAD: [Vul.] *s.* Persona sumamente desagradable cuya presencia pone a prueba la paciencia de un santo. *Ej.* "I can't believe you invited that dick head here. He'll ruin the party!"

DIDDLY: (sin. diddly-squat) *s.* 1) Una cantidad mínima o sin valor. *Ej.* "They're paying me diddly for all the work I do." 2) (sin. zilch, jack) Nada, cero. *Ej.* "Your opinion means absolutely diddly to me."

DIDDLY-SQUAT: VER *diddly*.

DIE (TO): *v.* 1) Tener una gran deseo con respecto a algo. *Ej.* "Oh, Jim is simply dying to meet her." Or "I'm dying to see the new Brad Pitt movie." 2) Estar muy decepcionado o descontento a cerca de una situación o evento. *Ej.* "Oh Jane will just die when she finds out you came by and she wasn't here."

DIFFERENT STROKES FOR DIFFERENT FOLKS: *exp.* Lo que sea que lo haga feliz a uno. Se dice de extrañas preferencias personales de alguien que dice o hace algo excéntrico pero inofensivo. *Ej.* "So she likes to cook in her birthday suit. Hey, different strokes for different folks." VER *each his own /to/*.

DIG: 1) *v.* Gustar, apreciar. *Ej.* "Hey, I dig those pants. Where did you buy them?" 2) *v.* Entender, comprender. *Ej.* "Alright, I dig where you're coming from." 3) Fijarse, mirar. *Ej.* "Dig that chick walking by." 3) *digs: s.pl.* Residencia, domicilio. *Ej.* "Check out my new digs!"

DIG IT: VER *get it*.

DIG ONE'S OWN GRAVE: *exp-vi.* Abrir la boca y crearse problemas y más problemas. *Ej.* "It just got worse as I tried to explain the lipstick on my shirt. I ended up digging my own grave."

DIME: VER *on someone's dime; nickel(s)-and-dime(s); worth a dime /not/*.

DIMWIT: (sin. dip, meathead, knucklehead) *s.* Una persona torpe, tonta, estúpida. *Ej.* "You'll never learn anything working for that dimwit!"

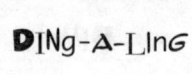

DING-A-LING

DING-A-LING: VER *dingbat*.

DINGBAT: (sin. ding-a-ling) s. Persona estúpida y hueca. Ej. "No you dingbat, you're putting it in backwards."

DIP: s. Una persona socialmente inepta y poco atractiva. Ej. "You're a real dip to ask that girl to dance while blowing your nose."

DIPSHIT: [Vul.] s. Una persona tonta o estúpida, con una dosis adicional de pesadez. Ej. "You are a real dipshit to pick on little kids."

DIRT: s. Detalles poco favorables y/o muy privados sobre alguien o algo. Ej. "I've got the dirt on Marilyn's affair with Tom."

DIRT CHEAP: adj. Muy barato. Ej. "This shirt was dirt cheap. It only cost five bucks."

DIRTBAG: s. Una persona despreciable, censurable, a quien nadie quiere. Ej. "You need to get your head examined if you think I'd ask that dirtbag to baby-sit our kids."

DIRTY: 1) adv. Circunstancia de poseer o consumir drogas prohibidas. Ej. "If they test me I'm busted 'cause I've been dirty for months." 2) Culpable, implicado en actividades ilegales. Ej. "We know he's dirty, but we still lack the smoking gun to bring him in." VER TAMBIEN *do someone dirty; hang out the dirty laundry; play dirty*.

DIRTY MIND: s. Mal pensado. La mente de alguien que siempre piensa en sexo y transforma comentarios inocentes en alusiones sexuales. Ej. "All I said is, 'I like it a lot' and he turns it into some sexual connotation. What a dirty mind he's got!"

DIRTY POOL: exp. Acciones que son ilegales o inmorales. Ej. "That's dirty pool bringing in a ringer."

DIRTY TRICK: exp. Una mala jugada. Ej. "It was a dirty trick telling them I wasn't interested in the job when I was."

DIRTY WORK: s. 1) (sin. grunt work) Tareas desagradables y aburridas. Ej. "We're partners, but you get all the glory and leave me the dirty work." 2) Hechos inmorales o ilegales generalmente efectuados por ciertos elementos criminales de nuestra sociedad. Ej.

DO BUNNY

"Knocking people off is dirty work, but it sure does pay well."

DISH: s. Persona de buena apariencia, atractiva, esp. una mujer. Ej. "Who's the dish in the waiting room?"

DISS: v. Insultar, burlarse. Ej. "Yo, diss my mother and I'll smack you upside the head."

DITCH: v. 1) Deshacerse de algo, desecharlo. Ej. "Ditch the evidence before the cops get here." 2) Deshacerse o alejarse de alguien, esp. un acompañante. Ej. "After being stuck with him all day, I finally managed to ditch him." 3) Faltar a clases o a la escuela. Ej. "Hey man, let's ditch. I don't feel like going to school today."

DITZY: adj. Ligero de cascos, enajenado, entre poco y nada entre los oídos. Ej. "You know, you're so ditzy, I worry about you sometimes."

DIVE: s. 1) Bar que sirve de lugar de reunión muy informal para tomar alcohol. Ej. "It may be a dive, but they make a great Martini." 2) Vivienda en estado de gran descuido (ej. departamento, casa, etc.). Ej. "He's living in a real dive. There are roaches everywhere!" VER TAMBIEN *take a dive*.

DIVE IN HEAD FIRST: exp-vi. Sumergirse totalmente en algo. Ej. "The first day on the job, I dove in head first and tried to learn everything."

DIVVY: v. Dividir. Gen. se dice divvy up. Ej. "Let's say we divvy up the loot and then cut out of here."

DO: 1) s. Peinado, estilo de peinado. Ej. "That's the funniest do I've ever seen!" 2) vi. Usar, ingerir. Ej. "Do you do broccoli?" 3) vi. Tener relación sexual. Ej. "He said he did her, but I know he's lying." 4) vi. Matar a alguien. Ej. "The mob did him for not paying on time." VER *waste*.

DO A JOB ON: (sin. do a number on) exp-vi. Dañar física o mentalmente. Regañar severamente o dar una dura paliza, esp. de manera planificada y a conciencia. Ej. "My grandmother did a job on my brother when he was little by always dressing him as a girl." Or "The bully threatened to do a job on me if I didn't give him money."

DO A NUMBER ON: VER *do a job on*.

DO BUNNY: exp-vi. Hablar por mu-

cho rato, gen. sobre nada en especial. (Ing.) Ej. "I was on the horn doing bunny with an old friend."

DO ONE'S PART: *exp-vi.* Trabajar o esforzarse en una asociación o compromiso. Ej. "We'll get this job done a lot quicker if everyone does their part."

DO PORRIDGE: *exp-vi.* Estar preso. (Ing.) Ej. "He's doing porridge for stealing inflatable dolls."

DO SOMEONE DIRTY: *exp-vi.* Hacerle algo censurable a alguien, gen. engañar o calumniar. Ej. "You do me dirty telling my wife I fool around."

DODGE: VER *out of Dodge.*

DOG: *s.* 1) Persona que no es atractiva, más bien fea. Ej. "You're such a dog your own mother can't stand to look at you." 2) Producto de calidad realmente inferior, o simplemente malo. Ej. "That car you bought is a dog. It's always in the shop." 3) Persona mala o inmoral. A menudo se dice como broma entre amigos. Ej. "You dog! Trying to pick up that school girl." 4) Cecina. Ej. "We'll eat some dogs at the game." 5) *dogs: s.pl.* Pies. Ej. "I've been pounding the pavement all day. My dogs are killing me!" 6) Persona, gen. un hombre. Ej. "You dog, I knew you'd get the promotion!" VER TAMBIEN *hair of the dog that bit you; work like a dog; you can't teach an old dog new tricks; rain cats and dogs; barking dogs seldom bite.*

DOG IT: *exp-v.* Gastar intencionalmente el mínimo de energía y/o esfuerzo físico al hacer algo. Ej. "My partner is such a loser! He's always dogging it on the job so that I end up doing all the work."

DOG SOMEONE: *exp-v.* 1) Criticar a alguien severamente. Ej. "Hal's been dogging your girlfriend. He says she's ugly and real stupid." 2) Hacerle algo injusto o desagradable a un amigo. Ej. "My best friend dogged me by not coming to my b-day party."

DO-HICKEY: *s.* Algo que se dice en lugar del nombre real del objeto. Ej. "Pass me that do-hickey over there."

DOPEY

DOING /BE/: *exp-vi.* Estar ocurriendo o sucediendo. *Ej.* "What's doing at the disco tonight?"

DOLL: *s.* 1) Persona atractiva, esp. una mujer. *Ej.* "Your wife is a real doll." 2) Una persona gentil y amable. *Ej.* "You are such a doll for bringing me flowers."

DOLLED UP: *exp.* Vestido en forma mejor de lo corriente, gen. para una ocasión especial. *Ej.* "Where are you going all dolled up like that?. Do you have a date?" VER dressed to kill.

DON'T GIVE A DAMN: *exp.* No importarle nada alguien o algo. *Ej.* "I don't give a damn what he thinks, my opinion stands."

DON'T GO DOWN THAT ROAD: *exp.* Expresión con la cual se advierte a alguien que no siga adelante con una opinión, idea o línea de pensamiento. *Ej.* "You, Mr. different girl every weekend, are you preaching to me about fidelity? Don't go down that road man, just don't do it!"

DOO-DOO: *s.* Excremento. *Ej.* "Do you have to go doo-goo?" VER poo.

DOORMAT: *s.* ¿Sabes lo que es un doormat de verdad? Es un alfombrilla, un felpudo de puerta. Entonces, ¿te imaginas una persona así? Es sumisa, dispuesta a aceptar todo tipo de tratamiento. ¡Pobrecito/a! *Ej.* "What are you a doormat? Are you just going to accept that crap from him?"

DOOZIE: *s.* Algo extraordinario, inesperado o insólito. *Ej.* "What a doozie of a surprise! She gave me a car for my birthday!"

DOPE: 1) *adj.* Excelente, fantástico, buenísimo *Ej.* "You're getting hitched. That's dope, man. I'm totally psyched for you." 2) *s.* La verdad, información con-fidencial. *Ej.* "Who's got the dope on the bank merger?" 3) *s.* Una droga narcótica, gen. marihuana o heroína. *Ej.* "Let's get some dope for the weekend." 4) *s.* Persona tonta. *Ej.* "Ha, you have to work with the dope. You'll be doing all the work."

DOPEY: *adj.* 1) Atontado o desganado, que actúa o se siente como si se hubiera tomado un sedante o alguna droga. *Ej.* "I feel dopey after that nap." 2) Tonto,

DORk

lerdo, poco inteligente. Ej. "He'll never make it to college, he's too dopey."

DORK: s. Una persona rara, poco querida e inelegante a quien se le considera tanto ridículo como irritante. Ej. "Only a dork like you still watches those kiddy programs when he's sixteen."

DOUBLE: VER on the double.

DOUBLE EDGED SWORD /A/: exp. Una situación que tiene dos alternativas igualmente indeseables. Ej. "If I take revenge, I'll get arrested, but if I do nothing, I'll have no respect. Either way, it's a double edged sword."

DOUBLE-GATED: (sin. bi, swing both ways, AC/DC, switch hitter) s. Bisexual. Ej. "He's not gay, he's double-gated."

DOUCHE BAG: [Vul.] exp. Una persona muy poco querida, despreciable. Ej. "If I catch that douche bag messing with my sister, I'll break his face!"

DOUGH: (sin. bread, green stuff, moola, scratch,) s. Dinero. Ej. "Damn, I've got a hot date and no dough."

DOWN IN THE DUMPS: exp. Estar desganado, sin energía, deprimido. Ej. "He's been down in the dumps ever since he was cut from the baseball team."

DOWN ON ONE'S LUCK: exp. Constante mala suerte, esp. experimentar una racha de mala suerte. Ej. "First I get fired, then my girl leaves me, then I get beat up for looking at this guy the wrong way. Yeah, I guess you could say I'm down on my luck."

DOWN THE TUBE(S): exp. Quedar arruinado o perdido. Ej. "It's a year's work down the tube if they reject our proposal." Or "Don't join that team, they're going down the tubes."

DOWN UNDER: s. Australia o Nueva Zelandia. Ej. "We should go down under for our honeymoon."

DOWN WITH SOMETHING/SOMEONE /BE/: exp-vi. Estar de acuerdo sobre algo o tener amistad con alguien. Ej. "I'd be down with going to Florida for a few days." Or "It's cool, I'm down with Fred, we've been friends for a long time."

DOWNER: s. 1) Una droga sedante o calmante, como una pastilla para dormir. *Ej.* "I'm so wired I need a downer." 2) Una situación deprimente. *Ej.* "It was a real downer being alone for the holidays." 3) Una persona deprimente, aquella cuya compañía no se busca. *Ej.* "That dude's a downer man, he's always so pessimistic about everything."

DOWNSHIFT: *v.* Cambiar las prioridades en la vida al decidir que más tiempo libre o una mejor calidad de vida son más importantes que el dinero. *Ej.* "I was into the pressure job and earning lots of money till I just got sick of it and decided to downshift."

DRAG: *s.* 1) (sin. bummer). Algo o alguien odiosamente desagradable y/o aburrido y/o cansador. *Ej.* "School is such a drag." Or "She's a drag to be with." 2) (sin. toke, hit*) Una bocanada o chupada de cigarrillo, pipa o cigarro. *Ej.* "I don't want a whole cig, just give me a drag." 3) Una calle o camino. *Ej.* "This is the main drag in town. It's where all the shops are." 4) La vestimenta de un sexo usada por alguien del sexo opuesto. *Ej.* "You know Ted, you look good in drag!" VER TAMBIEN *main drag*.

DRAG ONE'S BUTT: (sin. drag one's heels) *exp-v.* Actuar o trabajar lentamente, por cansancio; moverse con lentitud y sin apuro. *Ej.* "I'm dragging my butt today 'cause I only slept three hours last night."

DRAG ONE'S HEELS: La forma más educada de *drag one's butt*.

DRAG QUEEN: *s.* Un travestista masculino (i.e. un hombre que viste como mujer). *Ej.* "He was the big jock in high school, so it was a surprise when we discovered that he's now a drag queen."

DRAIN THE LIZARD: *exp-vi.* Mear. *Ej.* "Harry's out draining the lizard, he'll be back in a sec."

DREAMBOAT: *s.* Persona sexy, atractiva, gen. un hombre. *Ej.* "I'd marry that dreamboat any day!"

DRESSED TO KILL: (sin. dolled up, duded up) *exp.* Andar muy bien vestido, esp. en forma llamativa. *Ej.* "Wow, you're dressed to kill! Who's the hot date?"

DRINK: (sin. booze, sauce) *s.*

DRINK LIKE A FISH

Bebida alcohólica. Ej. "I need a drink to settle my nerves."

DRINK LIKE A FISH: exp-vi. Beber mucho alcohol con frecuencia. Ej. "Ted drinks like a fish, he must suck down ten beers a day."

DRINK SOMEONE UNDER THE TABLE: exp-vi. Ser capaz de beber más alcohol que otra persona. Ej. "He may be a top student, but I can drink him under the table any day!"

DRIP: s. Una persona aburrida, irritante, que es tan querida como una gotera lenta en la noche cuyo sonido 'drip, drip' retumba como descarga de artillería. ¿Te imaginas cómo es esta persona? Ej. "I dated the biggest drip last night. He talked about his ant farm for two hours!"

DRIVE SOMEONE UP THE WALL: exp-vi. Irritar a alguien a un grado extremo. Ej. "His inability to make even the smallest decision drives me up the wall!"

DROP: v. Gastar dinero, esp. en grandes cantidades. Ej. "I dropped a few c-notes on this bike."

DROP DEAD: int. Expresión de gran rabia o desprecio, que implica el deseo de que la persona a quien se dirige se vaya. Ej. "After stealing my boyfriend you still want to be friends? Drop dead Susan!" VER TAMBIEN drop-dead.

DROP IT: int. Orden o exigencia de abandonar un tema. Ej. "Drop it, okay? I don't want to talk about this anymore."

DROP OUT: exp-v. 1) Dejar de asistir o participar, gen. refiriéndose a un partido, un club, una escuela, etc. Ej. "He dropped out of school when he was 12 years old." 2) Retirarse de la sociedad establecida, gen. porque se está cansado y desilusionado de los valores convencionales, a menudo materialistas. Ej. "He hated the materialism of the city, so he dropped out and moved to a cabin in the woods."

DROP-DEAD: adj. Muy impresionante, espectacular, para nunca olvidarlo. Ej. "The actress is not only drop dead beautiful, but she also gives a drop dead performance." VER TAMBIEN drop dead.

DUCK: VER dead duck; lame duck.

DWEEB

DUDE: s. Macho. Una palabra usada frecuentemente por la juventud de hoy en día, que se repite en forma impresionante y molesta. Se ocupa como un puente o relleno entre dos palabras. Ej. "So dude, like check it out, I met this dude who introduced me to this other dude who's super tight with this dude who works at a radio station who said he'd check out our sound."

DUDED UP: exp. Vestido en forma elegante, gen. con la mejor ropa y esp. diferente de la ropa diaria de uno. Ej. "Where are you going all duded up like that?" VER *dressed to kill*.

DUFF: s. Las nalgas. Ej. "Get off your duff and clean this place up!"

duh: VER *no duh*.

DUKE: 1) v. Pelear, esp. a puñetes. Ej. "It's time we duked it out and put an end to this bickering." 2) **dukes:** s. Puños. Ej. "Put up your dukes, we're gonna fight."

DUMB: VER *play dumb*.

DUMB AS A DOORKNOB: exp. Se emplea para describir a una persona muy estúpida. Ej. "He's not just dumb, he's as dumb as a doorknob."

DUMBO: s. Un idiota, un estúpido, en el lenguaje de los niños. Ej. "Only a dumbo would stick his finger in an electric socket."

DUMP: (sin. break-up with) exp. Dar calabazas; Terminar una relación romántica de modo abrupto y desagradable. Ej. "Just when I thought he was going to ask me to marry him, he dumps me!" VER TAMBIEN *down in the dumps; take a dump*.

DUMP ON: exp-v. 1) Contar todos los problemas de uno, esp. hacerlo sin considerar si la otra persona quiere escucharlos (nota de ed.: gen. no quiere escucharlos). Ej. "Why does everyone always dump on me with their problems?" 2) Criticar en forma severa y brutal. Ej. "The professor dumped on my presentation."

DUST: v. Matar, asesinar. Ej. "Pay him back or he's gonna dust your ass." VER *waste*. VER TAMBIEN *bite the dust*

DWEEB: (sin. twit) s. Una persona despreciada, o al menos no

querida, por considerársele rara, poco elegante y/o demasiado diferente a uno. Ej. "That kid is a dweeb. He only plays with his little sister."

DYKE: [Vul.] (sin. lesbo) s. Lesbiana. Ej. "You'll never guess who's a dyke? Remeber Roberta? Well, she came out of the closet to her parents." VER TAMBIEN *bull dyke*.

DYNAMITE: *adj.* Buenísimo, fantástico. Ej. "That was a dynamite gift you gave him. He never expected a week's vacation in the Caribbean."

EACH HIS OWN /TO/: (sin. different strokes for different folks) *exp.* Lo que sea que lo haga feliz a uno. Se dice de extrañas preferencias personales de alguien que dice o hace algo excéntrico pero inofensivo. Ej. "You shouldn't criticize him just because his interest in insects seems a little odd and excessive. You just have to say, hey, to each his own."

EARLY BIRD GETS/CATCHES THE WORM: *exp.* Aquel que se sacrifica, esp. en ser el primero en llegar, o hace un gran esfuerzo, consigue sus metas. Ej. "I get the tickets because I was here first. Hey, the early bird gets the worm."

EARS: VER *be all ears; play it by ear; prick up one's ears; stick it in one's ear; wet behind the ears*.

EASY: *adj.* Sexualmente licencioso o demasiado dispuesto a conceder favores sexuales. Ej. "He only dates easy girls." VER TAMBIEN *get off easy*.

EASY STREET: *exp.* Algo muy fácil que generalmente incluye mucho dinero. Ej. "If I win the lottery, we're talking easy street baby: piña coladas in the Caribbean and shrimp on the barbie!"

EAT AND RUN: *exp-vi.* 1) Ir a cenar con alguien y partir en el momento de terminar de comer. Ej. "That's the last time I invite John over. He always eats and runs." 2) Comer muy rápido para ir a alguna parte y/o continuar trabajando. Ej. "I'll have to eat and run if I want to catch the bus."

EAT HUMBLE PIE: *exp-v.* Sentirse humillado por algún acontecimiento.

ENCHILADA

Ej. "He talked and talked about how great he is at tennis, but I made him eat humble pie on the court."

EAT LIKE A BIRD: *exp-vi.* Comer muy poco. *Ej.* "Are you on a diet or do you always eat like a bird?"

EAT ONE'S CAKE AND HAVE IT TOO: (sin. have one's cake and eat it too) *exp-v.* Querer dos cosas diferentes que se oponen intrínsecamente de tal manera que es muy difícil lograrlas. *Ej.* "You want to get married, but you still want to play the field. That's the typical attitude of someone who wants to eat his cake and have it too."

EATS: *s.* Comida. *Ej.* "Where can we get some good eats around here?"

EDGE: VER *on the edge.*

EDUCATED GUESS: *s.* Conjetura sin tener 100% de seguridad, pero creyendo que es cierto. *Ej.* "I can't say for certain, but an educated guess places him at his favorite watering hole by this time."

EENCY-WEENCY: *adj.* Muy pequeño. *Ej.* "The baby's toes are eency-weency."

EGG: VER *good egg; goose egg; put all one's eggs in one basket; walk on egg shells.*

EGG ON ONE'S FACE: *exp.* Situación o sensación de gran vergüenza o humillación. *Ej.* "He had egg on his face after the boss yelled at him in front of us."

EGGHEAD: *s.* Una persona demasiado intelectual, una persona sólo interesada en lo esotérico y no en lo mundano. *Ej.* "She may be an egghead, but at least she's happy."

EGO TRIP: *s.* Gratificación extrema del ego, que se convierte en una onda de presunción. *Ej.* "He's been on an ego trip ever since he won that prize for best student."

EIGHT BALL: VER *behind the eight ball.*

ELBOW GREASE: *s.* Labor física y esfuerzo agotador/a. *Ej.* "You'll need some elbow grease to get those rusted bolts off."

ELBOWS: VER *rub elbows with.*

EMPTY: VER *that empty feeling.*

ENCHILADA: VER *the whole enchilada.*

END OF ONE'S ROPE

END OF ONE'S ROPE/TETHER/AT THE/: *exp.* Al punto de agotamiento, paciencia o frustración con alguien o con una situación dada. *Ej.* "I'm at the end of my rope with him. If he doesn't start cleaning up his act I'm gonna…I don't know what I'm gonna do, but I'm gonna do something."

ENOUGH: *int.* ¡Basta!, un pedido a otro para que deje de hablar o hacer algo. *Ej.* "Enough! more bickering between the two of you."

EVEN OUT IN THE WASH: *exp.* Un adagio que, en una situación desigual e injusta, implica que a pesar de las circunstancias y después de todo, la justicia y el karma arreglarán las cosas para que se equiparen. *Ej.* "I know he's got the better of you now, but you're a good person and it'll even out in the wash."

EVEN: VER *not even.*

EVEN STEVEN: *exp.* Intercambiar o haber intercambiado favores. *Ej.* "You did me a favor and I did you a favor. Now we're even Steven."

EVERLOVING: *adj.* Irritante, maldito, muy molesto. *Ej.* "Get your everloving hands off me!"

EVERY TOM, DICK AND HARRY: *exp.* Como si fueran muchos. *Ej.* "I only invited 50 people to the party, but it seemed like every Tom, Dick and Harry came."

EX: *s.* Cónyuge o pareja anterior. *Ej.* "My ex called the other day to remind me of the alimony payment."

EYE: VER *apple of one's eye; catch a little shut-eye; catch one's eye; give the evil eye; hit the bull's eye; in a pig's eye; keep an eye on; more to something/someone than meets the eye; mud in your eye /here's/;.*

EYEBALL: *v.* 1) Examinar, escudriñar. *Ej.* "Look at that creep eyeballing that gal! It's like he's undressing her with his eyes." 2) Medir o calcular en forma aproximada a simple vista. *Ej.* "Eyeballing it, I'd say there are 32 people here."

EYES PEELED: *exp.* Mantenerse totalmente alerta. *Ej.* "Keep your eyes peeled for a pharmacy. I need some Pepto Bismo fast!"

FAB: *adj.* Excelente, fantástico, buenísimo. *Ej.* "I had a fab time at the beach."

FACE: VER blue in the face; break someone's face; egg on one's face; fall flat on one's face; in someone's face; in-your-face; lose face; out of someone's face; pizza-face; shut one's face; stuff one's face; suck face; what's his/her face.

FACE THE MUSIC: *exp-v.* Aceptar las consecuencias desagradables que resultan de una acción, esp. la acción propia. *Ej.* "I told you not to fight again, but you didn't listen, so now it's time to face the music."

FAG: [Vul.] (sin. queer, fairy, faggot, fruitcake*, homo) *s.* 1) Homosexual masculino. *Ej.* "Are you a fag, or do you just act like one?" 2) Hombre que demuestra cualidades femeninas. *Ej.* "You look like a fag in those tight shorts."

FAGGOT: VER fag.

FAIRY: VER fag.

FAKE (SOMEONE) OUT: *exp-v.* Engañar o embaucar, esp. simular una acción y realizar otra. *Ej.* "He faked me out by pretending to go left and then going right." Or "I got faked out."

FALL: *s.* Culpa o castigo por un crimen u ofensa. *Ej.* "I'll always owe Joe. He took the fall for me on that robbery."

FALL FLAT ON ONE'S FACE: *exp-vi.* Fallar miserablemente en un intento. *Ej.* "He got stage fright and forgot all of his lines. It was sad seeing him fall flat on his face."

FALL FOR SOMETHING: *exp-vi.* Creer una mentira o tragarse un cuento. Ser ingenuo. *Ej.* "You're pretty darn gullible to have fallen for the old switcheroo."

FALL GUY: *s.* 1) Un chivo expiatorio. *Ej.* "The boss says we need a fall guy to get the cops off our case." 2) Una víctima crédula. *Ej.* "There are always enough fall guys to make a scam work."

FALL THROUGH: *exp.* Algo que se planea y no resulta. *Ej.* "We had plans to go to the movies and to dinner, but they fell through."

FALSIES: *s.pl.* Rellenos que se usan

FAMILY JEWELS

dentro de un sostén para aparentar tener senos mayores. Ej. "Are those real or is she wearing falsies?"

FAMILY JEWELS: s.pl. Los genitales masculinos. Ej. "He cried when she hit him in the family jewels."

FAMILY WAY /BE IN THE/: (sin. bun in the oven /have a/) exp-vi. Estar embarazada. Ej. "She's not overweight, she's in the family way."

FANNY: s. 1) Las nalgas. Ej. "Would you mind scooting your fanny over so I can get past?" (en los EE.UU.) 2) La vagina. Ej. "Some bloody American had the gall to ask me to move my fanny!" (en Ingl.)

FAR-OUT: 1) adj. Maravilloso, estupendo, excepcional. Ej. "That was a far-out concert." Or "It'd be far-out travelling through Africa." 2) int. Extraordinario, fuera de lo común, único y sorprendente. Ej. "Far-out! He just jumped over a car on a bicycle."

FART: 1) s. Un pedo; escape de gas del ano. Ej. "Who let out the fart?" 2) v. Expulsar gases intestinales. Ej. "Sorry, I farted."

FART AROUND (WITH): exp-v. 1) Tratar sin respeto o sin el cuidado merecido. Ej. "Don't fart around with that machine. It's worth more than your life!" 2) Malgastar o perder el tiempo. Ej. "We'll never finish if you don't stop farting around."

FAST: (sin. easy) adj. Suelta, esp. dispuesta rápidamente para la actividad sexual; se dice de una mujer. Ej. "I like fast cars and fast women!"

FAST BUCK: s. Dinero que se ha conseguido fácilmente y a menudo inescrupulosamente. Ej. "You go looking for a fast buck and you'll end up in jail."

FAST ONE: s. Un truco o engaño furtivo, astuto. Ej. "He thought he could pull a fast one on me, but I wasn't so easily fooled."

FAT: VER phat.

FAT CAT: s. 1) Una persona adinerada y/o altamente privilegiada. Ej. "The golf club is where the fat cats hang out." 2) Una persona adinerada que contribuye significativamente a una campaña política. Ej. "The fat

FIGHT SOMEONE

cats are supporting the Republicans again."

FAT CHANCE: *exp.* Poca o ninguna posibilidad, a menudo usado en el imperativo. *Ej.* "You a doctor? Fat chance!"

FAT LOT /A/: *exp.* Muy poco o nada. *Ej.* "A fat lot of good saying sorry is after you hit him."

FATSO: *s.* Una persona gorda. *Ej.* "Hey fatso, stop eating so much candy."

FED: *s.* Un agente u oficial federal. *Ej.* "This is a job for the feds, not the local police."

FED UP WITH /BE/: *exp-vi.* Estar muy molesto con alguien o algo. *Ej.* "I'm fed up with your complaining. Just shut up and do your work!"

FEEL SOMEONE UP: *v.* Tocarse con caricias apasionadas, esp. los senos de una mujer. *Ej.* "Just when I started to feel her up, my mom walked in."

FEET: VER *keep one's feet wet; hold one's feet to the fire; cold feet; grovel at one's feet.*

FESS UP: *v.* Reconocer o confesar una acción. *Ej.* "It'll be better for you to fess up and tell us how you pulled the bank job."

FIELD: VER *play the field.*

FIEND: *s.* 1) Una persona adicta a algo. *Ej.* "Tony has been a dope fiend since he was 21." 2) Persona totalmente absorta u obsesionada por un determinado trabajo o pasatiempo. *Ej.* "Paul is a computer fiend, he spends all day surfing the net."

FIERCE: VER *something fierce.*

FIGHT SOMEONE/SOMETHING TOOTH AND NAIL: *exp-vi.* Defenderse con todas las

FAT CAT

FINe

fuerzas. *Ej.* "They were fighting each other tooth and nail for child custody."

FINE: *adj.* Atractivo, de buena apariencia, para persona u objeto. *Ej.* "That's one fine man you married!" Or "I'll buy a fine car if I win the lottery."

FINGER: 1) *v.* Informar sobre alguien. *Ej.* "He went to the cops and fingered his pals." 2) *v.* Escoger, esp. la víctima intencional de un crimen. *Ej.* "The trick to a good scam is to finger the right victim." 3) *finger /the/:* s. La expresión física para *fuck you*. *Ej.* "That guy just gave you the finger for cutting him off." Ver *bird /the.*

FINK: s. 1) (sin. *rat, tattle tale*) Delator: persona que informa sobre la actividad secreta o las actividades de otros (etim. rompehuelgas). *Ej.* "If we catch the fink, he's history." 2) Persona detestable, despreciable. *Ej.* "You're just a fink and you'll always be a fink, so buzz off!"

FINK ON: (sin. *rat on*) *exp-v.* Informar sobre alguien. *Ej.* "It breaks my heart to think Joey would fink on us!"

FINK OUT: *exp-v.* Fallar al no completar una acción prometida. *Ej.* "He promises and promises, but he always finks out."

FIRE: *v.* Despedir del trabajo. *Ej.* "If they fire me, my wife will kill me!" VER TAMBIEN *hold someone's feet to the fire; frying pan into the fire; nothing to set the world on fire; play with fire.*

FIRE AWAY: *exp-v.* Comenzar a hacer preguntas, esp. en forma rápida y seguida. *Ej.* "After the controversial lecture, the audience started firing away with their questions."

FIRE UP: *exp-v.* Hacer partir un motor. *Ej.* "Fire up the engine and let's get moving."

FIRED UP: *adj.* 1) (sin. *amped*) Sumamente entusiasmado. *Ej.* "I got fired-up for the big game." 2) Abandonarse a excesos de alcohol o de drogas. *Ej.* "Hal was fired up last night. He was dancing with a floor lamp."

FIREWORKS: *s.pl.* Exabruptos, explosiones en el sentido de fuertes discusiones, escándalos o

FIXER-UPPER

fuegos cruzados. *Ej.* "There's gonna be fireworks galore when the mayor finds out about this bribery thing." Or "When those two argue, it's like fireworks going off."

FIRST BASE: *exp.* Besarse. (etim. Del béisbol, donde hay cuatro bases que van en importancia desde la primera hasta la última – la base meta.) *Ej.* "She's a prude, She'll only go to first base."

FIRST RATE: *exp.* De primera, sobresaliente *Ej.* "This book is first rate. It's sure to become a classic."

FISHY: *adj.* Una situación o una persona sospechosa, esp. que no es lo que aparenta. *Ej.* "There's something fishy about that guy, I just don't trust him." Or "I get a fishy feeling about this."

FIST FIGHT: *s.* Pelea a puñetes. *Ej.* "They got into a fist fight over the last slice of pizza."

FISTED: VER *tight fisted*.

FIVE: VER *give someone five; high-five; nine to five; take five*.

FIVE FINGER DISCOUNT: *exp.* Obtenido por robo. *Ej.* "I don't like to accept his presents because I know he gets them with a five finger discount."

FIVE FINGER: (sin. *shop lift*) *v.* Robar, escamotear, hurtar de una tienda. *Ej.* "My first bust was catching a kid five fingering a candy bar."

FIVE O'CLOCK SHADOW: *exp.* Comienzos de barba en la cara de un hombre que no se ha afeitado durante varias horas. *Ej.* "I'll need to shave before we go to dinner, I've got a five o'clock shadow."

FIVE SPOT: VER *fiver*.

FIVER: (sin. *five spot*) *s.* Un billete de cinco dólares. *Ej.* "Lend me a fiver." Or "It'll cost you a five spot."

FIX: *s.* 1) Una dosis, gen. tomada a través de inyección endovenosa, de un narcótico, gen. heroína. *Ej.* "This is my last fix before I go clean." 2) Una dosis de algo que se necesita o se desea mucho. *Ej.* "I need my sports fix every day."

FIX SOMEONE'S WAGON: *exp-v.* Desquitarse o vengarse de alguien *Ej.* "He thinks he can insult me in public, well, I'll fix his wagon soon enough!"

FIXER-UPPER: *s.* Casa o departamento a bajo precio y en

mal estado esperando que una mano solícita la/lo embellezca. *Ej.* "Don't say the house is a dump, say it's a fixer-upper."

FLAKE: s. 1) Persona en quien no se puede confiar. *Ej.* "You're such a flake. You always say you'll do something, but you never do it." 2) Persona que cambia en forma caprichosa de intereses o gustos. *Ej.* "She's a flake. First she was into transcendental Buddhism, then it was crystal power and now it's the Virgin Mary cult." 3) Cocaína. *Ej.* "You want to try some flake?" VER *coke*.

FLAKE OUT: v. No cumplir un plan convenido, esp. a último minuto. *Ej.* "Fred, we've already made all the arrangements. Come on man, don't flake out on us."

FLAMER: s. Hombre homosexual que declara su homosexualidad con orgullo. (Desp.) *Ej.* "Them flamers are having a parade to celebrate gay pride."

FLAP: s. Crítica, comentario negativo con muestra de desaprobación. *Ej.* "I got a lot of flap for dating my friend's ex."

FLASH: v. Revelar las partes pudendas de uno en un lugar público para escandalizar y ser indecente (y nos preguntamos qué gracia tiene). *Ej.* "I was walking down the street when this pervert flashed me."

FLASHER: s. Persona que se exhibe de manera indecente. *Ej.* "They finally arrested the flasher who had been terrorizing young girls."

FLASHY: adj. Un despliegue llamativo u ostentoso de riqueza. *Ej.* "These neuveaux riche are so flashy it's embarrassing."

FLAT BROKE: (sin. *not have a red cent, tapped out*) exp. El estado de no tener dinero en un momento dado o estar en una grave situación económica. *Ej.* "Me lend you money? No way, I'm flat broke."

FLAT-OUT: adj. 1) Totalmente, enteramente, completamente. *Ej.* "I'm just flat-out tired of your excuses." 2) A máxima velocidad. *Ej.* "He was going flat-out when the tire exploded."

FLEABAG: s. Un lugar de hospedaje a maltraer, destartalado, casi arruinado (ej. hotel, motel,

FLY LIKE THE WIND

departamento, etc.) a menudo con una buena población de pulgas. Ej. "How can you live in that fleabag hotel? It's disgusting!"

FLICK: s. Película. Ej. "Let's say we catch a flick tonight."

FLIP OFF: exp-v. Hacer un gesto obsceno con la mano, gen. el finger. Ej. "He punched him for flipping off his mother."

FLIP ONE'S LID: VER flip one's wig.

FLIP ONE'S WIG: (sin. flip one's lid) exp-v. 1) Perder control emocional, esp. enojarse mucho. Ej. "He simply flipped his wig when his parrot flew away." 2) (sin. lose one's marbles) Volverse loco, demente. Ej. "Poor lady, she flipped her wig one day and was never the same afterwards."

FLIP OUT: exp-v. 1) Perder control emocional, esp. enojarse mucho. Ej. "My mom will flip out if she sees the mess we made." 2) (sin. lose [all] one's marbles) Volverse loco, trastornarse. Ej. "He flipped out after too many drugs." 3) flip out over: Entusiasmarse mucho con algo o alguien. Ej. "You know there's a problem with today's youth when they flip out over something like the Spice Girls."

FLIP-FLOPS: s. 1) Sandalias. Ej. "Bring your flip-flops to the beach." 2) Un retroceso, un viraje, en cuanto a la opinión o posición de uno frente a un tema o cuestión. Ej. "No more flip-flops on abortion. Where do you stand?"

FLOAT ONE'S BOAT: (sin. each his own/to/) exp-v. Provocar o estimular el interés de alguien. Ej. "You like cross-dressing? Well, whatever floats your boat I guess."

FLOOZY: s. 1) Una mujer llamativa, cuya apariencia es vulgar o barata. Ej. "Only a floozy would wear plastic jewelry to the opera." 2) Una mujer suelta. Ej. "Why did he marry that floozy?"

FLY: 1) s. Bragueta, o cremallera; cierre ubicado adelante en pantalones. Ej. "Hey, your fly is down." 2) vi. Ser aceptado o aprobado, ser convincente. Ej. "Do you think my alibi will fly in court?" 3) adj. Atrayente. Ej. "It's a fly new sound they're playing."

FLY LIKE THE WIND: exp-vi. Ir muy

FOLKSY

rápido, en auto, corriendo, etc. Ej. "No one will ever catch him. He flies like the wind."

FOLKSY: VER *hippie*.

FOLLOW THE LEADER: *exp.* Juego infantil en que se imitan las acciones y palabras del líder. Ej. "Let's have the kids play follow the leader."

FOOT: VER *touch something/someone with a ten-foot pole /not/; put one's foot in one's mouth; put one's foot down; put one's best foot forward; shoot oneself in the foot; lead foot*.

FOOT OUT THE DOOR: *exp.* Listo para partir. Ej. "I'm so tired of these arguments. I tell you, I've already got one foot out the door."

FOR REAL: *exp.* VERdadero. Ej. "Is this place for real?" Or "Are you for real?"

FOR THE BIRDS: *exp.* Desagradable o sin valor. Ej. "Working on Sunday is for the birds."

FOR THE HECK OF IT: *exp.* Hacer algo puramente por diversión. Ej. "Why did you hit him?" "Oh, just for the heck of it I guess."

FOR THE HELL OF IT: *exp.* El equivalente vulgar de *for the heck of it*.

FORGET ONE'S PLACE: *exp-vi.* Hacer algo absolutamente desatinado, que no corresponde a la condición de uno. Ej. "You are forgetting your place telling the boss what to do."

FORK OVER: *exp-v.* Entregar algo contra la voluntad, esp. el dinero para pagar por algo. Ej. "Come on, you owe me ten bucks, so fork it over."

FOUR-EYES: *s.* Persona que usa lentes. (Desp.) Ej. "Hey four-eyes, watch where you're going!"

FOUR-LETTER WORD: *s.* Se usa en vez de decir un garabato. (etim. La garabatos estadounidenses más comunes tienen cuarto letras.) Ej. "He was suspended from school for using a four-letter word in class."

FOX: *s.* Una persona atractiva, gen. una mujer. Ej. "That actress is a fox!"

FOXY: *adj.* Atractiva, seductora. Ej. "I'd like to get stuck in an elevator with that foxy mama!"

FRAME: *v.* Inventar testimonios o

FRUITCAKE

falsificar pruebas para incriminar falsamente a alguien. Ej. "It's so obvious they framed him since he wasn't even in town the night of the murder."

FREAKING OUT: (sin. bugging) adj. Actuando de manera irracional o descontrolada. Ej. "Yo man you're freakin' out. Take it easy."

FREAKY: adj. 1) Extraño, raro, sobrenatural. Ej. "It was a freaky sensation. I felt like I'd died, gone to heaven and had come back again". 2) Aterrador, esp. excéntricamente peligroso. Ej. "I had this freaky dream last night that I was being chased down a dark alley in my undies."

FREEBIE: s. Un artículo gratis, esp. uno incluido con una compra o al inscribirse con una compañía o institución. Ej. "They're giving out freebies at the bank to all new customers."

FREELOAD: VER mooch.

FRENCH KISS: s. & v. Beso/besar con lengua. Ej. "Can you believe they French kissed?!"

FRENCHIE: s. Francés, alguien de Francia. (Desp.) Ej. "With that accent, he must be a Frenchie."

FRESH: adj. 1) Alguien que no respeta ni las normas sociales ni los límites ajenos. Ej. "She's so fresh she'd talk back to a nun." 2) Excelente, fantástico. Ej. "That's fresh you got a scholarship to the University." VER awesome.

FRIDAY THE 13TH: exp. Día de mala suerte y espíritus malévolos. Ej. "They went and saw a horror movie on Friday the 13th."

FRIGGING: adj. & adv. 1) Una expresión de sumo enojo o frustración. Ej. "My frigging car broke down again!" 2) Una expresión de sumo regocijo o maravilla. Ej. "This is the best frigging party I've ever been to!"

FRISCO: s. San Francisco. Ej. "I live in Frisco."

FRITZ: VER on the fritz.

FROG: s. Persona francesa. (Desp.) Ej. "Them frogs make good food."

FROM THE TOP: exp. Desde el principio. Ej. "That was all wrong. We'll have to start again from the top."

FROSTY: s. Cerveza. VER brew.

FRUITCAKE: s. 1) Homosexual.

FRYING PAN INTO THE FIRE

(Desp.) 2) Hombre que demuestra caracteríticas femeninas. (Desp.) Ej. "With those limp wrists and high voice he seems like a fruitcake to me." VER fag. 3) Persona alocada o muy excéntrica. Ej. "I can't believe that fruitcake made a bomb in his house."

FRYING PAN INTO THE FIRE: *exp.* Pasar de una mala situación a una peor. Ej. "First I forgot her b'day, then I called her my ex-girlfriend's name. Talk about going from the frying pan into the fire!"

FUCK: [Vul.] 1) *v.* Copular; Tener relaciones sexuales. Ej. "They were fucking in the attic." 2) *int.* Exclamación de rabia o desagrado. Ej. "Fuck! I'm late again!" 3) *s.* Persona despreciable o censurable. Ej. "Tell that fuck to get the hell out of here!" 4) *v.* Maltratar, esp. perjudicar por engaño o medios ilegales/inmorales. Ej. "The guy fucked me on the deal!"

FUCK AROUND: [Vul.] *exp-v.* 1) Tener contacto sexual, esp. ser promiscuo. Ej. "That guy has fucked around with every cute chick in school." 2) Estar sin hacer nada productivo o sin esforzarse. Ej. "When are you going to stop fucking around and get a job?"

FUCK OFF: [Vul.] 1) *exp-v.* Estar sin hacer nada productivo o sin esforzarse. Ej. "That guy is such a loser, he just fucks off all day long." 2) *int.* Expresión enojada de rechazo. Ej. "Fuck off José!"

FUCK UP: [Vul.] 1) *v.* Estropear, chapucear. Ej. "You fuck up this job and you're fired." 2) *v.* Actuar descuidadamente, tontamente o equivocadamente. Ej. "I really fucked up when I told my mother-in-law she could come live with us." 3) *v.* Dañar, herir. Ej. "I fucked up my hand playing baseball." 4) *v.* Volver neurótico/a, dañar psicológicamente. Ej. "She got fucked up as a child from always being told she'd be a failure in life." 5) *s.* Una persona considerada un fracaso. También una persona inmadura y necia. Ej. "He's a real fuck up. He can never hold a job for more than a week."

FUCK YOU: [Vul.] (sin. screw you) *int.* Para expresar el gran disgusto que le provoca alguien. ¡Insulto mayor! Ej. "Fuck you Paul! Fuck you and your whole stupid fucking family!"

FULL OF BEANS

FUCKED UP: [Vul.] *adj.* Pésimo estado, esp. después de una pelea, accidente o exceso de drogas y/o alcohol. *Ej.* "I don't know what happened last night. I was so fucked up I don't remember a thing." Or "She got fucked up in the car crash."

FUCKER: [Vul.] *s.* 1) Insulto mayor, describe a alguien muy desagradable, desconsiderado, abusador, etc. *Ej.* "I wouldn't work for that fucker for a million dollars!" 2) Cosa, objeto, esp. algo que causa molestias. *Ej.* "I can't get this fucker to work."

FUCKING: [Vul.] *adj. & adv.* Adjetivo o adverbio usado para acentuar o enfatizar, que no tiene un significado específico. Sirve de relleno o como puente entre palabras. *Ej.* "This fuckin' thing doesn't work." Or "He's a fuckin' pain in the ass."

FUCKING A: [Vul.] *int.* Expresión que significa 'por supuesto', 'definitivamente'. *Ej.* "Fucking A I'd like a free beer!"

FUCKUP: [Vul.] (sin. screwup) *s.* 1) Persona descuidada o tonta, esp. una que constantemente crea problemas. *Ej.* "He's a fuckup that will never amount to a hill of beans." 2) Un disparate, error, equivocación. *Ej.* "One more fuckup and you're history at this firm."

FUDDY-DUDDY: *s.* Persona considerada muy tensa, muy empaquetada, demasiado consciente de los normas sociales y/o demasiado conservador. No es el tipo de persona que bailará sobre la mesa en una fiesta. *Ej.* "Don't invite that fuddy-duddy or he'll insist we all play Scrabble."

FUDGE: *v.* 1) Timar un poco en cuanto a una medida o cantidad. *Ej.* "So who doesn't fudge their tax returns just a little bit?" 2) Distorsionar la verdad un poco. *Ej.* "Don't fudge, tell me what really happened."

FUGLY: *abr.* Fucking ugly = Sumamente feo. *Ej.* "Dude, I've got news for you. Your new jacket is fugly."

FULL OF BEANS: *exp.* 1) Mintiendo, exagerando a un grado extremo, o, simplemente, equivocado. *Ej.* "That gal is full of beans. I wouldn't believe a word she says." 2) Lleno de energía. *Ej.* "What's gotten into

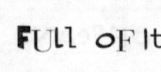

Full of It

you? You're normally so mellow, but today you're full of beans."

FULL OF IT: *exp.* Muy exagerado, esp. errar, equivocarse, o mentir. *Ej.* "She's so full of it I don't think she even knows the difference between the truth and her lies."

FULL OF SHIT: [Vul.] *exp.* Forma grosera y poco diplomática para referirse a alguien como un mentiroso. *Ej.* "He's full of shit if he says I stole your money."

FUNERAL: *s.* Una causa de gran preocupación, esp. implicando que uno debe asumir las consecuencias. *Ej.* "It's his funeral if he doesn't deliver on time."

FUNKY: *adj.* Algo original, refiriéndose esp. a ropa, comida, o gustos en general, que demuestran una personalidad poco convencional. *Ej.* "He's a corporate lawyer, but he wears funky suits to work." Or "Wow, this food has a really funky taste. I've never tried anything like it before."

FUNNY FARM: *s.* Un manicomio o "servicio de salud mental" – hablando *politically correct*. *Ej.* "They finally sent that loony to the funny farm."

FUNNY MONEY: *s.* 1) Moneda falsificada. *Ej.* "Are these real greenbacks or is this funny money?" 2) Dinero de origen dudoso (léase ilícito). *Ej.* "I'd rather be honest and poor than accept your funny money."

FUSE: VER *blow a fuse; short fuse.*

FUTZ AROUND: *exp-v.* 1) Hacer algo sin ánimo; dejar pasar el tiempo sin hacer nada. *Ej.* "I spent the day futzing around the house." 2) Tratar sin respeto o sin cuidado apropiado. *Ej.* "Hey, don't futz around with those machines!"

FUZZ /THE/: *s.* Policía. (Desp.) *Ej.* "You'd better scram before the fuzz gets here." VER *cop.*

F-WORD: *s.* Un eufemismo para 'fuck' o cualquiera de sus derivados. *Ej.* "My mommy was so angry at the man that she used the f-word."

Gab

GAB: *v.* Hablar libremente y socialmente esp. sobre temas triviales. *Ej.* "My darn sister can gab on the phone for hours!"

GABFEST: *s.* Reunión para hablar

sobre temas sin importancia, especialmente para hablar sobre el último chisme. *Ej.* "When they get together, it's a regular gabfest."

GAGA: *adj.* 1) Loco, demente. *Ej.* "He got hit in the head and has been gaga ever since." VER *bats.* 2) Muy entusiasta, muy interesado. *Ej.* "I'm gaga about the Rollings Stones new album."

GAL: (sin. dame, chick, skirt, broad) *s.* Mujer, tipa. *Ej.* "She's a nice gal, you'd like her."

GAME: VER *name of the game; play the game.*

GANGBANG: *v.* 1) El que varios hombres tengan forzadamente relación sexual con una mujer (lo que, en general, implica violación). *Ej.* "They all got arrested for gangbanging that poor girl." 2) Pertenecer a una pandilla de maleantes y dedicarse a actividades ilegales y/o peligrosas. *Ej.* "From choir boy to gangbanging; it's a story of moral decay."

GANGBUSTERS /LIKE/: *exp-vi.* Realizando algo con mucho intensidad, ímpetu. *Ej.* "They were working like gangbusters trying to finish the house on time."

GANGIA: *s.* Marihuana. *Ej.* "It's illegal to buy gangia in the U.S."

GAS: *s.* Algo o alguien muy entretenido y divertido. *Ej.* "The amusement park was a gas." Or "He's a gas. He makes me laugh really hard." VER TAMBIEN *run out of gas.*

GAZILLION: (sin. bazillion) *s.* Numero inventado, mucho de, muchos veces. *Ej.* "It's a great song, but I've heard it like a gazillion times so I'm sick of it."

GAZONGAS: *s.pl.* Senos de mujer, gen. muy grandes. *Ej.* "There's no way those gazongas are real. She must've had implants."

GEE: *s.* 1) (sin. grand, thou) Mil dólares. *Ej.* "I pull down a gee a week at my job." 2) Amigo. *Ej.* "Hey gee, what's up?"

GEEK: (sin. nerd) *s.* 1) Una persona con un sólo propósito o demasiado comprometida con un interés científico, esp. la computación. *Ej.* "He doesn't care if people thinks he's a geek, because he knows that

he's going to make tons of money in Silicon Valley someday." 2) Una persona socialmente inepta y poco atractiva. *Ej.* "It used to be that only geeks used computers, but now everyone uses them."

GEEZER: *s.* Un viejo, esp. uno raro o excéntrico. *Ej.* "Don't go near that geezer's house. He'll shoot at you if he thinks you're trespassing."

GENTLE AS A LAMB: *exp.* Describe a un ser inofensivo o tímido. *Ej.* "Even though he appears dangerous, he's gentle as a lamb."

GET: *vi.* 1) Entender. *Ej.* "Oh, I get you." Or "I don't get the question." 2) Vengarse, desquitarse. *Ej.* "You touch my sister and I'll get you!" 4) Observar, mirar, gen. algo o alguien fuera de lo común o raro. *Ej.* "Get that guy over there talking to the birds." 5) Matar, asesinar. *Ej.* "They got him in the back." VER *waste*. 6) Provocar dolor, pena. *Ej.* "It really gets me to see people starving in the world."

GET A KICK OUT OF: *exp-vi.* Disfrutar mientras se hace algo, o mientras se mira algo o a alguien. *Ej.* "I get a kick out of watching my kids play together." Or "She gets a kick out of driving fast."

GET A LIFE: *exp.* Expresión irónica para aconsejarle a alguien que deje de fijarse en forma obsesiva en un aspecto de su vida y comience a comportarse como una persona normal. *Ej.* "Get a life pal, you spend all day watching TV!"

GET A LOAD OF: *exp-vi. & int.* VER, examinar o escuchar a alguien/algo muy divertido, terrible o vil. *Ej.* "Did you get a load of the pick-up lines he was laying on that chick?" Or "Get a load of that guy over there."

GET AWAY WITH MURDER: *exp-vi.* Hacer algo malo sin castigo. *Ej.* "He got away with murder not being expelled from school after stealing the principal's car."

GET CANNED: VER *get the ax*.

GET DOWN: *exp-vi.* 1) Bailar. *Ej.* "Get down Fred! Way to shake that thing!" 2) Actuar libremente, esp. dejar a un lado la tendencia conservadora normal de uno y actuar sin inhibiciones. *Ej.* "It's good to see him get down and have

GET OFF ONE'S HIGH HORSE

fun for a change."

GET INTO IT: *exp-vi.* 1) Comenzar a luchar. *Ej.* "If you want to get into it with me, you'd better have health insurance." 2) Comenzar a discutir acaloradamente. *Ej.* "When my parents get into it, it's time to leave the house."

GET INTO SOMEONE'S PANTS: [Vul.] *exp-vi.* Tener relaciones sexuales con alguien. *Ej.* "He's really cute. I'd like to get into his pants some night!"

GET IT INTO ONE'S HEAD: *exp-vi.* Comprender totalmente o aceptar un hecho, una orden o una realidad de la vida. *Ej.* "Just get it into your head, you are not going to be the next President of the United States without a college degree."

GET IT ON: [Vul.] *exp-vi.* Tener relación o actividad sexual. *Ej.* "I was shocked when she asked me if I wanted to get it on."

GET IT UP: [Vul.] *exp-vi.* Lograr una erección. *Ej.* "You'd better see a doctor if you cannot get it up."

GET IT: *exp-vi.* Ser castigado o retado. *Ej.* "You're gonna get it from your father for hitting your sister."

GET LAID: [Vul.] *exp-vi.* Tener relación sexual. *Ej.* "If you can get laid, anyone can."

GET LOCKED UP: (sin. get sent away, send up) *exp-vi.* Ir a la cárcel. *Ej.* "With the life he's leading, it's a sure thing he'll get locked up one day."

GET LOST: *int.* ¡Lárgate! *Ej.* "I told the bum to get lost." Or "Get lost you loser!"

GET NOWHERE FAST: (sin. go nowhere fast) *exp-vi.* Hacer algo sin lograr a nada. *Ej.* "You are getting nowhere fast with those lame excuses."

GET OFF EASY: *exp-vi.* Escapar o evadir castigo o serias consecuencias. *Ej.* "You got off easy not having to go to jail."

GET OFF ON: *exp-vi.* Experimentar gran placer o deleite, a menudo ilícitos. *Ej.* "You're sick to get off on child pornography."

GET OFF ONE'S ASS: Forma vulgar de *get off one's rear*.

GET OFF ONE'S HIGH HORSE: *int.* Se le dice a alguien de manera insultante para que deje de

GET OFF ONE'S REAR

creerse tan altanera. Ej. "Oh, get off your high horse Sarah. Stop being Miss Upper Crust and just accept people for what they are."

GET OFF ONE'S REAR: *exp-vi.* Ponerse a trabajar, comenzar a hacer algo, esp. decir adiós a la flojera y hola a la productividad. Ej. "It's time you get off your rear and get a job."

GET OFF: *exp-vi.* 1) [Vul.] Tener un orgasmo. Ej. "It felt so good to get off last night." 2) Experimentar gran placer o deleite, a menudo ilícitos. Ej. "She gets off watching other couples having sex." 3) Sentirse eufórico, esp. como resultado de tomar una droga. Ej. "Watch out for that stuff, it'll really get you off."

GET OLD: *exp-vi.* Tornarse aburrido. Ej. "It gets old hearing you complain all the time."

GET ON ONE'S HIGH HORSE: *exp-vi.* Asumir un actitud altanera. Ej. "When my mom gets on her high horse, no one I date is good enough for the family."

GET ON THE STICK: *exp.* Apurarse. Ej. "You'd better get on the stick, or we'll miss the movie."

GET ONE'S ACT TOGETHER: *exp-vi.* Organizarse; dejar de comportarse en forma vaga. Ej. "You had better get your act together and start studying or I'm gonna tan your hide!" Or "I have to get my act together or I'll never finish this project."

GET ONE'S GOAT: *exp-v.* Molestar o causarle enojo a alguien. Ej. "It gets my goat when people try to cut in front of me."

GET ONE'S HOOKS INTO: *exp-vi.* Dominar a alguien, poner a alguien en una situación comprometedora. Ej. "Once these crooks get their hooks into you, you're history."

GET ONE'S REAR IN GEAR: *exp-vi.* Entrar en movimiento, iniciar una acción. Ej. "I better get my rear in gear if I'm going to finish painting the house."

GET ONE'S ROCKS OFF: *exp-vi.* Sentirse estimulado, excitado; sentir placer por algo, esp. un placer ilícito. Ej. "I cannot believe people get their rocks off being peed on!"

GET ONE'S SHIT TOGETHER: [Vul.]

GET tHE BrEAKs

exp-vi. Organizarse o lograr control sobre los asuntos o la vida de uno. Ej. "You better get your shit together if you want to succeed in life."

GET ONE'S: exp-vi. Recibir el castigo merecido. Ej. "You've been screwing people over for a long time, but someday you're going to get yours."

GET REAL: int. Significa dejar de bromear, dejar de actuar como un tonto y volver a la realidad. Ej. "Get real, I would never do such a juvenile prank." Or "Get real Sam, you're not a teenager any more."

GET SENT AWAY: (sin. get locked up, send up) exp-vi. Ir a la cárcel. Ej. "She got sent away for organizing a prostitution ring."

GET SOME: exp-vi. Obtener algo, gen. referente a actividad sexual. Ej. "I'm going to get some this weekend!"

GET (SOME)ONE'S DRIFT: exp-vi. Comprender la perspectiva, idea, sugerencia, etc. de otro. Ej. "Get my drift?" Or "I get your drift."

GET SOMETHING OFF ONE'S CHEST: exp-v. Desahogarse, contar un problema, una queja o fuente de frustración a otra persona. Ej. "Is there something bothering you? Tell me, it'll be good to get it off your chest." Or "I have to get this off my chest. It really hurt me when you didn't say anything about my new hairdo."

GET THE AX: (sin. get canned) exp-vi. Perder el trabajo o ser despedido abruptamente. Ej. "Poor Ted, he got the ax for the third time this month."

GET tHE Ax

GET THE BREAKS: exp-vi. Persona que tiene mucha suerte; para

GET tHE BuLL By tHE hoRNs

quien todo se resuelve en su favor. *Ej.* "Joe is so lucky, he always gets the breaks."

GET THE BULL BY THE HORNS: *VER* take the bull by the horns.

GET THE CAT BY THE TAIL: *exp-vi.* Dominar totalmente una situación. *Ej.* "There's no way you're going to control this situation until you get the cat by the tail."

GET THE DROP ON: *exp-vi.* Lograr una definitiva ventaja sobre algo/alguien. *Ej.* "He got the drop on you by arriving earlier."

GET THE HOOK: *exp-vi.* Ser despedido, o echado inesperadamente y sin ceremonia. *Ej.* "Once again, Al had gotten the hook for propositioning his boss's wife."

GET THE JUMP ON SOMEONE: *exp-vi.* Anticipar la acción de alguien y actuar antes. *Ej.* "She got the jump on me and dumped me before I could dump her."

GET THE LAST LAUGH: (sin. have the last laugh, one who laughs last, laughs longest) *exp-vi.* Proverbio que significa que la persona que tiene la última jugada disfruta más. *Ej.* "Yeah, you've gotten the better of me for now, but I'll get the last laugh if it's the last thing I do!"

GET THE LEAD OUT: *exp-vi.* Ponerse en marcha. Comenzar a moverse, o moverse más rápido; también se usa relacionado con el trabajo (trabajar más rápido). *Ej.* "Hey, let's get the lead out or we'll never make it to the movies on time."

GET TO THE POINT: (sin. get to the heart of the matter) *exp-vi.* Llegar a la esencia de una idea o conversación. *Ej.* "Get to the point, Hal. How much money do you need?"

GET TOGETHER: *s.* Reunión social informal con algo de comida y/o tragos. *Ej.* "It's not a big party, it's just a get together at Phil's place."

GET WHAT ONE PAYS FOR: *exp.* Dicho como advertencia que comprar lo más barato es a menudo más caro porque luego habrá que reponerlo. *Ej.* "You shouldn't have bought the cheapest brand. You always get what you pay for."

GIVE AN INCH AND ONE TAKES A MILE

GET WITH IT: *exp-vi.* Fijarse en los eventos que lo rodean y comprometerse. *Ej.* "Get with it Stanley, everyone else is ready to go except you."

GET WITH THE PROGRAM: *exp-vi.* Estar atento a los acontecimientos que afectan la vida de uno, participar en lo que se pueda. *Ej.* "We're all waiting for you, so how about getting with the program?"

GET YOUR KNICKERS IN A TWIST: *exp-vi.* Ponerse nervioso en una situación. (Ing.) *Ej.* "Don't get your knickers in a twist. It's only an informal interview."

GETTING BY: *exp.* Una respuesta a "¿Cómo estás?" que significa bien pero no demasiado bien. *Ej.* "How's it going Fred?" "Oh, I'm gettin' by."

GHETTO BLASTER: (sin. boom box) *s.* Un aparato estereofónico portátil capaz de producir sonido muy fuerte. *Ej.* "Damn, that ghetto blaster makes a lot of noise."

GIG: *s.* Un trabajo, esp. un contrato para músicos. *Ej.* "I got you guys a gig at a new club."

GIMP: *s.* Una persona que cojea. *Ej.* "I've been a gimp since my knee operation."

GIRLY: 1) *adj.* Mujeres con poca ropa o desnudas que figuran en películas, revistas pornográficas o en bares. *Ej.* "You must be sexually frustrated looking at those girly magazines all day." 2) *s.* Femenino. *Ej.* "I don't want to belong to your girly club anyway!"

GIT-GO /FROM THE/: *adv.* Desde el comienzo, al empezar. *Ej.* "He played well from the git-go."

GIVE A CRAP: [Vul.] *exp-vi.* Importarle a uno, pero gen. se usa en forma negativa para expresar una falta de preocupación. *Ej.* "I don't give a crap about your excuses, it's over between us!"

GIVE A SHIT: [Vul.] *exp-vi.* No importarle algo a uno, no estar interesado. También se usa en forma negativa para significar lo mismo. *Ej.* "As if I give a shit what he does at home."

GIVE AN INCH AND ONE TAKES A MILE: *exp.* Se dice de alguien que se aprovecha de la generosidad de otro. *Ej.* "She was really stressed

GIVe GOOd SOMeTHInG

so I told her to take some time off. She's been gone two months! I tell you, I gave an inch and she took a mile."

GIVE GOOD SOMETHING: *exp-vi.* Hacer algo esmeradamente. Ej. "She's a successful telemarketer because she gives good phone."

GIVE IT ONE'S ALL: VER *give it one's best shot.*

GIVE IT ONE'S BEST SHOT: (sin. *give it one's all*) *exp-vi.* Esforzarse al máximo con algo. Hacer algo con toda la energía y esfuerzo. Ej. "I didn't win the competition, but at least I gave it my best shot."

GIVE IT UP: *int.* Dejar de hacer algo o rendirse ante algo. Ej. "Give it up, Dave. You're never going to be a professional athlete."

GIVE ME A BREAK!: *int.* Decirle a una persona que desista con un argumento irracional, una exageración, o mentira. Ej. "Give me a break! I know you didn't go to Turkey last week."

GIVE SOMEONE (SOME) LIP: *exp-vi.* Hablarle a alguien en forma irrespetuosa. Ej. "That jerk tried to give me some lip, but I set him straight." Or "Give me lip and you'll be sorry!"

GIVE SOMEONE A HARD TIME: (sin. *give someone grief*) *exp-v.* Molestar o sacar de quicio. Ej. "My friends have been giving me a hard time for hanging with my girlfriend and not with them."

GIVE SOMEONE FIVE: *exp-vi.* Palmotear con alguien como seña de saludo o para felicitar. Ej. "Hey Joe, give me five."

GIVE SOMEONE GRIEF: (sin. *give somone a hard time*) *exp-vi.* Acosar, molestar a alguien. Ej. "My husband has been giving me grief all week for no reason."

GIVE SOMETHING A REST: *exp-vi.* Dejar de hablar o de comportarse en forma molesta o fastidiosa. Ej. "Why don't you give it a rest Bob, you've been complaining for an hour."

GIVE THE EVIL EYE: *exp-vi.* Desearle el mal a otra persona. Maldecir a alguien. Ej. "Everything was going great for Tim till she gave him the evil eye. Now he's alone and begging for change on street corners".

GO AT IT

GIVE THEM HELL: Hablado: give 'em hell. 1) *int.* Palabras de aliento para infundir entusiasmo y éxito a alguien. *Ej.* "Give 'em hell tonight Joey, show 'em your stuff!" 2) *exp-vi.* Regañar o criticar fuertemente. *Ej.* "He gave 'em hell for picking on the younger kids."

GIZMO: *s.* Cosa, objeto, aparato cuyo nombre se ha olvidado o se desconoce. *Ej.* "I can't find that damn gizmo for the whatchamacallit."

GLAD RAGS: *s.pl.* Ropa a la moda, esp. las que se usan para una fiesta. *Ej.* "Look who's got their glad rags on tonight!"

GLAMOUR BOY/GIRL: *s.* Persona muy preocupada por su imagen que típicamente usa ropa cara y se da aires, esp. un hombre con chaqueta de cuero, anteojos de sol caros, etc. que trata de verse atrayente. *Ej.* "She's dating this total glamour boy. He's like so conceited that he has portraits of himself all over his place."

GLITZ: *s.* Ostentación de mal gusto, despliegue charro. *Ej.* "The movie was all glitz and no substance: million dollar sets and no plot."

GNARLY: *adj.* Excelente, fantástico. *Ej.* "That was a gnarly move dude! Do it again!" VER awesome.

GO: *s.* Aprobación, permiso. *Ej.* "We got the go on the parking lot project, but the no go on the skyscraper."

GO ALL OUT: *exp-vi.* Hacer un esfuerzo máximo para perseguir una meta o lograr algo. *Ej.* "Wow, they went all out on this wedding! No expense spared."

GO ALL THE WAY: *exp-v.* Tener relaciones sexuales, ir más allá de besarse y tocarse hasta el mismo acto sexual. *Ej.* "I didn't go all the way until I was married."

GO APE SHIT: [Vul.] *exp-vi.* 1) Perder control emocional, esp. enfurecerse. *Ej.* "I went ape shit when he told me that he had crashed my new car." 2) Entusiasmarse mucho con algo. *Ej.* "The kids will go ape shit when they find out we're taking them to Disney Land."

GO AT IT: *exp-vi.* Pelear. *Ej.* "It was

GO BALLISTIC

ugly when the two sisters went at it."

GO BALLISTIC: *exp-vi.* Perder la compostura y/o el control, esp. como resultado de enojo. Ej. "I went ballistic when she told me there was another man in her life."

GO BELLY UP: *exp-vi.* Como un pez muerto flotando en el mar, esta expresión significa quebrar económicamente. Ej. "The business went belly up after the president ran off to Mexico with all the money."

GO COLD TURKEY: *exp-vi.* Parar de un viaje. Abandonar un vicio totalmente, gen. alcohol, drogas, cigarrillos. Ej. "After smoking for ten years, I went cold turkey one day and haven't touched another cig since."

GO COLD: *exp-vi.* Tornarse inútil, esp. al estar rindiendo bien y repentinamente dejar de hacerlo. Gen. se dice con referencia a competencias. Ej. "He scored 20 points in the first half and then went cold, missing all his shots."

GO DOWN: *exp-vi.* Ocurrir, suceder. Ej. "Where were you when the burglary went down."

GO DOWN ON: [Vul.] *exp-vi.* Practicar sexo oral sobre alguien. Ej. "Is it true you went down on her?"

GO DUTCH: *exp-vi.* Pagar la mitad de algo, gen. la cuenta de un restaurante. Ej. "I'd like to go out with you, but only if we go Dutch."

GO FOR IT: *int.* Darle ánimo a alguien para que haga algo. Ej. "Go for it dude, you can make it." Or "Go for it, I think travelling around the world will be a profitable experience."

GO GIRL: *exp.* Palabras de aliento o felicitaciones, gen. entre mujeres. A menudo se dice you go girl. Ej. "You go girl, you deserved that promotion!"

GO IN TOGETHER: *exp-vi.* Ser socio de alguien. Ej. "It's too risky to do it alone, let's go in together on the deal."

GO NOWHERE FAST: (sin. get nowhere fast) *exp-vi.* Hacer algo sin llegar a nada. Ej. "He's going nowhere fast working at a gas station."

GO OFF ON: *exp-vi.* 1) Discutir algo

en gran detalle y durante demasiado tiempo. *Ej.* "The teacher went off on the importance of Napoleon's horse for like an hour." 2) Gritarle a alguien. *Ej.* "I was so angry at him for getting drunk before meeting my parents that I just went off on him."

GO OFF SOMEBODY/SOMETHING: *exp-vi.* Dejar de gustarle una persona o una idea. *Ej.* "I've gone off John; he's such a bore." Or "I've gone off meat." (Ing.)

GO OUT WITH: (sin. dating /be/) *exp-vi.* Estar saliendo con alguien. *Ej.* "She's been going out with him for a month now."

GO OVERBOARD: *exp-vi.* Exagerar, sobrepasarse. *Ej.* "Here's the credit card, but don't go overboard buying clothes."

GO STEADY: *exp-vi.* Tener una seria relación con alguien de carácter constante. *Ej.* "I just want an occasional roll in the hay, I don't want to go steady."

GO TO HELL: *int.* Para expresar el gran disgusto que le provoca alguien. *Ej.* "Go to hell Steve, you're worthless and you know it!"

GO TO MAN: *s.* La persona más confiable, esp. en momentos de gran presión. *Ej.* "At crunch time, you have to believe in your go to man."

GO TO POT: *exp-vi.* Deteriorarse, gen. muy rápidamente. *Ej.* "The team has really gone to pot. Champions last year, last place this year."

GOD'S GIFT TO MANKIND: *exp.* Tenerse en muy alta estima. Creerse superior a los demás. *Ej.* "You're so full of yourself, you act like you're God's gift to mankind."

GOFER: *s.* Persona de los mandados de una oficina, mal pagada, gen. masculino. *Ej.* "Get a gofer to photocopy these pages."

GOLD DIGGER: *s.* Una mujer que sale con o se casa con hombres ricos porque quiere algo de su fortuna. *Ej.* "They say she's a gold digger, but maybe she's just attracted to older, wealthy men."

GONE: *adj.* 1) Locamente enamorado, amartelado. *Ej.* "My sis is gone over Brad Pitt." 2) Embarazado. *Ej.* "How many

GONER

months gone is she?"

GONER: s. Un muerto o una persona condenada a morir o fracasar dramáticamente. Ej. "You're a goner if you don't meet this deadline."

GONNA: abr. Going to = Verbo en tiempo futuro. Ej. "I'm gonna go to college some day."

GONZO: adj. Excéntrico o poco convencional, casi loco. Ej. "He's been gonzo ever since the Gulf War."

GOOD EGG: s. Una muy buena persona, una persona honesta y confiable. Ej. "He's a good egg, you can definitely trust him."

GOOD OLD BOY: s. 1) Un hombre, típicamente blanco del sur rural de los Estados Unidos, que sigue el comportamiento estereotipado de sus pares, esp. en cuanto a intolerancia y compañerismo. Ej. "Be careful of the good old boys down south. They can turn a northerner's vacation into a nightmare lickety-split." 2) Un miembro masculino de un grupo cerrado que trabaja junto e intercambia favores para mantener control. Ej. "The good old boys will never let an outsider win a local election."

GOOD TO THE LAST DROP: exp. Algo sumamente deseable, apetecible y/o delicioso hasta el último momento. Ej. "This vacation has been good to the last drop."

GOOD TURN /A/: exp. Un favor. Ej. "Tom did me a good turn last year, and I haven't forgotten it."

GOODS: s.pl. Información o pruebas acusadoras. Ej. "The cops tried to get the goods on the crook."

Good old boy

GOODY TWO-SHOES: (sin. goody-goody) s. Una persona santurrona. Ej. "She's such a goody two-shoes she'll never go along with the prank."

GOODY-GOODY: (sin. goody two-shoes) s. Una persona santurrona. Ej. "That goody-goody cut class? Not likely!"

GOOF: 1) (sin. goof ball) s. Una persona ridícula, tonta, o necia. Ej. "I'm not inviting that goof over to my house." 2) s. Una falta, error, o equivocación. Ej. "That was a major league goof telling the teacher what you *really* thought of him." 3) s. Algo entretenido, divertido. Ej. "Let's go to the circus, it'll be a goof." 4) v. Equivocarse tontamente. Ej. "I goofed on my driving test by leaving the emergency brake on."

GOOF AROUND: exp-v. Chacotear, estar sin hacer nada productivo o estar traveseando. Ej. "Are you capable of being serious for even a moment, or do you always goof around?"

GOOF BALL: (sin. goof*) s. Una persona ridícula, tonta o necia. Ej. "He's such a goof ball he'll never do anything worthwhile with his life."

GOOF UP: exp-v. Equivocarse, hacer algo mal. Ej. "Sam goofed up big time. He forgot to turn off the gas and practically burnt down the house."

GOOF-OFF: (sin. mess around) v. Pasarlo bien esp. actuar con poca seriedad. Ej. "If you always goof-off in school you'll never learn anything."

GOOFY: adj. Tonto, ridículo, estrafalario. Ej. "She's in such a goofy mood, she's been laughing all day."

GOOK: s. 1) (sin. goop) Una substancia gruesa, desagradable, como lodo. Ej. "I can't get this gook off my hands!" 2) Persona asiática, esp. un soldado de Vietnam del Norte durante la Guerra de Vietnam. (Desp.) Ej. "Those gooks were a lot tougher than we thought."

GOON: s. Un hombre grande y amenazante, gen. un matón contratado. Ej. "You tell your goons to stay out of my casino,

GOONY

or there are going to be fireworks!"

GOONY: *adj.* Sin gracia y tonto. *Ej.* "He's still a goony guy no matter how nice you say he is."

GOOP: (sin. gook*) *s.* Substancia gruesa, pegajosa, mojada. *Ej.* "How do you clean this goop up?"

GOOSE: *v.* Pellizcar a alguien entre o en las nalgas. *Ej.* "She slapped him for goosing her." VER TAMBIEN *wild goose chase*.

GOOSE EGG: *s.* Cero, nada, gen. se usa para el resultado de un partido. *Ej.* "We scored a big goose egg in the game."

GOOSE IS COOKED /ONE'S/: *exp-v.* Perder o arruinar una oportunidad. *Ej.* "If they find out I'm an ex-con, my goose is cooked and I'll never get the job."

GORILLA: *s.* 1) Un hombre grande y amenazador. *Ej.* "Who let that gorilla out of the zoo? I wouldn't want to be in a dark alley with him!" 2) Un matón contratado. *Ej.* "Tell your gorillas to back off or there's gonna be trouble."

GOUGE: *exp-v.* Cobrar precios excesivos. *Ej.* "I don't shop at that store, they gouge you there."

GOURD: VER *out of one's gourd*.

GOY: *s.* Uno que no es judío. (Desp.). *Ej.* "Them goys will never understand our traditions."

GRAB THE HELM: *exp-v.* Tomar el mando o la responsabilidad en una situación en que, siguiendo la metáfora de un buque, no hay capitán. *Ej.* "If we're gonna salvage this business, someone needs to grab the helm."

GRABS: VER *up for grabs*.

GRAIN OF SALT: VER *pinch of salt*

GRAMPS: *s.* Abuelo. *Ej.* "Tell me a story gramps, please!"

GRAND: (sin. gee*, thou) *s.* Mil dólares. *Ej.* "I'm a grand short to buy the car. Can you spot me the gee"

GRANOLA: VER *hippie*.

GRAPES: VER *sour grapes*.

GRASS: (sin. reefer, weed*, hooch*, pot*, buddah, gangia, herb) *s.* Marihuana. *Ej.* "Do you want to smoke some grass?"

GRAVY: *s.* Dinero, ganancia o beneficios adquiridos inesperadamente o fácilmente. *Ej.* "Getting that bonus was gravy on

GREENBACK

top of his million dollar salary."

GRAVY TRAIN: s. Ingreso, gen. de un trabajo, que requiere poco trabajo y paga bien. *Ej.* "My new job is a gravy train. I make six figures just telling people where to put their money."

GRAZE: v. Comer grandes cantidades de todo lo que está a mano. (etim. *graze* es un verbo que describe cómo comen las vacas y otros animales herbívoros que se alimentan todo el día). *Ej.* "Billy Joe Bob doesn't eat, he grazes."

GREASE: VER *elbow grease; squeaky wheel gets the grease.*

GREASE MONKEY: s. Persona que trabaja con motores y que siempre tiene las manos y ropa manchadas con grasa. *Ej.* "If you have a car, it's great to have a grease monkey as a friend."

GREASE SOMEONE'S PALM/HAND: exp-v. Sobornar. *Ej.* "If you want the municipal contract, you'd better grease the right person's palm."

GREASER: s. 1) Un hombre macho y duro, esp. un blanco proveniente de la clase obrera que ama motocicletas o autos. *Ej.* "She started dating a greaser just to piss-off her dad." 2) Un latinoamericano, esp. un mexicano. (Desp.) *Ej.* "There's a lot of greasers living in LA nowadays."

GREASY SPOON: s. Un restaurante sucio y barato que gen. sirve porciones generosas de comida estadounidense. *Ej.* "I know a great greasy spoon where we can go for breakfast."

GREEN LIGHT /GIVE THE/: exp-vi. Aceptar, en el sentido de decirle 'sí' a una proposición. *Ej.* "After thrice being rejected, I was finally given the green light on my proposal."

GREEN STUFF: s. Dinero. *Ej.* "I like the look of the green stuff." VER *dough.*

GREEN: *adj.* 1) Característica de una persona joven y sin experiencia. *Ej.* "He's a little too green for that kind of responsibility." 2) Con nauseas, como a punto de vomitar. *Ej.* "That dude looks green. Someone should take him to the john before he yukes."

GREENBACK: s. Dólar. *Ej.* "Sammy's so tight, he wouldn't

GRIN AND BEAR IT

even lend a greenback to his own mom." VER buck.

GRIN AND BEAR IT: *exp-v.* Tolerar una situación mala o desagradable sin quejarse. *Ej.* "I know you despise your boss, but we need the money so you're just going to have to grin and bear it."

GRODY: (sin. icky, skanky) *adj.* Baboso, asqueroso, sumamente poco atractivo. *Ej.* "He's so grody even his mother won't kiss him."

GROOVE: 1) *s.* Rutina establecida. *Ej.* "I'm getting into the groove of a nine-to-five job." 2) *v.* Disfrutar, deleitarse. *Ej.* "I love just sitting around, grooving on the music." 3) (sin. hood) *s.* Barrio. *Ej.* "We come from the same groove."

GROOVY: *adj.* Muy agradable, excelente, maravilloso. *Ej.* "I love the groovy new sound of The Figments."

GROPE: *v.* Agarrar, tocar o acariciar para lograr estímulo sexual, gen. usado en forma peyorativa para expresar disgusto por tal acción. *Ej.* "She kicked him in the nuts for trying to grope her."

GROSS OUT: *exp-v.* Causar náuseas, hacer vomitar, dar asco. *Ej.* "I got so grossed out when this guy puked on the bus."

GROUND: *v.* Castigar a un niño, esp. restringir sus movimientos. *Ej.* "The next time you break curfew, you'll be grounded for a month."

GROUPIE: *s.* Un hincha, entusiasta o admirador que es fanático de un grupo musical, grupo, persona o profesional y lo/la/los sigue o asiste a funciones donde se encuentra tal foco de fanatismo. *Ej.* "She was a groupie of the Rolling Stones for years before having a change of life and becoming a fireman's groupie."

GROVEL AT ONE'S FEET: *exp-v.* Humillarse o rebajarse ante alguien. *Ej.* "I hate it when my children grovel at my feet, begging for candy."

GROW LIKE WILDFLOWERS: *exp-vi.* Crecer muy rápido. *Ej.* "When kids are young, they grow like wildflowers."

GROW ON ONE: *exp-vi.* Acostumbrarse a algo o alguien que al principio le era desagradable a uno. *Ej.* "I didn't like Susan the first few times I met her, but after a while she grew on me." Or "You may not like sushi at first, but it grows on you."

GRUB: 1) (sin. chow) s. Comida. Ej. "I need to get some grub. I'm starving!" 2) v. Obtener algo suplicando o pidiéndolo. Ej. "It's pathetic how these kids are always grubbing for money." VER TAMBIEN *rustle up some grub*.

GRUNGE: s. 1) Inmundicia, mugre. Ej. "Look at the grunge on your new clothes!" 2) Estilo o moda que se popularizó a fines de los 80 y comienzos de los 90 consistiendo en ropa muy informal a desgarbada y una apariencia que hasta cierto punto representa desilusión con las autoridades. Ej. "Are you going for the grunge look or are you just sloppy?" 3) Tipo de música (como Nirvana, Pearl Jam, Soundgarden, etc.) cuyas letras expresan una desilusión con la vida moderna y una falta de expectativas para el futuro. Ej. "I used to love disco, but now I love grunge."

GRUNGY: *adj.* Sucio, andrajoso, a maltraer. Ej. "I'm not eating in that grungy looking restaurant!"

GRUNT: s. "medio pollo" 1) Persona pagada para realizar tareas desagradables y aburridas para otro. Ej. "Be smart, hire a grunt to do the leg work for you." 2) Persona intermediaria; alguien considerado como de poca importancia. Ej. "He's just a grunt in the office, he'll be the first to be fired."

GRUNT WORK: (sin. dirty work) *exp.* Tareas desagradables y aburridas, que a menudo implican esfuerzo físico que provoca gruñidos. Ej. "It was some serious grunt work cleaning out that old barn."

GUFF: s. Tontera, insolencia. Ej. "Any guff from you and your grounded for a week."

GUILT TRIP: *exp.* Intencionalmente hacer que alguien se sienta culpable o se recrimine. Ej. "He gave me a big time guilt trip for forgetting his birthday."

GUM UP: *exp-v.* Arruinar, estropear, echar a perder. Ej. "If we get Dave in the deal, he's gonna gum

GUMSHOE

up the works with his insane demands."

GUMSHOE: (sin. dick) s. Un detective, un investigador. Ej. "We hired a gumshoe to find out who'd been sending us threatening mail."

GUN: VER *big gun; jump the gun; loose gun; smoking gun; stick to one's guns; under the gun.*

GUNG-HO: adj. Muy entusiasta. Ej. "Have a little patience, you don't have to be so gung-ho all the time."

GUT: 1) s. Estómago amplio. Ej. "You must've drunk a lot of beer to get a gut like that." 2) s. & adj. Instinto, intuición. Ej. "I'm gonna listen to my gut feeling on this and decide in favor of Jerry." Or "In her gut, she knew her parents were right, but her stubborn streak wouldn't allow her to listen to herself." 3) guts: s.pl. Valor, fortaleza. Ej. "Show some guts for a change. You can't be a pussy all your life." VER TAMBIEN *hate someone's guts; spill one's guts.*

GUT IT OUT: exp-v. Encarar la resistencia y adversidad con resolución y perseverancia. Ej. "I was so beat towards the end of the marathon, but I gutted it out and finished."

GUTLESS: adj. Cobarde. Ej. "You're really gutless if you can't tell him the truth."

GUTSY: adj. Muy fuerte y atrevido, a menudo en forma arriesgada o presumida. Ej. "You're gutsy to camp in the woods all alone."

GUY: 1) s. Hombre, tipo. Ej. "Would you ask that guy to come over here?" 2) guys: Hombres y mujeres. Ej. "What do you guys feel like doing?" VER TAMBIEN *bad guys; fall guy; tough guy; wise guy.*

GYP: 1) v. Defraudar, estafar, engañar. Ej. "He's so money hungry he'd gyp his own mother." VER *burn.* 2) (sin. rip-off) s. Una estafa o engaño. Ej. "It was a real gyp buying from that store."

HACK: 1) v. Reducir o mutilar cortando o quitando. Ej. "They hacked the proposal to bits." 2) v. Tolerar, aguantar, o manejar. Gen. se dice can hack. Ej. "Can he hack the pressure of the big leagues?" Or "She's so tough she can hack anything." 3) s. Persona que

HANd JOB

disfruta de un deporte, aunque no sea un experto; generalmente golf. Ej. "I have taken many lessons, but I'm still a hack." 4) v. Entrar sin permiso al computador de otra persona. Ej. "Joe was able to hack the CIA's computers." VER TAMBIEN *can hack*.

HACKER: s. Persona que, a través del internet, entra ilegalmente a los computadores de otros. Ej. "A hacker broke into Bill Gates' computer and stole his e-mail."

HAIR: VER *bad hair day; by a hair; let one's hair down; split hairs.*

HAIR OF THE DOG THAT BIT YOU: exp. Beber algo alcohólico al día siguiente de haber bebido demasiado, al sentirse con resaca. El supuesto propósito de este trago es sentirse mejor. Ej. "If you're badly hung over, you should start the day with the hair of the dog that bit ya'."

HAIRY: adj. Peligroso, difícil o alarmante. Ej. "It was a hairy situation when he pulled out a gun to rob us."

HALF-ASSED: [Vul.] adj. Actitud de alguien que realiza su trabajo a media máquina, sin cuidado ni esfuerzo. Ej. "He is a nice enough guy, but he does everything half-assed."

HALF-PINT: s. Un ser pequeño. Ej. "I am filled with natural empathy for all the half-pints of this world."

HAM IT UP: exp-v. Actuar deliberadamente en forma muy tonta o ridícula, esp. ser la entretención de amigos u otras personas. Ej. "All he needs is an audience of two or three people to start hamming it up."

HAMMERED: adj. Muy ebrio. VER *smashed.*

HAND JOB: s. Estímulo hasta orgasmo del pene con la mano de

HAIr OF THe DOg THAt BIT yoU

HANd

otra persona. *Ej.* "I was psyched that she gave me a hand job."

HAND: *VER* helping hand; have one's hands in many pots; live hand to mouth; play into one's hands; tip one's hand; better a bird in the hand than two in the bush; catch someone with one's hands in the cookie jar; grease someone's palm/hand.

HANDLE WITH KID GLOVES: *exp-v.* Tratar con mucho cuidado, esp. una persona que es en extremo sensible. *Ej.* "You have to handle him with kid gloves. The slightest annoyance sets him off."

HANG: *VER* let it all hang out.

HANG IN THERE: *exp-vi.* Perseverar o persistir a pesar de dificultades y/u obstáculos. *Ej.* "I know it's tough going to a new school, but just hang in there and eventually you'll make friends."

HANG IT UP: *exp-vi.* Abandonar, renunciar, dimitir. *Ej.* "It's a sad day when an athlete realizes that it's time to hang it up."

HANG LOOSE: *exp-vi.* Mantenerse tranquilo o relajado, esp. no permitir que algo/alguien lo perturbe a uno. *Ej.* "Don't let her get you down man, just hang loose and things'll work out for the best."

HANG OUT THE DIRTY LAUNDRY: *exp-vi.* Hablar de los detalles íntimos de la vida de otro o de uno. *Gen. don't hang out...*; una recomendación para no discutir problemas personales en público. *Ej.* "Please don't hang out your dirty laundry. I really don't want to hear about your impotency troubles."

HANG OUT: (sin. hang) *exp-vi.* Pasar mucho tiempo en un lugar o con amigos. *Ej.* "Those kids hanging out at the pool hall will get into trouble one day." Or "I like hanging out with John, he's a lot of fun."

HANG TOUGH: *exp-vi.* Mantener la resolución, no sucumbir frente a presiones, fatiga o dudas. *Ej.* "You need to hang tough if you're going to finish this long trial."

HANG WITH: *exp-v.* 1) Ser amigo de (alguien), pasar mucho tiempo con (alguien). *Ej.* "I started hanging with the older boys this summer." 2) Mantenerse a la par o al mismo nivel de otros. Ej. "I don't want anyone on the hike who can't hang with me."

HANG-OUT: s. Lugar frecuentado por una persona o grupo. Ej. "My favorite hang-out is this little bar called Brennan's."

HANG-UP: s. Neurosis, un complejo psicológico de algún tipo. Ej. "You have to get over your hang-up about feeling inferior to your sister."

HANKY-PANKY: exp. 1) Manera graciosa de referirse a actividad sexual real o sospechada. Ej. "I'm afraid the kids are already starting to get into some hanky-panky." 2) Actividad ilegal o inmoral, gen. refiriéndose a la política o a los negocios. Ej. "The scandal broke when the reporter caught the Senator in some hanky-panky." 3) Actividad engañosa o traviesa. Ej. "Keep an eye on the kids and make sure they don't get up to any hanky-panky."

HARD LIQUOR: s. Bebida de alto contenido alcohólico (ej. whisky, ron, gin, vodka, tequila etc. pero no vino, cerveza, etc.). Ej. "We started out on beer and then moved on to hard liquor."

HARD STUFF: s. Alcohol o drogas fuertes. Ej. "He started out smoking marijuana and then moved to the hard stuff."

HARD TIME: s. Una larga condena de cárcel. Ej. "You'll serve hard time for murder." VER TAMBIEN give someone a hard time.

HARD-ASS: [Vul.] s. Persona muy difícil e intransigente. Ej. "Don't even bother trying to explain why you're late to that hard-ass, he'll never buy it."

HARD-ON: [Vul.] s. Erección. Ej. "The worst part of puberty was I'd get a hard-on in the most inappropriate of circumstances." VER woody.

HASH: s. Hachís. Ej. "You want a hit of some killer hash?"

HAT: VER talk through one's hat.

HATCHET JOB: s. Destruir, despedazar, algo físico o no físico (como la reputación de uno). Ej. "The carpenters did a hatchet job on the renovation, so I'm going to do a hatchet job on their reputation."

HATE SOMEONE'S GUTS

HATE SOMEONE'S GUTS: *exp-v.* Aborrecer. Odiar visceralmente (en inglés, a diferencia del español, se llega a odiar las vísceras de la otra persona). *Ej.* "I hate his guts so much I wish he'd die!"

HAUL ASS: [Vul.] *exp-v.* Moverse, gen. manejando, o hacer algo muy rápido. *Ej.* "We'd better haul ass if we're going to get there on time."

HAUL OFF: *exp-v.* Retirar el brazo, listo para pegarle a alguien. *Ej.* "He was insulting me so I hauled off and punched him."

HAVE A BALL: *exp-vi.* Pasarlo muy bien. *Ej.* "We had a ball at our high school reunion."

HAVE A BUG UP ONE'S/THE BUTT: *exp-vi.* Estar, al parecer, siempre de mal genio. *Ej.* "What's your problem? You got a serious bug up your butt or what?!"

HAVE A COW: *exp-vi.* Desquiciarse, esp. enojarse mucho, mucho. *Ej.* "My dad had a cow when I told him I wanted to start using the pill."

HAVE A WHACK AT: VER *take a whack at.*

HAVE IT MADE IN THE SHADE: *exp-vi.* Estar en una posición envidiable (ref. tranquilidad y éxito). *Ej.* "If I win the lottery I'll have it made in the shade."

HAVE IT OFF: *exp-vi.* Tener una relación sexual. *Ej.* "Do you think it's true they had it off?" (Ing.)

HAVE ONE'S CAKE AND EAT IT TOO: VER *eat one's cake and have it too.*

HAVE ONE'S EYES OPENED: *exp-vi.* Una revelación; darse cuenta de golpe de una verdad sobre alguien o algo. Esp. VER la real naturaleza de alguien o algo. *Ej.* "It was pretty unpleasant having my eyes opened to what a slimebag my fiancée really was."

HAVE ONE'S HANDS IN MANY POTS: *exp-vi.* Estar implicado en varias actividades o negocios a la vez. *Ej.* "The guy has his hands in so many pots I don't know how he keeps tracks of everything."

HAVE SOMEONE BY THE BALLS: [Vul.] *exp-vi.* Tener a alguien totalmente a la merced de uno o controlado. *Ej.* "With these nude pictures of him with another woman, I've got him by the balls."

HAVE SOMEONE'S NAME ON IT: *exp-vi.* Cosa deseada o anhelada

por alguien, esp. algo que posee una atracción magnética, como si dijera, 'tómame, soy tuyo/a!' Ej. "That guitar has my name on it. I just have to get the money to buy it." Or "Mercedes, come to the table, there's a plate of pancakes with your name on it."

HAVE THE LAST LAUGH: VER get the last laugh

HAY: VER hit the hay; roll in the hay.

HAYSEED: s. Un campesino, una persona poco sofisticada y gen. tonta. Ej. "The hustlers wait for the hayseeds to get off the bus in the big city and then rip them off for everything they've got."

HEAD: s. 1) Excusado. Ej. "I gotta use the head, where is it, man?" 2) Persona que usa drogas ilegales o farmacéuticas en forma habitual. Ej. "He's thirty and he's been a head since he smoked his first joint fifteen years ago." 3) s. Felonía. Ej. "She gave me head in the movie theater." VER TAMBIEN acidhead; air-head; bonehead; dive in head first; dick head; egghead; get it into one's head; hit the nail on the head; knucklehead; meathead; muscle head; pinhead; pothead; shithead; soft in the head; talking head; where one's head is at.

HEAD SHRINKER: s. Psiquiatra o psicoanalista. Ej. "My head shrinker attributes my problem to a domineering mother."

HEADHUNTER: s. Persona que busca trabajo o ubica gente altamente educada, comúnmente abordando un empleado de una empresa con una oferta para trabajar en otra. Ej. "Some headhunter called today with an offer for a higher paying job at another company."

HEAD-TRIP: s. Sensación en que el ego crece de tal manera que la persona se "cree la muerte". Ej. "She's been on this major head-trip since being voted the prom queen."

HEADY: adj. Motivador, muy inspirador, gratificador para el ego. Ej. "It was a heady experience being honored by my peers."

HEAP: 1) s. Un auto viejo y en mal estado. Ej. "It may be a heap, but

it still runs." 2) *heaps*: (sin. beaucoup) *adv.* Mucho, gran cantidad, harto. *Ej.* "I've got heaps of work to do." VER TAMBIEN *top of the heap.*

HEART: VER *warm the cockles of one's heart.*

HEART OF THE MATTER /GET TO/: VER *get to the point.*

HEAT: *s.* 1) Presión, tensión. *Ej.* "They're giving me a lot of heat to get the project done." 2) Un aumento en presión de parte de la policía para ponerle fin a la actividad criminal o persiguiendo a un criminal. *Ej.* "The heat is on. We'd better split town." 3) Crítica negativa y hostil. *Ej.* "The mayor took a lot of heat for implementing a pro gay policy during her administration." 4) Una arma, gen. un revólver. *Ej.* "We'll need some heat for this bank job." 5) *heat /the/*: Policía. (Desp.) *Ej.* "I hear sirens. We better beat it before the heat gets here." VER *cop.* VER TAMBIEN *in the heat of the moment; take the heat.*

HEAVE-HO: (sin. *boot**) *s.* Un despido sin gloria de un trabajo o una destitución abrupta de un lugar. *Ej.* "When the cutbacks began, I was the first to get the old heave-ho."

HEAVY: 1) *adj.* Importante, de gran profundidad, impresionante. *Ej.* "There were a lot of heavy insights made by the philosopher." 2) *adj.* Influyente, importante. *Ej.* "He's a heavy in the music business." 3) *s.* Un maleante, el culpable. *Ej.* "Don't try to make me the heavy for your problems."

HEAVY-DUTY: *adj.* Muy importante o intenso. *Ej.* "Bring tissues, it's a heavy-duty movie."

HEAVY-HITTER: *s.* Persona importante o con poder; del tipo que toma decisiones que afectan la vida de muchos. *Ej.* "You'd better have some leverage when you negotiate with the heavy-hitters."

HECK: (sin. *heckuva, helluva*) *s.* Se usa para enfatizar. *Ej.* "What the heck are you two doing in there with no clothes on?"

HECKUVA: (sin. *heck, heckuva*) *s.* Forma cortés de decir *helluva.* (ety. *heck of a = heckuva*). *Ej.* "I had a heckuva time finding this

I got lost three times!"

HEEBIE-JEEBIES: s. Susto, inquietud, sensación de incomodidad que algo está mal en cuanto a una situación o persona. Ej. "Let's get out of here, this place gives me the heebie-jeebies."

HEINIE: s.pl. Las nalgas. Ej. "Our baby has such a cute heinie!" VER bum.

HEIST: s. Un robo, hurto. Ej. "Did you read about the diamond heist?"

HELL: s. Se usa para enfatizar. Ej. "That was one hell of a good time!" VER TAMBIEN come hell or high water; give them hell; raise hell; what the hell; catch hell; like a bat out of hell; for the hell of it; go to hell.

HELL ON: exp. Que dañan o maltratan. Ej. "Bumpy roads are hell on a car's suspension."

HELL TO PAY: exp. Muchas molestias, muchos problemas y desgracias. Ej. "You'll have hell to pay if you disobey me."

HELLACIOUS: adj. Notable, extraordinario. Ej. "We had a hellacious good time at the beach."

HELLUVA: (sin. heck, heckuva) s. Se usa para enfatizar. (ety. hell of a = helluva) Ej. "We had a helluva good time bowling last night!"

HELM: VER grab the helm.

HELPING HAND: s. Un favor, ayuda. Ej. "Mary could really use a helping hand getting things ready for the party."

HEN PARTY: s. Reunión de mujeres que se juntan para hablar sobre temas sin importancia, especialmente para hablar sobre el último chisme. Ej. "Oh jeezums, the Tupperware ladies are with my wife having one of

HEP

their hen parties. Guess I'll go get a beer with the boys."

HEP: VER *hip*.

HERB: s. Marihuana. Ej. "You're nuts to try and smuggle herb into China." VER *grass*.

HEY: int. Saludo informal o modo de interrumpir o comenzar una conversación. Generalmente no se usa con un desconocido. Ej. "Hey, how ya' doing?"

HIDE: VER *tan someone's hide*.

HIGH: adj. Los efectos de tomar drogas. Ej. "She got high on one puff."

HIGH ROLLER: s. 1) Persona que gasta dinero a manos llenas y sin moderación, esp. en cosas caras, lujosas y/o entretención. Ej. "You're acting like a high roller with your fancy restaurants and clothes. But just remember who changed your diapers!" 2) Apostadero de grandes sumas de dinero. Ej. "The high rollers are in town for the big poker game."

HIGH-FIVE: s. Un gesto de saludo, regocijo o victoria en que una persona palmotea la mano de otra. Ej. "The players gave each other high-five's after winning the game."

HIGHLIGHT REEL: s. Los mejores momentos de nuestra vida o de algún período particular. Ej. "That road trip we took to Mexico is definitely on my highlight reel."

HIGHTAIL IT: exp-v. Moverse lo más rápido posible, esp. para escaparse rápidamente. Ej. "I was hightailing it out of the house when the phone rang."

HIKE: VER *take a hike*.

HILL OF BEANS: exp. Poco, una cantidad mínima, algo con poco valor. Ej. "The truth is that your excuses aren't even worth a hill of beans to me."

HIP: adj. 1) (sin. *with it*) Muy entendido en, o preocupado por la moda y/o tendencias. Ej. "You need to spend less time finding out what's hip and more time studying." 2) Bien informado. Ej. "Is he hip to the party tonight?" VER TAMBIEN *shoot from the hip*.

HIP-HOP: s. El estilo joven de *cool* que se capta en el canal MTV de televisión. Ej. "Hip-hop is more popular than grunge at my school."

HIT iT

HIPPIE: (sin. folksy, granola) s. Una persona que rechaza y se opone a muchas convenciones y costumbres de la sociedad, especialmente una que defiende un liberalismo extremo en cuanto a actitudes y modos de vida. *Ej.* "My dad has been a hippie for like 50 years or something. He still drives a VW Bug and rags on Nixon."

HIPSTER: s. Persona joven que habla en jerga y tiene aplomo. *Ej.* "Look who's becoming the little hipster! And to think you were a complete geek last year."

HISTORY /BE/: *exp-vi.* Ser algo del pasado, esp. cuando se es despedido, destituido u olvidado. *Ej.* "If you mess up again, you're history."

HIT: s. 1) (sin. drag*, toke) Una dosis o bocanada de una droga narcótica. *Ej.* "I need a hit to get me through the day." 2) Un asesinato planificado, gen. realizado por el miembro de una pandilla o gángster. *Ej.* "It was the fifth hit this week in the escalating gang war."

HIT A HOME RUN: *exp-vi.* Hacer algo con mucho éxito. *Ej.* "If I hit a home run with just one of my ideas, I'll be a rich man."

HIT AND MISS: *exp.* Imposible de predecir, incalculable, esp. en el sentido de calidad variable. *Ej.* "This director is really hit and miss. Sometimes his movies are pure genius, but other times, they're the pits."

HIT IT BIG: *exp-vi.* Tener mucho éxito, esp. tener éxito y ganar mucho dinero. *Ej.* "She hit it big with her new single."

HIT IT HARD: (sin. hit the bottle, pound, throw them back) *exp-vi.* Beber mucho alcohol esp. *hard liquor* durante una fiesta o una tomatera, cuyo efecto es una resaca al día siguiente. *Ej.* "She used to drink, but after she got fired, she started hitting it hard."

HIT IT OFF: *exp-vi.* Conocer a otra persona y avenirse. *Ej.* "I'm so happy my friends from work and school hit it off."

HIT IT: *int.* Activar o poner algo en movimiento rápidamente, como un motor. *Ej.* "When I say 'three', hit it."

HIT LIST

HIT LIST: s. Una lista de víctimas designadas para asesinato o para ataque. *Ej.* "The mob had two hit lists: one for politicians they wanted out of office, and the other for people they wanted rubbed out."

HIT MAN: s. Un asesino profesional. *Ej.* "He was the highest priced hit man in town, charging $100,000 a hit."

HIT ON: *exp.* Perseguir a un hombre o a una mujer con la esperanza de tener una relación romántica. *Ej.* "I can't stand Ed, he's always hitting on my wife."

HIT ONE: *exp-vi.* Repentinamente ocurrírsele algo o recordarse de algo. *Ej.* "I was walking down the street when it suddenly hit me — I'll just quit my job, sell my house and move to the South Pacific."

HIT ROCK BOTTOM: *exp-vi.* Estar muy bajo de ánimo en un momento de la vida. *Ej.* "When even my kids said they didn't want to see me anymore, I felt like I'd hit rock bottom."

HIT SOMEONE UP: *exp-vi.* Pedirle algo a alguien, gen. dinero. *Ej.* "My kids must think I'm a bank, the way they always hit me up for money." VER *put the bite* ON.

HIT SOMEONE WITH SOMETHING: *exp-v.* Proponer un tema, sugerencia o idea a alguien, esp. cuando no se espera. *Ej.* "When he hit me with the marriage proposal, I nearly fainted!"

HIT THE BOOKS: *exp-vi.* Estudiar con diligencia. *Ej.* "I've been hitting the books all week, preparing for the exam." Or "No more TV, it's time to hit the books."

HIT THE BOTTLE: VER *hit it hard.*

HIT THE BULL'S EYE: *exp-vi.* Dar en el blanco. Adivinar algo sin saberlo. *Ej.* "You hit the bull's eye! How did you know that's my favorite color?"

HIT THE CEILING: (sin. hit the roof) *exp-vi.* Estar sumamente enojado, tan enojado que pareciera que la cabeza está a punto de explotar y *hit the ceiling* = estrellarse contra el cielo. *Ej.* "My dad hit the ceiling when I told him I flunked out of school."

HIT THE DECK: (sin. hit the dirt) *exp-vi.* Rápidamente tenderse

HOG hEAVEN

boca abajo, postrarse. *Ej.* "When my old man goes on a rampage, it's best to just hit the deck until the fireworks are over."

HIT THE DIRT: VER *hit the deck*.

HIT THE FAN: *exp-vi*. Esto tendrá serias consecuencias, esp. el brote inminente de un escándalo. *Ej.* "When the press finds out about the mayor's involvement in the sex scandal, the shit's going to hit the fan!"

HIT THE GROUND RUNNING: *exp-vi*. Comenzar un intento con gran energía y entusiasmo. *Ej.* "He always hits the ground running, but then he runs out of steam."

HIT THE HAY: (sin. *hit the sack*) *exp-vi*. Irse a la cama, irse a dormir. *Ej.* "Okay kids, it's time to hit the hay."

HIT THE JACKPOT: *exp-vi*. Inesperadamente ganar una gran cantidad de dinero o experimentar algún gran éxito. *Ej.* "You really hit the jackpot with this book."

HIT THE NAIL ON THE HEAD: *exp-vi*. Acertar total y absolutamente en cuanto a algo o alguien. *Ej.* "I thought he was a good guy, but you hit the nail on the head when you said he wasn't to be trusted."

HIT THE ROAD: *exp-vi*. Irse, esp. una orden para partir o alejarse inmediatamente. *Ej.* "When I caught him looking in my purse, I told him to hit the road."

HIT THE ROOF: VER *hit the ceiling*.

HIT THE SACK: VER *hit the hay*.

HIT THE SPOT: *exp-vi*. Satisfacer un deseo completamente, gen. refiriéndose a comida o bebida. *Ej.* "A dog and a cold one would really hit the spot right now."

HITCHED: *Verbo en pasado*. Casado. *Ej.* "We're going to get hitched in a Synagogue."

HOCK: *v*. Empeñar, o estar en una casa de empeños. *Ej.* "I was so desperate, I hocked my wedding ring."

HOE: (sin. *hooker, working girl*) *s*. Prostituta. *Ej.* "He got busted picking up a hoe."

HOG: *s*. Una motocicleta grande. *Ej.* "That hog makes a lot of noise. It must have a big engine."

HOG HEAVEN: *s*. Un estado de felicidad total. *Ej.* "He was in hog

HOKEY

heaven with all the praise he received for his book."

HOKEY: *adj.* 1) Necio, exageradamente sentimental o saturado de clichés. *Ej.* "I know he's trying to be romantic, but when he recites his hokey poetry, it's all I can do to not crack up." 2) Fabricado, artificial. *Ej.* "It was such a hokey speech that no one thought he was sincere."

HOLD DOWN THE FORT: *exp-v.* Mantener el orden y el control de un lugar, esp. cuando el jefe/dueño no se encuentra presente. *Ej.* "Who's holding down the fort at work while you're on vacation?"

HOLD ONE'S FEET TO THE FIRE: *exp-vi.* Presionar a alguien para que haga o termine de hacer algo. *Ej.* "You've gotta hold his feet to the fire or he'll never get the project done."

HOLD THE PHONE: *exp.* Expresión usada para decirle a alguien que deje de hacer algo, generalmente hablar. *Ej.* "Hold the phone, I've got something to say."

HOLDING SOMEONE BACK /NO/: (sin. all the way, full blast) *exp.* Hacer algo con gran entusiasmo y energía. *Ej.* "There's no holding me back when I decide to do something."

HOLDING: *adj.* En posesión de algo ilegal, esp. narcóticos o armas. *Ej.* "They caught him holding five keys of heroin."

HOLY COW: (sin. holy mackerel, holy moly, holy smokes) *int.* Expresión que denota una gran sorpresa, esp. después de ver algo extraordinario. (nota de ed.: los norteamericanos usan mucho la palabra *holy* = "santo") *Ej.* "Holy cow, did you see that gal punch him?"

HOLY MACKERAL: VER *holy cow*.

HOLY MOLY: VER *holy cow*.

HOLY SHIT: versión vulgar de *holy cow*.

HOLY SMOKES: VER *holy cow*.

HOME: VER *nothing to write home about; hit a home run; bring home the bacon; come home*.

HOME RUN: *exp.* Tener relaciones sexuales. (etim. Del béisbol; un jonrón - cuando uno llega a la base meta de un viaje.) *Ej.* "He was the

HOOk SOMEONE uP

first guy in our group of friends to get a home run with his girlfriend. Lucky bastard!"

HOMEBOY: s. 1) Un amigo que proviene, como lo implica el término, del pueblo o barrio de uno. Ej. "Leave my homeboy alone or you'll have to mess with me." 2) Un compañero de pandilla. Ej. "The homeboys got together for some gangbanging."

HOMO: VER fag.

HONCHO: s. La persona a cargo o al mando. Ej. "He stepped over a lot of people to become head honcho of the corporation."

HONEY: (sin. pumpkin, sugar) int. Expresión afectuosa para tratarse en pareja. Ej. "Honey, would you bring me a coffee?"

HONKER: s. Nariz, esp. una nariz muy grande. Ej. "Poor guy, he must get a lot of jokes about his honker." Ver beak.

HONKY: (sin. whitey) s. Una persona blanca. (Desp.) Ej. "Get that honky out of my face!"

HOOCH: s. 1) Alcohol, esp. alcohol de contrabando. Ej. "We brew some fine hooch down at the farm." 2) Marihuana. Ej. "Let's smoke some hooch before the movie." Ver grass.

HOOD: s. 1) Barrio. Ej. "We come from the same hood." 2) Un maleante, un matón, un rufián. Ej. "Get that hood out of here before he steals something."

HOOF IT: exp-v. Caminar, esp. cuando no hay un vehículo disponible u otro medio de transporte. Ej. "When I was a kid, I used to have to hoof it ten miles to school every day."

HOO-HAH: exp. Un alboroto, un disturbio, un tumulto. Ej. "What's all the hoo-hah about?"

HOOK: v. 1) Cautivar, interesarse totalmente u obsesionarse por algo. Ej. "I got hooked on football the first time I played it." 2) Lograr, obtener, por astucia. Ej. "How, without any qualifications, did he hook that great job?" 3) Trabajar como prostituta. Ej. "She was out hooking by the time she was 16." VER TAMBIEN get one's hooks into.

HOOK SOMEONE UP: exp-v. Proporcionar, dar, arreglárselas

HOOk uP

para tener algo. Ej. "Yo, can your brother hook me up with a job at his garage?" Or "Hey man I want some too, hook me up."

HOOK UP: *exp-v.* 1) Asociarse con, formar un lazo. Ej. "You have to hook up with the right guys to make it in this town." 2) Conocer y tener un encuentro romántico o sexual con alguien. Ej. "I hooked up with this really nice chick last night." 3) Encontrarse, juntarse con alguien. Ej. "Let's hook up at the game."

HOOK, LINE, AND SINKER: *exp.* Como un pescado que traga el anzuelo completamente, la expresión significa hacer o pensar algo en su totalidad, completamente, sin cautela. Ej. "He's so gullible, he bought my explanation hook, line and sinker."

HOOKER: (sin. hoe, working girl) *s.* Una prostituta. Ej. "He got V.D. from a hooker."

HOOKY: VER play hooky.

HOOPS: *s.* Baloncesto. Ej. "Let's go play some hoops."

HOPPING: *exp.* Muy entretenido. Ej. "The disco was hopping."

HORIZONTAL MAMBO: *exp.* Forma graciosa para describir o referirse a una relación sexual. Ej. "This tacky guy asked me if I wanted to get together for the horizontal mambo."

HORIZONTAL MAMBO

HORN: *s.* Teléfono. Ej. "Get me my lawyer on the horn."

HORNY: *adj.* Lascivo, deseoso de actividad sexual, o sexualmente

HOT BEEF INJECTION

excitado. *Ej.* "Two months alone in the woods and I was as horny as I've ever been."

HORSE: (sin. junk, smack) s. Heroína. VER TAMBIEN *get off one's high horse; get on one's high horse; look a gift horse in the mouth; take someone off someone's high horse.*

HORSESHIT: [Vul.] s. 1) Trabajo, tarea o pedido irritante. *Ej.* "I cannot believe the amount of horseshit they make me do at work." 2) Hablar sin sentido, hipócrita, o sencillamente mentiroso. *Ej.* "After listening to his horseshit for five minutes I told him to go 'f' himself."

HOT: *adj.* 1) Creando gran conmoción o controversia. *Ej.* "So what's the hot gossip?" 2) Deseoso, ansioso. *Ej.* "I'm hot to try that new video game." 3) Sexualmente excitado/excitante o estimulado/estimulante. *Ej.* "Go for it man, I think she's hot for you." 4) Robado. *Ej.* "I bought a hot car radio for half the store price." 5) Más reciente, actualmente popular. *Ej.* "Check out this hot new single by <u>The Figments</u>." 6) Muy bueno, muy bien o impresionante. A menudo se usa en sentido negativo. *Ej.* "She hasn't been feeling so hot since the last operation." 7) Con suerte descomunal, con una racha ganadora. *Ej.* "I got hot at the race track today." 8) Caracterizado por gran actividad o energía. *Ej.* "I'm exhausted after a hot day at the office." 9) Muy atractivo/a, esp. sexy, refiriéndose a una persona. *Ej.* "Now that's a hot babe!" Or "What a hot bod he has!" 10) Arriesgado, peligroso, difícil. *Ej.* "It was hot on the battlefield; bullets were flying everywhere." 11) *hots /the/:* adv. Atraído sexualmente por o deseoso de. *Ej.* "I'm embarrassed to admit that I've got the hots for my boss." VER TAMBIEN *make it hot; sell like hot cakes; blow hot and cold.*

HOT AIR: *exp.* Habla, conversación vacía y sin sentido. *Ej.* "Don't listen to him, he's just filled with hot air."

HOT BEEF INJECTION: *exp.* Una manera humorística pero cruda de describir el acto sexual. *Ej.* "What kind of pick-up line is, 'Hey, do you want the hot beef injection?'"

HOT NUMBER

HOT NUMBER: s. Una mujer muy atractiva y sexy. *Ej.* "He's dating a hot number." VER *babe*.

HOT PANTS: s.pl. Sexualmente excitado o deseoso. *Ej.* "He's so conceited that he thinks all women have hot pants for him."

HOT POTATO: s. Un objeto, problema, o tema que es peligroso e indeseable. *Ej.* "When there's a screw up, everyone passes around the responsibility like a hot potato. No one fesses up!"

HOT STUFF: s. Persona o cosa que excita o gusta en seguida a alguien, esp. en sentido sexual. *Ej.* "That bathing suit she's got on is hot stuff!"

HOT TO TROT: exp. Lascivo, excitado sexualmente y deseoso. *Ej.* "I was hot to trot after my boyfriend had been away a month."

HOT UNDER THE COLLAR: exp. Enojado, furioso. *Ej.* "Wow, did mom ever get hot under the collar when my brother got kicked out of school!"

HOTDOG: s. Persona que ejecuta pruebas llamativas y peligrosas que requieren habilidad atlética. *Ej.* "I told my son that hotdogs belong in a roll with mustard, not out doing crazy stunts."

HOTSHOT: s. Una persona de gran habilidad, esp. una que es detestablemente confiada. *Ej.* "Why is it that we root for hotshots to fall flat on their face?"

HOT-WIRE: v. Hacer partir un vehículo, gen. un auto, sin llave, haciendo un corto circuito en el sistema de arranque. *Ej.* "I thought every New Yorker knew how to hot-wire a car?"

HOW COME: int. ¿Por qué? *Ej.* "You can't go? How come?"

HOW DO YOU LIKE THEM APPLES: exp. Afirmación, a manera de pregunta, usada en forma sarcástica después de presentar los hechos de un asunto, esp. cuando dichos hechos tienen por objeto molestar o causar envidia. Poner énfasis en *them*. *Ej.* "You think you're so great, well, not only did I also get accepted to the University, but they also gave me a full scholarship. So how do you like them apples!?"

HURTING

HOW GOES IT?: *exp.* Un saludo informal. *Ej.* "How goes it Ted? What ya been up to?"

HOW'S IT HANGING?: *exp.* Un saludo informal. *Ej.* "Man, how's it hanging? Where you been hiding yourself lately?"

HOWL: 1) *v.* Reírse desmesuradamente fuerte. *Ej.* "I was howling when he told me the story about his grandmother's cat." 2) *s.* Algo muy divertido. *Ej.* "The class reunion was a howl."

HUCK A LUGI: *exp-v.* Escupir. *Ej.* "Oh gross! He hucked a lugi on her skirt."

HUMDINGER: *s.* Algo/alguien extraordinario, excelente o sobresaliente. *Ej.* "You'd better have one humdinger of an excuse for why you're late again."

HUMP: [Vul.] *v.* Tener una relación sexual. *Ej.* "She slapped me just because I asked her if she liked to hump!"

HUMUNGOUS: *adj.* Tremendo, enorme, muy grande. *Ej.* "I had one humungous hangover after my bachelor's party."

HUNG: *adj.* Con un pene grande. *Ej.* "You have to be hung to work in porno films."

HUNG UP ON: *adj.* 1) Obsesionado o envuelto en, esp. hasta un grado malsano o poco recomendable. *Ej.* "She's been hung up on her old boyfriend all winter." 2) Con trancas psicológicas o complejos. *Ej.* "He's been hung up on issues of sexuality for over a year."

HUNGOVER /BE/: *exp-vi.* Sufrir de resaca. Sentirse muy mal como resultado de beber demasiado alcohol la noche o día anterior. *Ej.* "She was so hungover she was green."

HUNK: *s.* Un macho muy atractivo. *Ej.* "She married a hunk. He used to be a Playgirl centerfold!"

HUNKY-DORY: *exp.* Regio, fantástico, sin razón para quejarse. *Ej.* "Everything's been hunky-dory ever since I started taking lithium."

HURL: *v.* Vomitar. *Ej.* "You loser, you hurled on my new rug!" VER chuck up.

HURTING: *adj.* Muy malo. *Ej.* "That's one hurtin' looking jacket you've got on. Where did you find

HUSH MONEY

it, in the garbage?"

HUSH MONEY: s. Un soborno que se paga para mantener secreto algo ilícito. Ej. "The administration had a secret fund to pay out hush money."

HUSTLE: 1) v. Vender agresivamente. Ej. "The cops caught him hustling stolen goods." 2) v. Robar, obtener ilegalmente o por medios dudosos. Ej. "Out on the streets, you've got to hustle just to get something to eat." 3) v. Presionar para comprar o hacer algo. Ej. "The worst is when your supposed 'friends' try to hustle you into doing something bad." 4) v. Engañar, estafar u obtener algo por medios ilegales. Ej. "On these mean streets everyone is trying to hustle you." 5) v. Practicar la prostitución o solicitar clientes para una prostituta. Ej. "Nothing sadder than seeing children out on the streets hustling." 6) v. Entablar una conversación como preludio para un encuentro sexual. Ej. "I hate going out to eat with Fred. He's always trying to hustle the waitress." 7) s. Un fraude o engaño. Ej. "There's a new hustle invented everyday."

HUSTLER: s. 1) Persona que estafa a otros. Ej. "Don't bet him in pool, he's a hustler." 2) Persona que trabaja en forma ardua y con gran energía. Ej. "With two kids and a full-time job, she's become a real hustler."

HYPE: 1) s. Publicidad, propaganda excesiva, que a menudo trae afirmaciones espectaculares y excesivas, y la reacción de pánico del consumidor que la sigue. Ej. "With all the hype surrounding the movie, I'm certain it'll be sold-out." 2) v. Promover, publicar, esp. con afirmaciones espectaculares y excesivas. Ej. "If we hype his candidacy, we can probably get him elected."

HYPER: adj. Demasiado activo, muy excitado y agitado. Ej. "Take a chill pill man! Stop being so hyper."

I HEAR THAT: (sin. I'm down with that) exp. Estoy de acuerdo; comprendo. Ej. "I hear that, I could definitely do with some chow right now."

I MEAN BUSINESS: *exp.* Hablo en serio, no estoy hablando en broma. Gen. se usa esta expresión cuando uno no está hablando de negocios. *Ej.* "Listen little girl, I mean business, alright? So stop fooling around and get in bed."

I'M OUT: *int.* Adiós. *Ej.* "I'm out man, I've got to go see my old lady."

ICE: 1) *v.* Asegurar la victoria de un concurso, gen. un juego, partido. *Ej.* "He iced the game with another goal in the last minute." 2) *v.* Matar, asesinar. *Ej.* "We're gonna ice Joey to teach the others a lesson in respect." VER *waste*. 3) *s.* Diamantes. *Ej.* "That's some piece of ice on your finger." VER TAMBIEN *break the ice; walk on thin ice*.

ICING ON THE CAKE: *exp.* Lo mejor de algo, especialmente si se logra sin esfuerzo. *Ej.* "He got a sweet deal with a six figure salary, but the icing on the cake is the two months paid vacation."

ICKY: (sin. *grody, skanky*) *adj.* Baboso, asqueroso, sumamente poco atractivo. *Ej.* "He's like a worm he's so icky."

IDIOT BOX: (sin. *tube /the/, boob tube*) *s.* Televisión. *Ej.* "You're gonna rot your brain if you watch the idiot box all day."

IDIOT-PROOF: *adj.* Algo hecho para gente tonta, torpe; a prueba de tontos; así, algo fácil de usar/operar que no se rompe ni estropea con facilidad. *Ej.* "Even you can use this microwave Susan, it's idiot-proof."

IF PUSH COMES TO SHOVE: (sin. *when push comes to shove*) *exp.* Momento en el cual, habiendo tomado en consideración todas las posibilidades, se debe enfrentar una situación de una u otra forma. *Ej.* "I'd like to avoid a lawsuit, but if push comes to shove, we'll go to court."

IF YOU SNOOZE, YOU LOSE: VER *one who snoozes, loses*.

IFFY: *adj.* Dudoso, incierto, que aún se debe decidir. *Ej.* "I'm still feeling kind of iffy about marrying him."

IN /AN/: (sin. *connection*) *s.* Un contacto que le permite a uno recibir un trato especial o ciertos privilegios. *Ej.* "Don't worry about tickets. I've got an in at the ballpark who lets me in for free."

IN A hOLE

IN A HOLE: *exp.* En desventaja, esp. referente a deudas. *Ej.* "Once you get in a hole, it's hard to get out."

IN A PIG'S EYE: *exp.* Bajo ninguna condición, nunca, esp. algo que nunca sucederá. *Ej.* "In a pig's eye I'd rat on my own brother."

IN A TIZZY: *exp.* En un estado avanzado de nerviosismo, emoción, agitación o confusión. *Ej.* "My mom was in a tizzy over the Christmas preparations."

IN SOMEONE'S FACE: *exp.* Presionando o molestando a alguien. *Ej.* "Don't get in my face about buying your car."

IN THE BAG: *exp.* Casi asegurado o cierto. *Ej.* "The game is in the bag; I paid off the referee."

IN THE DOGHOUSE: *exp.* Con graves problemas o que alguien está molesto con uno. Encontrarse fuera de gracia o muy criticado/a. *Ej.* "I'm in the doghouse for not having cleaned my room again."

IN THE GROOVE: *exp.* 1) Funcionando a un nivel muy alto. *Ej.* "Once I get in the groove, all my shots go in." 2) A la moda, elegante. *Ej.* "You've got to get in the groove and buy some cool threads."

IN THE HEAT OF THE MOMENT: *exp.* Un momento de fuerte emoción en que se actúa con gran impulsividad. *Ej.* "In the heat of the moment, I passionately kissed my boss' wife. The next day I was fired."

IN TOP FORM: *exp.* Estar muy bien o esforzarse y obtener estupendos resultados. *Ej.* "If she finishes her last year in university in top form, she'll get into the best law school."

IN YOUR DREAMS: *exp.* Afirmación que indica que de ninguna manera se hará realidad un deseo. *Ej.* "You, President? In your dreams pal!"

INDIAN GIVER: *exp.* Persona que regala algo a alguien para después quitárselo o usarlo uno mismo. (nota del ed: Una expresión irónica si se considera que el gobierno de los EE.UU. regularmente rompía los acuerdos, y no los indios.) *Ej.* "It's mine now, you said I could have it so don't be an Indian giver."

INJUN: *s.* Indio, nativo de los Estados Unidos. (Desp.) *Ej.* "I buy my cigs from the Injuns 'cause they're tax free."

INNIE: *s.* Ombligo aplanado. *Ej.* "My

Jack of All Trades

sister's got an innie."

INSIDE TRACK: s. La mejor posibilidad de lograr algo. Ej. "Sarah's got the inside track on getting the promotion."

INTO SOMEONE FOR: exp. Endeudarse. Ej. "I'm into my bookie for 10 gees."

IN-YOUR-FACE: exp. Burla o desafío expresada/o a/por un adversario. Ej. "In your face, I scored again!"

IS THE POPE CATHOLIC?: exp. La contestación a una pregunta cuya respuesta es obvia. También relacionado con algo con lo cual uno está muy familiarizado. Ej. "Do you want another beer?" "Is the Pope Catholic? Of course I do!" (nota del ed: existen numerosas variaciones a este comentario, todas expresando lo obvio.)

ITEM /BE AN/: exp-vi. Forma adulta y humorística para describir una relación romántica. Ej. "I think Charlie is more than a friend to our daughter. I think they're an item."

IVORIES: s.pl. 1) Teclado del piano. Ej. "It's a treat to hear him tickle the ivories." 2) (sin. pearly whites) Dientes, gen. dientes humanos. Ej. "I'm going to the dentist to get my ivories cleaned."

JACK: (sin. diddly*, zilch) s. Nada, ni lo más mínimo. Ej. "You don't know jack about what's going on in my head!"

JACK: s. Amigo, amigote. Ej. "Yo Jack, what you doing?"

JACK AROUND: exp-v. Tratar sin cortesía ni honestidad, esp. no ser directo y engañar para retrasar algo. Ej. "My mechanic has been jacking me around as to what's wrong with my car. I wish he'd just tell me straight up."

JACK OF ALL TRADES: s. Describe a una persona que trata de hacer arreglos sin saber cómo, esp. una

JACK OFF

persona capaz de hacer una gran variedad de cosas, pero ninguna bien. Ej. "My dad can probably fix it. He's a Jack of all trades."

JACK OFF: [Vul.] *exp-v.* Masturbarse. Ej. "Is it true he got caught jacking off in the bathroom?" VER *beat off*.

JACK SHIT: [Vul.] *exp.* Absolutamente nada, incluso menos que nada si fuera posible. Ej. "I give jack shit about your problems."

JACKOFF: [Vul.] *s.* Persona excesivamente improductiva y floja; el tipo de trabajador que uno odiaría contratar; persona que sólo es buena para una sola cosa: coloque un espacio entre la letra "k" y la "o" - ¡busque en el diccionario y lo encontrará!. Ej. "That jackoff has wasted enough of my time. He's fired!"

JAG: *abr.* Jaguar; un auto deportivo lujoso. Ej. "She's so spoiled her parents gave her a Jag for her b'day."

JAILBAIT: *s.* Persona, gen. una mujer, bajo la edad mínima para tener relaciones sexuales. Entones, tener relaciones sexuales con tal persona, llevaría a la cárcel. Ej. "Don't do it John, she's definite jailbait. I don't even think she's fourteen!"

JAM PACKED: *adv.* Apelotonado, lleno, repleto. Ej. "I hate taking the subway in the morning, it's always jam packed."

JAP: *abr.* Jewish American Princess = Princesa norteamericana judía. Judía que actúa como princesa. Ej. "She's such a JAP the way she prances about in her designer clothes and acts so snobby."

JAP: *s.* Japonés. (Desp.) Ej. "He's a Jap."

JAVA: *s.* Café (bebida). Ej. "I'm a java junkie and proud of it."

JAZZ: *s.* 1) Disparate, tontería o una historia exagerada. Ej. "Don't give me that jazz about car trouble again, where were you?" 2) Cosas, elementos en general. Ej. "Stanley brought the beer and the other jazz to the party."

JAZZ UP: *exp-v.* Animar, decorar, alegrar un lugar. Ej. "We need to jazz up this place, it's too dark and

JOCK

depressing."

JAZZY: *adj.* Ostentoso, muy decorativo y colorido. *Ej.* "That was some jazzy tie Zach wore to work."

JEEZUM: *int.* Expresar sorpresa, confusión o temor reverente. *Ej.* "By jeezum, that sure is great news!"

JERK: (sin. wanker) *s.* Sujeto desagradable. *Ej.* "I can't stand that jerk, she's always talking about how much money she has."

JERK AROUND: *exp-v.* 1) (sin. jack around) Tratar sin cortesía ni honestidad, esp. no ser directo y engañar para retrasar algo. *Ej.* "The boss has been jerking me around about the raise I asked for." 2) Hacer algo sin ánimo; dejar pasar el tiempo sin hacer nada. *Ej.* "No jerking around here, just get the cleaning done right away."

JERK OFF: *exp-v.* Masturbarse. VER *beat off.*

JEW DOWN: *exp-v.* Regatear para bajar el precio de algo. (Desp.) *Ej.* "The bastard tried to jew me down on the car so I told him to take a walk."

JIM DANDY: *int.* Una respuesta a "¿Cómo estás?" que significa fantástico, regio. *Ej.* "How ya doing John?" "Oh, I'm just Jim Dandy!"

JIMMY: (sin. johnson, pecker, wiener, cock, prick*, weenie*, dick*) *s.* Pene. Uno de los tantos sinónimos para referirse a esta obsesión universal. *Ej.* "Stop thinking with your jimmy and wise up!"

JIVE: 1) *s.* Discurso engañoso, absurdo, sin sentido. *Ej.* "He tried to lay this jive on me that even a bonehead wouldn't believe." 2) *v.* Bromear, hablar sin sinceridad. *Ej.* "My older brother is always jiving me about something." 3) *v.* Engañar, o llevar a conclusiones erróneas mediante adulaciones, halagos repetidos. *Ej.* "It's a riot listening to Tom try and jive the ladies." 4) *adj.* Engañoso, falso. *Ej.* "She's just a jive talking fool."

JOB: *s.* Un delito, acto delictivo, gen. un robo. *Ej.* "They pulled a bank job last week." VER TAMBIEN *blow job; do a job on; hand job; hatchet job; snow job.*

JOCK: *s.* Atleta excesivamente concentrado en su deporte hasta

JOE

el punto de no interesarse en nada más. *Ej.* "She's not just a jock, she's also a good student."

JOE: VER *ordinary Joe.*

JOE BLOW: *s.* Un norteamericano típico; persona común y corriente. *Ej.* "It's easy, any Joe Blow could do it."

JOE SCHMO: *s.* Un norteamericano típico; persona común y corriente. *Ej.* "Cancun is where every Joe schmo goes. I'm going to the jungle."

JOHN: *s.* 1) Hombre que paga para tener sexo con una prostituta. *Ej.* "Arrest the hoe and the john." 2) *john /the/:* Excusado. *Ej.* "Where's the john?" VER *throne /the/.* VER TAMBIEN *Dear John Letter.*

JOHN HANCOCK: *s.* Firma, rúbrica. (etim. Proviene del gran tamaño de la firma de John Hancock en la Declaración de Independencia). *Ej.* "Just put your John Hancock here and we'll be done with the contract."

JOIN THE CLUB: *int.* Ser incluido en un grupo, esp. en circunstancias negativas. *Ej.* "You're also divorced? Join the club!"

JOINT: *s.* 1) Lugar de reunión, a menudo mal decorado y poco salubre. *Ej.* "Let's get a beer at the joint on the corner." 2) Cigarrillo de marihuana. *Ej.* "Let's go smoke a joint." 3) Residencia. *Ej.* "How much are you paying for this joint?" 4) *joint /the/:* Prisión, cárcel. *Ej.* "If you step out of line, we're going to send you to the joint." VER *clink /the/.* VER TAMBIEN *case the joint.*

JOKER: *s.* Un bromista, una persona molestosa, fastidiosa. *Ej.* "Who's the joker that took my pen?" Or "Let's split, there are too many jokers at this party."

JOLLIES: *s.pl.* Diversión; generalmente, fuente de alegría y diversión extraña. *Ej.* "He gets his jollies watching kids play in the park."

JONES: *v.* Tener un enviciamiento o fuerte deseo de algo. *Ej.* "I'm jonesing for a beer."

JOSÉ: VER *no way, José.*

JUICE: *s.* 1) La habilidad para lograr hacer algo, esp. tener la autoridad para lograr un fin deseado. *Ej.* "I don't want to mess around, just

KEEP AN EYE ON

tell me who has the juice to get this project through." 2) Corriente eléctrica. Ej. "Don't touch that wire, it's loaded with juice."

JUMP: *v.* 1) Estar animado, ruidoso y lleno de actividad. Ej. "The place was jumping to the rhythm of Dr. Groove." 2) Atacar sorpresivamente, tender una emboscada. Ej. "The thug jumped him coming out of an ATM machine."

JUMP DOWN SOMEONE'S THROAT: *exp-v.* Criticar o censurar de improviso y en forma severa, esp. en respuesta a un comentario ofensivo. Ej. "My wife jumped down my throat for insulting her friend."

JUMP SOMEONE'S BONES: *exp-v.* Forma graciosa para describir el acto sexual, y esp. ganas de hacerlo con alguien. Ej. "I'd love to jump her bones, but she doesn't like me."

JUMP THE GUN: *exp-v.* Reaccionar o responder a algo antes que suceda. Ej. "I think you're jumping the gun, buying a wedding dress before he asks you to marry him."

JUMP THROUGH HOOPS: *exp-v.* Cumplir una serie de requisitos aparentemente superfluos para lograr algo (etim. Del circo, como un animal que literalmente salta a través de un aro). Ej. "These damn bureaucrats always make you jump through hoops to get anything done."

JUNK: (sin. horse, smack) *s.* Heroína. Ej. "You're going to nowheresville messing with junk."

JUNKIE: *s.* 1) Un drogadicto, especialmente a la heroína. Ej. "Get off the horse man, before you become a junkie." 2) Aquel que tiene un interés o devoción insaciable por algo. Ej. "My husband is such a sport's junkie he even watches bowling on TV."

KAPUT: *adj.* Destruido, fuera de servicio, que no funciona; generalmente refiriéndose a un motor, máquina. Ej. "His engine went kaput because he forgot to add oil to it."

KEEP AN EYE ON: *exp.* Ponerle atención a algo o alguien, esp. para evitar algo negativo. Ej. "Keep an eye on that guy. I don't trust him."

KEEP ON TRUCKING

KEEP ON TRUCKING: *exp-vi.* Seguir adelante, continuar, esp. persistir y perseverar en momentos difíciles. *Ej.* "Keep on trucking baby and you'll get it done."

KEEP ONE'S CARDS CLOSE TO ONE'S CHEST: (sin. play one's cards close to one's chest) *exp-vi.* No divulgar los planes y/o intenciones de uno. *Ej.* "You'll never know what Tom is up to till the last minute because he always keeps his cards close to his chest."

KEEP ONE'S CHIN UP: *exp-vi.* Palabras de aliento para alguien que no está logrando gran éxito con algo pero que necesita continuar intentándolo. *Ej.* "I admire her for keeping her chin up even in the worst of circumstances."

KEEP ONE'S COOL: *exp-vi.* Permanecer tranquilo, no perder la compostura. *Ej.* "Hey, keep your cool or you'll do something you regret later."

KEEP ONE'S FEET WET: *exp-vi.* Quedar involucrado en o mantenerse informado sobre alguna actividad del pasado, esp. una antigua profesión. *Ej.* "He left the publishing business, but kept his feet wet by talking with his former co-workers on a regular basis."

KEEP ONE'S SHIRT ON: *exp-vi.* Mantener la compostura, la calma, la paciencia. *Ej.* "Keep your shirt on Teddy, don't blow a fuse before you even hear her explanation."

KEEP THE WOLF FROM THE DOOR: *exp-v.* Evitar las consecuencias negativas (ej. hambre, desalojo, quedarse sin cerveza, etc.) que provienen de la falta de dinero. *Ej.* "I had to work three jobs just to keep the wolf from the door."

KEEPER: *s.* Algo/alguien que vale la pena no perder; algo/alguien que se debe cuidar para no perderlo. *Ej.* "She's a keeper and you'd be a fool not to marry her."

KEY: *s.* Un kilogramo de marihuana, cocaína, o heroína. *Ej.* "He was busted carrying five keys of smack across the border."

KEY UP: *exp-v.* Estar o volverse nervioso, emocionado. *Ej.* "Sarah was keyed up for her first TV appearance." Or "He got me all keyed

KICK (SOME) ASS

up by telling me the big boss was going to review my work."

KIBITZ: *v.* Ofrecer consejos, ya sean queridos o no, sobre cómo hacer algo. Esp. hacerlo durante un juego o partido. *Ej.* "Hey no kibitzing, let her do it on her own."

KICK: 1) *s.* Fuerza, potencia. *Ej.* "Whiskey sure has a kick." 2) *s.* Interés pasajero pero absorbente. *Ej.* "First he was on a health food trip and now he's on an aerobic kick." 3) *s.* Diversión, entretención, complacencia. *Ej.* "I always get a kick out of seeing my children play together." 4) *v.* Dejar un vicio/enviciamiento. *Ej.* "He finally kicked cigarettes with hypnosis."

KICK AROUND: *exp-v.* 1) Abusar de, tratar a alguien en forma grosera y sin interés. *Ej.* "He's been kicking you around for a year so when are you going to leave him?" 2) Cambiar de un trabajo a otro, o de un lugar a otro. *Ej.* "She was kicking around the Caribbean before settling in Barbados." 3) Tomar en consideración, pensar en algo. *Ej.* "I've been kicking around a few different ideas about what to do with my life."

KICK BACK: *exp-v.* Pagar para poder trabajar, llevar a cabo una actividad comercial en forma segura y sin molestias. *Ej.* "In this business you have to kick back to the mob and the cops."

KICK IN THE TEETH /A/: *s.* Insulto; actuar en forma extremadamente irrespetuosa con alguien que merece respeto, esp. en una traición. *Ej.* "After I got Charlie invited to the party, it was a kick in the teeth for him to insult me in front of everyone."

KICK IN: (sin. pitch in) *exp-v.* Compartir los gastos de algo. *Ej.* "Everyone has to kick in for the present."

KICK (SOME) ASS: [Vul.] 1) *exp-v.* Lograr algo, tener éxito en algo. *Ej.* "The test was difficult, but I still kicked ass on it." 2) *exp-v.* Derrotar en forma decisiva. *Ej.* "Our team is gonna kick some ass tonight!" Ver smear. 3) *adj.* Excelente, realmente bueno o increíble. *Ej.* "We had a kick ass time at the party." 4) *exp-v.* Hacer un llamado de alerta a quienes están

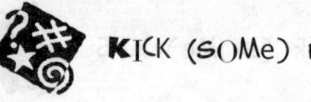
KICK (SOMe) BUTt

haraganeando y así infundir disciplina y castigar a quienes no cambien de actitud. *Ej.* "It's time to kick some ass and tell those lazy bastards what's what."

KICK (SOME) BUTT: *exp-v.* Forma educada de decir kick (some) ass.

KICK SOMEONE WHEN SOMEONE IS DOWN: *exp-v.* Aprovecharse de alguien cuando se encuentra en mala situación. *Ej.* "I learned what a scumbag he was when I was in financial trouble. Instead of helping, he kicked me when I was down and forced me into bankruptcy."

KICK SOMEONE'S ASS: [Vul.] *exp-v.* Golpear a alguien hasta dejarlo gravemente herido. *Ej.* "The gang kicked his ass just for fun." VER *beat someone up*.

KICK SOMEONE'S BUTT: *exp-v.* Forma cortés de decir kick someone's ass.

KICK THE BUCKET: (sin. *cash in one's chips, croak, buy the farm*) *exp-v.* Forma sarcástica de referirse a la muerte. Morirse. *Ej.* "We all have to kick the bucket sometime, Al."

KICK UPSTAIRS: *exp-v.* Ascender en lugar de despedir (que sería preferible) a una persona no precisamente productiva a un puesto de mayor rango que, sin embargo, conlleva menos responsabilidades. *Ej.* "They kicked the old man upstairs to make room for some aggressive youngsters in sales."

KICKBACK: *s.* Dinero pagado como soborno o como porcentaje de alguna actividad ilegal. *Ej.* "The contractors were paying kickbacks to the inspectors to get the building permits."

KICKING AROUND: *exp.* Estar sin nada que hacer y sentirse frustrado. Típico de los desempleados disconformes. *Ej.* "What's John doing these days?" "Oh, he got fired last week so he's just kickin' around looking for trouble."

KICKS: *s.pl.* Diversión, entretención más bien perjudicial. *Ej.* "It's strange, but she gets her kicks watching professional wrestling."

KIDDO: *s.* 1) Niño/a. *Ej.* "Hi kiddo, how was school today?" 2) Amigo. *Ej.* "Hey kiddo, how's the family?"

KISS UP TO

KIKE: s. Judío. (Desp.) Ej. "The fight started when he called her a kike."

KILL: v. 1) Doler, sentir dolor. Ej. "My foot kills me." 2) Terminar, tomar la última porción. Ej. "Is it cool for me to kill the salad?"

KILL FOR: v. Querer a un grado extremo. Ej. "It's so hot out I'd kill for a cold soda right now."

KILL TWO BIRDS WITH ONE STONE: exp-v. Lograr dos metas o propósitos a la vez. Ej. "I'll bring him the box. I have to see him anyway so I might as well kill two birds with one stone."

KILLER: adj. Excelente, fantástico. Ej. "Killer car dude!" VER awesome.

KINKY: adj. Sexy o erótico, esp. relacionado con la ropa o comportamiento sexual pervertido. Ej. "He had some rather kinky toys in his closet."

KISS ASS: [Vul.] exp-v. Congraciarse con alguien con fines interesados, generalmente con el jefe. Ej. "He'd kiss ass with a gorilla if he thought it'd get him a promotion."

KISS MY ASS: [Vul.] int. Insulto mayor que denota odio o desprecio por otro. Ej. "That jerk can kiss my ass if he doesn't like my offer."

KISS OFF: 1) v. Aceptar, dar por perdido, rendirse a pesar de los deseos de uno. Ej. "You're just gonna have to kiss off your vacation, we've got work to do." 2) int. Pedirle a alguien que se retire de inmediato o que desista/deje de molestar. Ej. "She told him to kiss off." VER TAMBIEN kiss-off.

KISS SOMEONE'S ASS: Forma vulgar de kiss someone's butt.

KISS SOMEONE'S BUTT: exp-v. Congraciarse con alguien por motivos ulteriores, interesados. Gen. el jefe. Ej. "It's not worth the job if I have to kiss her butt all the time."

KISS SOMETHING GOOD-BYE: exp-v. Despedirse o decir adiós a algo querido y perderlo. Ej. "It's time you kissed that dream good-bye and wake up to reality."

KISS UP TO: exp-v. Congraciarse con alguien por motivos ulteriores, interesados. Ej. "How can he kiss up to that conceited jerk?"

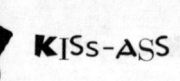

KISS-ASS

KISS-ASS: [Vul.] s. Persona que kiss ass. Ej. "That kiss-ass would do anything to ingratiate himself with the boss."

KISSER: s. 1) (sin. trap, yap*) La boca. Ej. "Plant one on the kisser baby!" 2) La cara. Ej. "He had a big zit right in the middle of his kisser."

KISS-OFF: s. Despido, rechazo, generalmente de un trabajo o relación amorosa. Ej. "She gave him the big kiss-off after he fooled around with her friend." VER TAMBIEN kiss off.

KLEPTO: abr. Kleptomaniac = Cleptómano. Ej. "Don't leave anything valuable out when Tim the klepto is around."

KLUTZ: s. Persona desgarbada, torpe, propensa a los accidentes. Ej. "She's such a klutz and yet she dances the tango beautifully."

KLUTZY: adj. Torpe, lerdo, propenso a los accidentes. Ej. "My mom is so klutzy she breaks something everyday."

KNEE DEEP IN IT: exp. Totalmente implicado en algo desagradable. Ej. "There's no pretending you're not involved, we know you're knee deep in the drug business."

KNEE-JERK: adj. Reacción o actitud pronosticable, gen. proveniente de un tipo de filosofía profundamente arraigada. Ej. "Those knee-jerk liberals will never accept any infringement on civil liberties."

KNOCK: 1) v. Criticar, poner peros a algo. Ej. "No matter what I do, she always knocks me." 2) s. Crítica, reparo. Ej. "Any more knocks about my cooking and I'll never cook again!"

KNOCK BACK: exp-v. Beber, normalmente bebidas alcohólicas. Ej. "He knocked back six beers before it struck noon."

KNOCK DOWN: exp-v. 1) Disminuir el costo de algo. Ej. "He knocked down the price of dresses by 20%." 2) Percibir como ingreso. Ej. "It's a good job that knocks down sixty gee a year."

KNOCK FOR A LOOP: exp-v. Asombrar, abrumar con sorpresa. Ej. "The news of my friends death knocked me for a loop."

KNOCK IT OFF: int. Orden para

KNOCK-OFF

dejar de hacer algo molestoso. *Ej.* "I told you kids to knock it off and get some sleep." Or "Knock it off! Now get back to work!"

KNOCK OFF: *exp-v.* 1) Dejar de trabajar, tomarse un descanso. *Ej.* "The workers knock off at five o'clock sharp." 2) Terminar o completar, generalmente con cierta facilidad. *Ej.* "It's amazing how many plays Shakespeare knocked off." 3) Disminuir la cantidad de algo, o eliminar. *Ej.* "She's so fat she could knock off ten pounds and you wouldn't even notice it." 4) Matar, asesinar. *Ej.* "They knocked him off in the woods." VER *waste.* 5) Robar. *Ej.* "The hoodlums knocked off a liquor store." 6) Reducir el costo de algo. *Ej.* "Because you're Tony's friend, I'll knock off an extra fifty dollars." 7) Comer con muchas ganas. *Ej.* "He knocked off six pancakes and then ordered four eggs."

KNOCK ONESELF OUT: *exp-v.* 1) Servirse todo lo que uno quiera de algo. *Ej.* "Can I have some cake?" "Sure, knock yourself out." 2) Trabajar demasiado para algún fin y experimentar una gran fatiga. *Ej.* "She knocked herself out preparing for the music recital."

KNOCK SOMEONE DEAD: *exp-v.* Afectar/conmover, especialmente con sorpresa y encanto. *Ej.* "Before she went on stage, her father would always say, 'Knock them dead tonight!'"

KNOCK SOMEONE'S SOCKS OFF: (sin. knock the socks off of) *exp-v.* Asombrar, sorprender, especialmente con una actuación/ejecución maravillosa. *Ej.* "He knocked their socks off with his Elvis impression."

KNOCK THE SOCKS OFF OF: VER *knock someone's socks off.*

KNOCK THE WIND OUT OF SOMEONE'S SAILS: VER *take the wind out of one's sail.*

KNOCK UP: *exp-v.* Quedar embarazada/ embarazar(se). *Ej.* "What luck! She got knocked up the first time she did the horizontal mambo."

KNOCKERS: *s.* Senos femeninos, gen. grandes. *Ej.* "I didn't know there was a bra size for knockers that big."

KNOCK-OFF: *s.* Imitación o copia no

141

KNOCKOUT

autorizada. *Ej.* "The company loses millions a year in knock-off software."

KNOCKOUT: *s.* Una mujer muy atractiva. *Ej.* "Wow, she's a knock-out!" VER *babe*.

KNOT: VER *tie the knot*.

KNOW SHIT FROM SHINOLA: [Vul.] *exp.* Conocer, ser entendido en cosas básicas. *Ej.* "Don't even bother asking him, he doesn't know shit from shinola about economics."

KNUCKLE SANDWICH: *s.* Golpe, puñetazo en la boca. *Ej.* "Any more wisecracks and you'll get a knuckle sandwich."

KNUCKLEHEAD: *s.* Persona torpe, tonta. *Ej.* "I'm such a knucklehead for forgetting my wife's birthday." Ver *dimwit*.

KOOK: *s.* Persona excéntrica, estrafalaria. *Ej.* "What kind of a kook would build a house out of garbage?"

KOOKY: *adj.* Una pizca excéntrico o loco. *Ej.* "She's a little kooky, what with ten cats and all, but I like her anyway."

KOSHER: (sin. *legit*) *adj.* Legítimo, permitido, justo. *Ej.* "Is it kosher for me to take an extra week of vacation?"

KRAUT: *s.* Alemán. (Desp.) *Ej.* "Them Krauts sure make good cars."

L.A.:

L.A.: *abr.* Los Angeles. *Ej.* "Them celebrity types live in L.A.."

LADY-KILLER: *s.* Un hombre que hace que las mujeres se vuelvan locas pero que, a menudo, las deja emocionalmente turbadas. *Ej.* "Resist the temptation, he's a lady-killer who will make you sorry."

LAID-BACK: *adj.* Relajado, calmado, despreocupado (actitud, carácter, ambiente). *Ej.* "We had a laid-back weekend at the beach." Or "I like Jim's laid-back approach to life."

LAM: VER *on the lam*.

LAME: (sin. *sucky*) *adj.* Mala calidad, sin gracia, aburrido. *Ej.* "This party is lame. Let's beat it."

LAME DUCK: *exp.* Se refiere a alguien en una posición de autoridad, gen. un personaje político cuyo período está a punto de vencerse y que no tiene

LAY OFF

posibilidad de continuar más allá. Ej. "Clinton's a lame duck now that he's been re-elected. Now we'll see if he takes any unpopular actions."

LAND: *v.* 1) Ganar, obtener, lograr. Ej. "He landed a big contract that saved the company." 2) Dar, propinar un golpe con el pie o la mano/puño. Ej. "He landed a hard right smack in the kisser."

LATER: *int.* Adiós. Ej. "Later bud, I'll catch you downtown tonight."

LAUGH: VER *get the last laugh; not in a laughing mood; one who laughs last, laughs longest.*

LAUNDRY LIST: *s.* Lista extensa de quehaceres o de cosas deseadas. Ej. "She brought a laundry list of demands to the interview." Or "Now that my mom is working, I've got a laundry list of things to do around the house."

LAW: VER *lay down the law.*

LAY: [Vul.] 1) *vi.* Tener relaciones sexuales. Ej. "I got laid last night." 2) *s.* Una relación sexual. Ej. "I need a lay so bad I'm ready to burst!" 3) *s.* Con quien se tiene una relación sexual. Ej. "He was a good lay."

LAY BACK: *exp-vi.* Relajarse y tomárselo con calma. Ej. "With all the stress at work, I just need to lay back for a few days."

LAY DOWN THE LAW: *exp-vi.* Definir, en forma clara y precisa, los términos y parámetros de comportamiento. Ej. "After she caught the workers slacking off, she laid down the law."

LAY INTO: *exp-vi.* 1) Retar, reprender, o regañar oralmente. Ej. "He laid into his son for getting drunk." 2) Dar una paliza. Ej. "He had to be taken to the emergency room after the gang laid into him."

LAY IT ON THICK: *exp-vi.* Exagerar, mentir imaginativamente; adular, halagar, casi siempre con la intención de lograr algo. Ej. "He tried to lay it on thick with her about her beauty and intelligence, but she figured out the motive behind it."

LAY OFF: *exp-vi.* 1) Dejar de hacer algo, esp. algo dañino. Ej. "You better lay off the booze before you become an alky." 2) Dejar a uno en paz; dejar de tratar o hablar a uno

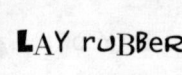
LAY RUBBER

en forma negativa. *Ej.* "Why don't you lay off Tim for a while. You've been on his back for a month now."

LAY RUBBER: *exp-vi.* Acelerar un vehículo motorizado de improviso, de manera que los neumáticos giren a una gran velocidad y dejen una marca en el pavimento. *Ej.* "They left in a hurry. Look at how they laid rubber."

LAY (SOMETHING) ON: *exp-vi.* Decir, revelar algo, esp. algo negativo, insospechado o desagradable. *Ej.* "All right, lay it on me; how much are they suing me for?" Or "Dave can really lay on the charm when he wants to."

LAYOUT: *s.* Establecimiento o propiedad, y todas las atracciones que se encuentren ahí. *Ej.* "You've made a real nice layout for yourself here."

LAZY BONES: (sin. couch potato) *s.* Persona muy perezosa o desganada. *Ej.* "Come on lazy bones, let's get moving."

LEAD FOOT: *s.* Inclinación a conducir rápidamente. *Ej.* "My grandma thinks I have a lead foot, but I'm not even breaking the speed limit."

LEAK: VER *take a leak.*

LEAVE SOMEONE HANGING: *exp-vi.* Dejar esperando a alguien, o no cumplir un compromiso de juntarse. *Ej.* "You bastard, you left me hanging Saturday night."

LECH: *s.* Persona, gen. un hombre, lascivo, despreciable y censurable. *Ej.* "He's such a lech he's probably a peeping Tom."

LEG: VER *charge an arm and a leg; pull someone's leg; stretch one's legs; with one's tail between one's legs.*

LEG WORK: *s.* El trabajo arduo y aburrido, gen. la investigación dentro de un gran proyecto. Esp. el trabajo que implica mucho tiempo caminando o trasladándose a diferentes lugares. *Ej.* "We're a team; he does the thinking and I do the leg work."

LEGIT: (sin. kosher) *adj.* Legítimo, permitido, justo. *Ej.* "Are you certain it's legit for me to take the car for the night?"

LESBO: (sin. dyke) *s.* Lesbiana. (Desp.) *Ej.* "Man, you're not wanted in there, it's a lesbo bar."

LIE THROUGH ONE'S TEETH

LET IT ALL HANG OUT: *exp-vi.* Ser totalmente relajado, cándido o libre de inhibiciones. *Ej.* "You can't pretend you are someone else, you've just got to let it all hang out."

LET OFF STEAM: *exp-vi.* Expresar enojo o frustración de manera benigna o no tan benigna. *Ej.* "He boxes to let off steam."

LET ONE'S HAIR DOWN: (sin. loosen one's tie, cut loose*) *exp-vi.* Hacer algo inusitado o que normalmente no corresponde a la edad que se tiene. *Ej.* "Mom, you need to relax. Let your hair down and have some fun."

LET ONESELF GO: *exp-vi.* Volverse desenfrenado (en la manera de actuar) o desaseado (en aspecto). *Ej.* "She really let herself go after her husband left her."

LET RIP: *exp-vi.* Comenzar algo y/o dejarlo avanzar a alta velocidad. *Ej.* "Let her rip, let's see what this baby can do." Or "In the middle of the meeting, he let rip a huge fart."

LET THE CAT OUT OF THE BAG: VER *spill the beans*.

LEVEL WITH SOMEONE: *exp-v.* Ser honesto y franco con alguien. *Ej.* "Just level with me; are they going to fire me or not?"

LIBERATE: *v.* Tomar, robar u obtener en forma ilegal. *Ej.* "I'm not robbing your jewels lady, I'm liberating them."

LICK: *v.* 1) Dar una paliza, a menudo como castigo por un delito. *Ej.* "I got licked for wising off to some jock" 2) Golpear, vencer a golpes. *Ej.* "Don't even think about fighting him, he could lick you one handed." VER *beat someone up*.

LICKETY-SPLIT: *exp.* En seguida, inmediatamente. *Ej.* "You'd better clean up that mess lickety-split, or else."

LICKING: *s.* Golpiza, zurra. *Ej.* "The team took a licking on Sunday." Or "My dad gave me some licking for hitting my sister!"

LID: *s.* Gorra de béisbol. *Ej.* "Get a load of the lid on that dude." VER TAMBIEN *flip one's lid; put a lid on it*.

LIE THROUGH ONE'S TEETH: *exp-v.* Mentir en forma descarada. *Ej.* "He was lying through his teeth when he said he was sick. I saw him

LIft

at a party."

LIFT: 1) s. Llevar a alguien (en un vehículo). Ej. "Can you give me a lift to the store?" 2) v. Robar, hurtar. Ej. "She lifted a piece of candy from the store." VER swipe.

LIGHT: VER green light; little light in the loafers; out like a light; see the light.

LIGHTEN UP: exp. Relajarse, dejar de sentirse tenso, nervioso o enojado. Ej. "You need to lighten up or you'll give yourself a heart attack."

LIGHTWEIGHT: s. 1) Persona que es afectado fácilmente por el alcohol. Ej. "She's such a lightweight. One beer and she's blitzed." 2) Persona de poca influencia o poca importancia. Ej. "He's a lightweight in the office. He's got no pull."

LIKE A BAT OUT OF HELL: exp-vi. Ir muy rápido, esp. conduciendo vehículo. Ej. "After breaking out of prison, he flew like a bat out of hell to cross the border."

LIKE NOBODY'S BUSINESS: exp. A nivel máximo, con gran esfuerzo e intensidad. Ej. "When Joey starts wailing on the guitar, he plays like nobody's business."

LIMEY: s. Inglés (persona). (Desp.) Ej. "I hear them limeys love fish and chips."

LIONS: VER throw to the lions.

LIP: VER bite one's lip; button one's lip; give someone (some) lip; pay lip service.

LIPS SEALED: (sin. button one's lip) exp-vi. Mantener silencio con respecto a un tema que se conoce o sobre el cual se tiene una opinión. Ej. "Hey, I can keep my lips sealed. I won't tell your wife about our affair."

LITTLE LIGHT IN THE LOAFERS: exp. Un modo delicado y gracioso de describir a alguien como homosexual, esp. cuando no se tiene certeza y sólo se supone. Ej. "In general I don't like to assume anything about anyone, but I'd say he's a little light in the loafers."

LITTLE SOMETHING ON THE SIDE: exp. Tener un enredo sexual o sentimental. Ej. "She dumped him. It turned out she wasn't too understanding about his having a little something on the side."

LIVE (FROM) HAND TO MOUTH: exp-v.

LOCAL YOKEL

Tener muy poco dinero, sin importarle demasiado la situación precaria. *Ej.* "Are you crazy? Work a 9 to 5 job? I'd rather live hand to mouth."

LIVE: *adj.* Mucha acción o emoción, gen. implica peligro también. *Ej.* "The movie was live, man: bullets flying, cars crashing. The shit was fresh!"

LIVE ONE: *s.* Tonto, persona a la que se puede engañar fácilmente. *Ej.* "There was a live one at the pool house last night. Boy, did he lose a bundle!"

LOAD: VER *get a load of; take a load off.*

LOADED: *adj.* 1) Adinerado, rico. *Ej.* "He married this gal who is loaded. Her dad is CEO of General Motors." 2) Ebrio, muy borracho. *Ej.* "He got loaded on whiskey last night." Ver *plastered.* 3) Que viene con todos los accesorios. *Ej.* "This car comes loaded. We're talking AC, radio, sun roof… the works."

LOAF: *exp-v.* Demorarse haciendo algo en el trabajo. *Ej.* "The biggest problem in this company is the workers loafing all the time."

LOAFERS: VER *little light in the loafers.*

LOAN SHARK: *s.* Prestamista. Persona que presta dinero cobrando altos intereses. El no pago a menudo significa la pérdida de miembro(s), vida, o ¡peor! *Ej.* "He had to split town because he owed the loan shark five gees."

LOCAL YOKEL: *s.* Residente local, esp. de una pequeña comunidad o área rural y que a menudo "el citadino" considera ignorante o

LITTLE LIGHT IN THE LOAFERS

LOCK UP

ingenuo. (Desp.) *Ej.* "The local yokels complain about us tourists being rude, but they sure don't complain about our money."

LOCK UP: *exp.* Prisión, cárcel. VER *clink /the/.*

LOOK: *s.* Apariencia física. *Ej.* "That's a new look for you, isn't it? I mean the purple hair and pierced nose?"

LOOK A GIFT HORSE IN THE MOUTH: *exp.* No quejarse de algo que es gratis, esp. en el sentido de exigirle más a algo o alguien. *Ej.* "Don't complain Tim. It may not be the greatest car in the world, but it's free. You should never look a gift horse in the mouth."

LOOK OUT FOR NUMBER ONE (1): *exp-v.* Preocuparse y proteger sólo los intereses propios, esp. a expensas de otros. *Ej.* "I wouldn't be partners with him, he only looks out for number one."

LOOK WHAT THE CAT DRAGGED IN: *exp-v.* Se dice cuando alguien llega inesperadamente o muy atrasado a una fiesta o donde hay un grupo reunido. *Ej.* "Look what the cat dragged in! Where have you been hiding for the last year?"

LOOKER: *s.* Persona muy atractiva y sexy. *Ej.* "Check out the looker John's dating!"

LOOKOUT: VER *on the lookout.*

LOOK-SEE: *s.* Vistazo, inspección rápida. *Ej.* "Give me a look-see at that <u>Playboy</u>."

LOONY: 1) *adj.* Loco, demente o, por lo menos, extremadamente absurdo. *Ej.* "He started acting loony after dropping acid one too many times." VER *bats.* 2) *s.* Persona loca, estúpida. *Ej.* "What kind of a loony marries a convicted murderer?"

LOONY-TUNE: *s.* Una persona loca, chiflada, que pareciera haber perdido alguna conexión cerebral vital (etim. Los dibujos animados de Warner Brothers, que se llaman "Looney Tunes"). *Ej.* "You must be a loony-tune to bungy jump from a bridge."

LOOP: VER *knock for a loop.*

LOOPED: *adj.* Intoxicado, ebrio. *Ej.* "Susan got looped last night."

LOOPY: *adj.* Un poco loco, casi demente. *Ej.* "He got a little loopy after sniffing too much glue." VER *bats.*

LOSE ONE'S MIND

LOOSE CANON: VER. *loose gun.*

LOOSE ENDS /THE/: *exp.* Detalles sin gran importancia pero que necesitan atención. *Ej.* "Why do I always have to tie up the loose ends in these contracts?"

LOOSE GUN: (sin. loose canon) *s.* Persona desequilibrada, esp. en cuanto a su comportamiento caprichoso. *Ej.* "Stay away from him. He's a loose gun just waiting to go off."

LOOSE TONGUE: *exp-v.* Hablar, esp. en el sentido de divulgar información indiscreta. *Ej.* "Give him a few cocktails and he'll loosen his tongue."

LOOSEN ONE'S TIE: (sin. let one's hair down) *exp-v.* Hacer algo inusitado o que normalmente no corresponde a la edad que se tiene. Se usa para un hombre. *Ej.* "Loosen your tie Hal, have a little fun in your life."

LOOT: (sin. mint /a/) *s.* Mucho dinero. *Ej.* "He must make some serious loot to buy a Ferarri."

LOSE (ALL) ONE'S MARBLES: (sin. flip out) *exp-vi.* Ser (totalmente) loco, volverse (totalmente) loco. *Ej.* "I'm worried about Jane. I think she's lost her marbles." Or "The guy lost all his marbles during the war."

LOSE FACE: *exp-vi.* Hacer algo o decir un comentario tonto o ridículo frente a los demás. *Ej.* "Sal got stupid drunk in front of his boss and completely lost face."

LOSE IT: *exp-vi.* Perder la compostura. Momentáneamente transformarse en otra persona, gen. una persona muy enojada. *Ej.* "I'm normally a very mellow person, but I lose it when I see people littering."

LOSE ONE'S COOL: *exp-vi.* Enojarse y/o alterarse. *Ej.* "The guy pissed me off so much I lost my cool and punched him."

LOSE ONE'S LUNCH: *exp-vi.* Vomitar. *Ej.* "It was terrible. I lost my lunch all over the President's pants." VER *chuck up.*

LOSE ONE'S MIND: (sin. lose one's head) *exp-vi.* Desequilibrarse mentalmente debido a una situación agobiadora o llena de tensiones. *Ej.* "She lost her mind from all the pressure of work and family."

LOSe ONE's SHIrT

LOSE ONE'S SHIRT: (sin. take to the cleaners) *exp-vi.* Perder todo el dinero o posesiones, esp. producto de las apuestas. *Ej.* "He lost his shirt in the futures market."

LOSER: *s.* Una persona considerada un fracaso. También una persona inmadura y necia. *Ej.* "The guy is such a loser. He's always trying to pick up girls ten years younger than him."

LOST IN SPACE: *exp-vi.* Estar momentáneamente distraído, sin ponerle atención a las personas o acontecimientos que lo rodean. *Ej.* "Are you lost in space or something? Didn't you see that car, it almost hit us!"

LOUNGE LIZARD: *s.* 1) Hombre que trata de actuar y vestir de manera atrayente o con donaire para seducir a mujeres, pero que generalmente se le ve como indigno de confianza y siútico. A menudo este tipo de hombre ha pasado demasiado tiempo en salones de hoteles baratos, escuchando o tocando piano o teclado electrónico y tomando tragos con paraguas multicolores. ¡Cuidado! *Ej.* "This total lounge lizard – I'm talking polyester suit, gold chains, the works — was trying to pick up on my mom." 2) Persona que pasa tanto tiempo en los bares que llega a ser una instalación fija, tan lubricada con trago que pareciera no tener columna, reclinado así sobre el amoblado y/o bar. *Ej.* "You can tell this is a serious drinking bar by the number of lounge lizards here."

LOUSE UP: *exp-v.* Arruinar, echar

LOUNGE LiZARd

LUNCH

a perder. Ej. "He loused up my birthday party by telling off-color jokes."

LOUSE: s. Persona despreciable, repelente, miserable. Canalla. (etim. De la palabra "louse": piojo.) Ej. "I wouldn't trust that louse with my kids."

LOUSY: adj. 1) Muy malo o sentirse muy mal. Ej. "I feel lousy after being out in the rain all night." 2) Abundancia, que tiene muchísimo. Ej. "That guy Bill Gates is lousy with money."

LOVE HANDLES: s. Gordura extra en las caderas, lo suficiente para que alguien agarre. Ej. "He's not fat, he just has love handles."

LOVER-BOY: s. Forma graciosa o sarcástica para referirse al novio, esp. usado por los padres o un adulto. Ej. "Are you going out with lover-boy again?"

LOW KEY: adj. Informal al vestirse y de actitud. Ej. "This is a low key affair, leave your tuxedo at home."

LOWDOWN/THE/: (sin. score /the/) s. Toda la verdad; información esencial y más importante. Ej. "Give me the lowdown on the deal and don't skip any important details."

LOW-LIFE: adj. Persona de bajo estándar moral. Esp. una persona que se aprovecha de la compasión de otros para lograr sus fines. Ej. "He's such a low-life for scamming money from old ladies."

LUCK: VER down on one's luck; push one's luck; shit out of luck.

LUCKY /GET/: exp-vi. Tener una experiencia sexual. Ej. "By the smile on his face this morning I'd say he got lucky last night."

LUG: s. Hombre torpe, lerdo y/o ingenuo. Ej. "That lug should do the world a favor and not propagate."

LUGI: VER huck a lugi.

LULU: s. Objeto o idea extraordinaria, notable o impresionante. Ej. "She comes up with some lulus. Yesterday, she told me she was starting a business selling used sneakers to Africa."

LUMP IT: int. Aceptar la realidad desagradable de una situación dada. Ej. "If you don't like it, lump it."

LUNCH: VER lose one's lunch; out

to lunch; no such thing as a free lunch.

LUSH: s. Borracho, bebedor. Ej. "Offer that lush a sip of your beer and he'll drink all of it."

MAC: s. Modo de dirigirse a un desconocido para caerle bien. Ej. "Pardon Mac, do you know where the bus station is?"

MAD MONEY: s. Dinero, gen. en pequeña cantidad, guardado para un caso de emergencia, o para darse un pequeño gusto. Ej. "My mom keeps some mad money, in case of an unexpected event."

MADAM: s. Dueña de un prostíbulo. Ej. "She made a lot of money as a madam."

MAIN: adj. Principal, primero, favorito. Ej. "I've got a lot of friends, but George is my main man."

MAIN DRAG: s. Calle principal de una ciudad o pueblo. Ej. "Let's go cruising on the main drag."

MAJOR: adj. Muy significativo o que implica/trae consecuencias. Ej. "It was a major error to insult the President of the company."

MAJOR LEAGUE: (sin. Big League) exp. Muy grande, afortunado o importante (etim. del baseball de Major League, la liga de béisbol más importante y prestigiosa del mundo). Ej. "Major League event in my life – I'm getting married!"

MAKE: 1) vi. Identificar a alguien o algo. Ej. "Can you make the person who robbed you? Did you see his face?" 2) s. Identificación de alguien o de algo. Ej. "Did he get a make on the license plate number?" VER TAMBIEN on the make; put the make on.

MAKE A LIVING: exp-vi. Trabajar, generalmente en algo poco glorioso, para poder sobrevivir. Ej. "Well, I'm not going to be rich and famous working here, but at least I'm making a living."

MAKE A MOVE: exp-vi. Actuar decididamente. Ej. "You can't just sit on your hands, you have to make a move."

MAKE A STINK: VER raise a stink.

MAKE A U-Y: VER pull a U-y.

MAKE BANK: exp-vi. Ganar mucho dinero, esp. en forma fácil. Ej. "I'm

MAKE OUT

making bank at my new job."

MAKE ENDS MEET: *exp-vi.* Ganar dinero justo para pagar las cuentas. *Ej.* "Even with both of us working it's still hard to make ends meet."

MAKE FUN OF: *exp-vi.* Burlarse de alguien. *Ej.* "She got pissed off when they made fun of her."

MAKE IT HOT: (sin. make it tough) *exp-vi.* Hacer que una situación o circunstancia se torne precaria, incómoda y/o peligrosa para alguien. *Ej.* "They'll make it hot for you to see if you can hack the pressure."

MAKE IT TOUGH: VER *make it hot*.

MAKE IT: *exp-vi.* 1) Tener éxito, lograr un objetivo. *Ej.* "For me, I'll have made it when everyone recognizes my genius." 2) Tener relaciones sexuales. *Ej.* "We made it in the back seat of my dad's car."

MAKE LIKE A BANANA AND SPLIT: *exp-vi.* Irse de algún lado, gen. por aburrido. *Ej.* "Let's say you make like a banana and split before I give you permanent brain damage."

MAKE LIKE: *exp-vi.* Imitar, personificar. *Ej.* "After insulting me behind my back, the jerk tried to make like he's my good friend."

MAKE MINCEMEAT OF: *exp-vi.* Derrotar total y despiadadamente o, deshacerse de una persona golpeándola en forma sostenida, o criticar en forma severa y brutal. En todo caso, nunca es bueno que alguien *make mincemeat of* algo tuyo. *Ej.* "What a lousy day! First the teacher made mincemeat of my presentation, and then Harry made mincemeat of me on the basketball court."

MAKE NO BONES ABOUT: *exp-vi.* Ser directo y sincero; actuar en forma abierta y sin reserva, o hablar las cosas claramente. *Ej.* "What I like about Ted is that he makes no bones about whether or not he likes someone."

MAKE OUT LIKE A BANDIT: *exp-vi.* Tener gran éxito y/o adquirir mucho de algo valioso a través de una actividad, esfuerzo o situación. *Ej.* "I made out like a bandit in the plastics business."

MAKE OUT: *vi.* Besarse y tocarse

MAKE TIME

con caricias apasionadas. *Ej.* "I'm sick of Ted! All he wants to do is make out. He's not interested in my mind!"

MAKE TIME: *exp-vi.* Viajar rápidamente para recuperar el tiempo perdido. *Ej.* "We had a slow start, but we made time on the highway."

MAKE TRACKS: *exp-vi.* Marcharse rápidamente, por lo general, no en el mejor momento. *Ej.* "When her dad found out I had been making it with her, I made tracks right quick."

MAKE UP: *exp-vi.* Reconciliarse después de una disputa. *Ej.* "You two have been fighting all week. It's time you made up."

MAKE WAVES: *exp-vi.* Causar alboroto o crear controversia. *Ej.* "The problem with Marco is he makes waves wherever he goes."

MAKE WHOOPEE: *exp-vi.* 1) Tener una gran fiesta o celebración con todo el ruido y festividad que ésta implica. *Ej.* "Are you planning on making whoopee tonight or is it going to be a quiet night at home?" 2) Tener relaciones sexuales. *Ej.* "You don't think he's making whoopee with our daughter, do you?"

MALARKEY: *s.* Habla exagerada o disparatada, generalmente con la intención de engañar. *Ej.* "Why are you telling me this malarkey? Do you think I was born yesterday?"

MAMA: *s.* 1) Madre, mamá. *Ej.* "Give mama a kiss before you go." 2) Mujer, generalmente sexy. *Ej.* "Check out that mama in the restaurant!"

MAMA'S BOY: *s.* Hombre, gen. joven, que se considera poco valiente o sumiso, como si aún necesitara la aprobación de la madre para hacer algo. *Ej.* "He's such a mama's boy that he never does anything without her say so."

MAN /ONE'S/: *s.* Amigo, esp. el mejor amigo, el más cercano a uno. *Ej.* "Don't mess with my man Charlie."

MAN EATER: *s.* Mujer que sale en son de conquista sexual por una noche. *Ej.* "You know he'll be on the bottom with that man eater."

MARBLES: VER *lose (all) one's marbles.*

MENtAL

MARK: s. Persona que es blanco de un robo o estafa. Ej. "The key to a good scam is to carefully choose the mark."

MASSACRE: v. 1) Golpear o pegar severamente. Ej. "The fighter got massacred in the last round." VER beat someone up. 2) Derrotar total y despiadadamente. Ej. "We're gonna massacre you guys in the championship!" VER smear.

MAX: s. & adv. Máximo. Ej. "I'll give you three grand max for the car." Or "She's the max!"

MAX OUT: v. Llegar al límite máximo de uno mismo o de algo. Ej. "I'm maxed out on my credit card."

McJOB: s. Un trabajo de bajo sueldo en el área de servicios. Ej. "I got a McJob flipping burgers."

McKOY: VER real McKoy.

MEAL TICKET: s. Apoyo financiero, esp. forma fácil para obtener ayuda financiera. Ej. "Instead of looking for a meal ticket, why don't you try working?"

MEAN: adj. Realmente bueno, muy atractivo. Ej. "That is a mean dress you have on!"

MEASLY: adj. Muy poco, una cantidad despreciable. Ej. "My boss gave me a measly 25 cents raise in my salary."

MEAT HOOK: (sin. mitt) s. Mano o puño, gen. dicho peyorativamente, como cuando un hombre manosea a una mujer. Ej. "You pig, keep your meat hooks to yourself!"

MEAT MARKET: s. Lugar donde hombres y mujeres buscan pasarlo bien sin ocultarlo (o sea, tener un intervalo romántico). Ej. "I hate going to that bar, it's like a meat market in there."

MEATHEAD: s. Una persona torpe, tonta, estúpida. Ej. "At best that meathead will get a job picking up trash." VER dimwit.

MEGABUCKS: s. Una gran suma de dinero. Ej. "He made megabucks playing the stock market."

MELLOW OUT: v. Relajarse, esp. deshacerse de preocupaciones. Ej. "I need to mellow out and forget about all the problems at work."

MENTAL: adj. Emocionalmente desequilibrada con aires de agresividad y/o violencia. Ej. "My sis will go mental on you if you

MENtAL BloCK

mess with her stuff."

MENTAL BLOCK: *exp.* Una parálisis temporal (¡por lo menos así se espera!) del proceso creativo. Gen. se refiere a los escritores. *Ej.* "What a mental block, I can't even think of how to start the paper."

MESS AROUND: (sin. goof-off) *exp-v.* Revolverla, ocasionar desorden pasándolo bien. *Ej.* "If you kids don't stop messing around, I'll have to beat you within an inch of your life!"

MESS (SOMEONE) UP: *exp-v.* Pegarle fuerte a alguien, golpear en forma sostenida a una persona. *Ej.* "They messed him up in the fight."

MESS WITH: *exp-v.* Implicarse con algo o alguien que se debería evitar. *Ej.* "Don't mess with drugs!" Or "Don't mess with me or I'll bust you upside the head!"

METAL: VER *pedal to the metal /put the/*.

MICKEY MOUSE: *adj.* Trivial, insignificante, simple. *Ej.* "I'm not interested in your Mickey Mouse concerns."

MIL: *s.* Un millón de dólares. *Ej.* "He's got over a mil in the bank."

MILE: VER *give an inch and one takes a mile*.

MENtAL BloCK

MILK RUN: *s.* Viaje de rutina, sencillo y seguro con paradas en diferentes lugares. *Ej.* "Don't worry kid, the job is basically a milk run. There shouldn't be any fireworks."

MILK SOMETHING: *exp-v.* Hacer algo lentamente para que dure y para sacarle máximo provecho. *Ej.* "This is the easiest job I've ever had. I'm going to milk it for as long as I can."

MILL: VER *run of the mill*.

MONEY GRUBBING

MINCE WORDS /NOT/: VER tell it like it is.

MINCEMEAT: VER make mincemeat of.

MIND ONE'S OWN BUSINESS: exp. No inmiscuirse en la vida de los demás. Ej. "In-laws should always mind their own business."

MIND-BLOWING: adj. Increíble, sorprendente, de gran impacto. Ej. "The teacher gave a mind-blowing lecture about evolution. It was simply fascinating."

MINT /A/: (sin. loot) s. Mucho dinero. Ej. "That mansion must've cost a mint."

MISS THE BOAT: exp-v. Llegar atrasado para aprovechar una oferta. Ej. "Sorry pal, you missed the boat. We gave the job away an hour ago."

MITT: VER meat hook.

MIX IT UP: exp-v. Pelear. Ej. "It was an ugly sight when the two brothers mixed it up."

MOBSTER: s. Persona que pertenece a la Mafia u otra forma de crimen organizado. Ej. "The mobsters are having a meeting at the Royal Inn."

MOFO: [Vul.] abr. Motherfucker. Ej. "Tell that mofo he better stay the fuck out of my face!"

MOI?: s. Forma graciosa de decir/preguntar "¿Yo?". (Fra.) Ej. "Take your shirt? Moi? Of course not!"

MOMENT OF TRUTH /THE/: exp. El momento en que hay que actuar o el momento más crítico. Ej. "It's the moment of truth; are you going to marry her or not?"

MONEY: 1) adj. Excelente, fantástico. Ej. "Yo, it's money you got that scholarship for college." VER awesome. 2) s. Alguien con quien se puede contar en una situación difícil o arriesgada. Ej. "He's money in the last minute of the game." VER TAMBIEN mad money; hush money; funny money; put one's money where one's mouth is; put money in the pot; throw money out the window; time is money.

MONEY GRUBBING: s. Persona reacia a gastar dinero, esp. una que trata de dar cuenta de cada peso. Ej. "He's so money grubbing he steals condiments from restaurants so he doesn't have to

MONiCKEr

buy them."

MONICKER: s. El nombre o apodo de alguien. Ej. "I know his name is Theodore, but doesn't he have a monicker?"

MONKEY BUSINESS: s. 1) Comportamiento poco serio o travieso. Ej. "All right kiddo, no monkey business while we're gone." 2) Comportamientos o actos engañosos. Ej. "I've got a feeling that there's some monkey business going on in accounting."

MONKEY ON ONE'S BACK: exp. Un problema muy grave y serio, esp. un problema personal, por ejemplo, una adicción que no se puede dejar. Ej. "Since he moved to New Orleans, drinking has become a real monkey on his back."

MONKEY SUIT: s. Un traje. Ej. "I hate having to wear this monkey suit to work every day."

MONTEZUMA'S REVENGE: s. Diarrea fulminante. Ej. "I needed three rolls of t.p. the last time I got Montezuma's revenge."

MONTH: VER *time of the month /that/*.

MOOCH: 1) (sin. freeload, sponge) v. Tener la costumbre de pedirles cosas a los amigos (ej. cigarrillos, bebidas, comida, etc.). Ej. "Why don't you try buying some of your own, instead of always mooching." 2) (sin. freeloader)s. Persona que hace esto. Ej. "Jerry's such a mooch, he asks for things even if he has his own."

MOOLA: s. Dinero. Ej. "Who's got the moola for the beer?" Ver *dough*.

MOON: v. Mostrar el trasero en público como broma o en señal de rebeldía. Ej. "The team mooned the pedestrians from the bus."

MOONLIGHT: v. Tener dos trabajos, o tener un segundo trabajo para aumentar los ingresos de uno. Ej. "She was moonlighting at the diner after finishing her shift at the mill."

MORE TO SOMETHING/SOMEONE THAN MEETS THE EYE: exp. Que tiene una característica no obvia a primera vista. Ej. "She seems meek, but there's a lot more to her than meets the eye. For instance, she's a black belt in karate."

MOST /THE/: adj. De la mejor calidad, superior al resto. Ej. "My

MUD iN YOUR EYe

boyfriend is the most."

MOTHER: s. 1) Algo grande o enorme. Ej. "He gave you one mother of a project for the weekend." 2) Persona mala, grosera o repugnante. Ej. "I wish that mother would get lost, he's spoiling all our fun."

MOTHER'S MILK: s. Alcohol, esp. se dice refiriéndose a una persona que toma mucho o que disfruta mucho el alcohol. Ej. "Does Joe drink beer? Are you kidding, it's mother's milk to him!"

MOTHERFUCKER: [Vul.] s. 1) Insulto muy pero muy feo que no se debe usar nunca entre amigos y, sin embargo, los amigos lo usan entre ellos. ¿Te das cuenta? Ej. "I could kill that motherfucker for messing with my girl!" Or "Yo motherfucker, how you been doing?" 2) Cosa, esp. algo que causa problemas. Ej. "I can't get this motherfucker to work!"

MOTOR MOUTH: s. Persona que habla mucho y sin parar hasta el punto en que los demás dejan de escucharla y/o pierden interés en lo que está diciendo. Ej. "Would someone please tell that motor mouth to shut up!"

MOUSE: VER Mickey Mouse; quiet as a mouse.

MOUTH: VER live from hand to mouth; look a gift horse in the mouth motor mouth; put one's foot in one's mouth; put one's money where one's mouth is; run off at the mouth; shoot one's mouth off; bad mouth; big mouth; born with a silver spoon in one's mouth; butter would not melt in one's mouth.

MOUTH OFF: exp-v. Hablar en forma grosera, irrespetuosa e imprudente. Ej. "He got smacked for mouthing off to the teacher."

MOVE IT: exp-v. & int. Apurarse, hacer algo rápido, esp. para ir a algún lugar. Ej. "If you don't move it we're gonna be late."

MOXIE: s. Valentía, iniciativa, empuje. Ej. "You have to like a kid that's got moxie, even if he is a bit presumptuous."

MUD: VER stick-in-the-mud.

MUD IN YOUR EYE /HERE'S/: exp. Saludo, un brindis gracioso. Ej. "To my son, who finally got a job. Here's mud in your eye John!"

MUG

MUG: s. La cara, el rostro. Ej. "Don't take this personally, but you really have an ugly mug."

MUG FOR THE CAMERA: exp-v. Posar, esp. hacer el ridículo para una fotografía. Ej. "My child just loves to mug for the camera."

MUG SHOT: s. Fotografía del rostro de una persona, generalmente tomada por la policía. Ej. "The guy is so vain, he combed his hair for the mug shot."

MUNCHIES: s. pl. 1) Bocadillo, tentempié (ej. papas fritas, palomitas de maíz, etc.). Ej. "Bring some munchies to the game." 2) *the munchies*: Antojo irresistible, gen. ganas de comer algo. Ej. "I've got the munchies. Let's get some ice cream."

MURDER: 1) s. Alguien o algo muy exigente, difícil, o que requiere de mucho esfuerzo. Ej. "It's been murder getting everything ready for the wedding." 2) v. Derrotar en forma terminante o despiadada. Ej. "The team got murdered last Sunday." VER smear. VER TAMBIEN *get away with murder; scream bloody murder.*

MUSCLE: VER *muscle man.*

MUSCLE HEAD: s. Hombre que se dedica demasiado a desarrollar su cuerpo, sin cultivar su mente. Ej. "Listen muscle head, try spending a little more time developing your brain instead of your biceps!"

MUSCLE MAN: (sin. *muscle*) s. Hombre fornido de aspecto amenazador contratado, a menudo, como guardaespaldas o matón. Ej. "The boss had a couple of muscle men for protection."

MUSCLE HEAD

NECK

MY DEAR: *exp.* Un término cariñoso. Una manera informal de dirigirse a alguien. *Ej.* "Oh hello my dear, what can I do for you?"

NAIL: *v.* 1) Arrestar. *Ej.* "They nailed him breaking into a drug store." 2) Poner al descubierto y divulgar. *Ej.* "The press tried to nail the politician in a lie." 3) Pegar, golpear, a menudo con asombrosa precisión. *Ej.* "I nailed the bus driver right between the eyes with a snow ball."

NAIL SOMEONE TO THE WALL: *exp-v.* Castigar a alguien severamente - o recibir el castigo máximo - esp. sentir satisfacción e incluso un poco de alegría al hacerlo. *Ej.* "The cops are gonna nail him to the wall for stealing a police car."

NAM: *abr.* Vietnam. *Ej.* "He's been a basket case ever since Nam."

NAME OF THE GAME /THE/: *exp.* El componente principal u objetivo de una empresa o actividad. *Ej.* "In business, the name of the game is to make money."

NARK: *s.* 1) Funcionario policial encargado del cumplimiento de la ley antinarcóticos. *Ej.* "The nark went undercover to break up the drug cartel." 2) Persona que delata, esp. a quienes son sus socios o amigos. *Ej.* "If you're a nark, you're a dead man!"

NARROW-MINDED: *exp.* VER la vida desde un punto de vista muy convencional y conservador. *Ej.* "Just because it seems...odd that she dresses in all men's clothes, doesn't mean there's a problem. We shouldn't be narrow-minded about these things."

NAW: (sin. nope) *adv.* No. *Ej.* "Naw, I don't want any."

NEANDERTHAL: *s.* Persona vulgar, muy poco refinada, a quien, en su caudal de genes, algo le faltó. *Ej.* "Who's the Neanderthal she's dating?"

NEAT: (sin. neato) *adj.* Atrayente. *Ej.* "Hey, what a neat place."

NEATO: (sin. neat) *adj.* Atrayente. *Ej.* "This club sure is neato!"

NECK: *v.* Besar y tocar con caricias apasionadas. *Ej.* "The teenagers were found necking in the car."

NECk OF The WOoDS

NECK OF THE WOODS: *exp.* Una comuna, un área o una región, gen. algún lugar muy remoto y lejano. Ej. "They live really far out of town in some neck of the woods."

NEED TO PUT SOME MEAT ON ONE'S BONES: *exp.* Describe a alguien muy flaco o débil que necesita comer más para engordar un poco. Ej. "My grandma always tells my girlfriend that she needs to put some meat on her bones."

NERD: VER *geek*.

NEST EGG: *exp.* Dinero guardado para usar cuando uno jubila. Ej. "I'm saving now so that I'll have a nice sized nest egg when I retire."

NEW AGE: *adj.* Característico del movimiento espiritual de los '80 que buscaba crear conciencia en una amplia gama de ámbitos, desde ecología hasta reencarnación, acentuando religiones indígenas y/o el Budismo, con una clara y marcada tendencia a comprender el verdadero ser interno. Ej. "Don't get New Age on me and tell me I need to get centered and in touch with my former selves."

NEW YORK MINUTE: *exp.* En muy poco tiempo. Ej. "I'll have that paper ready in a New York minute."

NICE: *adj.* Muy atractivo/a, esp. sexy. Ej. "Yo man, you got a nice sister. Is she going steady with anyone?"

NICK: *v.* Robar, hurtar. Ej. "Damn, somebody nicked my wallet!" Ver *swipe*.

NICKEL(S)-AND-DIME(S): *adj.* 1) Que involucra una cantidad pequeña de dinero, esp. en comparación con lo que uno acostumbra a manejar. Ej. "I'm not interested in nickel-and-dime businesses. I'm after the big bucks." 2) Despreciable, inferior, insignificante. Ej. "He's a pain to do business with because he'll nickel-and-dime you to death."

NIGGER: *s.* 1) Un afroamericano, una persona negra. (Desp.) Ej. "Tell that nigger to get out of here." VER *darky*. 2) Cualquier persona de tez oscura. (Desp.) 3) Amigo, compinche, se dice de una persona de tez oscura. (Nota del ed.: Bueno, realmente no entiendo de dónde provino esta última definición pero ahora está muy difundida. Sin embargo, cuidado, es muy probable que no sea bien recibida si se la usa). Ej. "Hey nigger, how's it going?"

NIGHT STICK: s. Un palo usado por la policía para "pacificar" a los civiles. Ej. "He got whacked on the head with a night stick for calling the cop a pig."

NIMBY: abr. Not in my backyard = No en mi patio. Ej. "You're so liberal until the government wants to put a drug rehabilitation center in your neighborhood, and then your Mr. NIMBY."

NINE: VER clound nine be on; sixtynine; stitch in time saves nine /a/.

NINE TO FIVE: exp. Trabajo, gen. uno que no entusiasma pero que paga las cuentas (etim. La mayoría de los trabajos en los EE.UU. comienzan a las 9.00 y terminan a las 5.00 de la tarde). Ej. "Ain't many career opportunities in this nine to five."

NITTY-GRITTY: s. La esencia de, los detalles específicos o esenciales de. Ej. "Let's forget the B.S. and get down to the nitty-gritty."

NIX: 1) adv. No, por ningún motivo. Ej. "He said nix to that idea." 3) v. Vetar, rehusar, o prohibir. Ej. "They've nixed all of my proposals!"

NO BRAINER /A/: exp. Algo sumamente obvio que no requiere el uso del cerebro. Ej. "Take it! It's a no brainer if they're offering you a promotion."

NO CAN DO: exp. Respuesta que denota algo imposible o que no está permitido. Ej. "He's mad because he asked if he could borrow my car and I told him, 'No can do'."

NO DUH: int. Significa: ¡Por supuesto, idiota! Ej. "No duh I'm late. Tell me something else I don't already know."

NO GREAT SHAKES: exp. Poco impresionante, común. Ej. "It's no great shakes to finally graduate from high school after six years."

NO SHIT: int. 1) Expresión de incredulidad. Ej. "No shit, they really won the championship?" 2) Expresión despectiva ante aquello que es obvio. Ej. "No shit I'm late for work. Tell me something I don't know."

NO SUCH THING AS A FREE LUNCH

NO SUCH THING AS A FREE LUNCH: *exp.* Refrán que significa que nada en este mundo, especialmente dentro de la sociedad estadounidense, es gratis y, en términos más específicos, que todo aquello que parece ser gratis a menudo tiene un costo oculto. *Ej.* "Listen Sam, there is no such thing as a free lunch. If he's inviting you out, there's something he wants from you."

NO SWEAT: *exp.* Realizado fácilmente, sin problema, sin necesidad de transpirar. *Ej.* "It was no sweat fixing the car, it just had a loose cable."

NO WAY, JOSÉ: *exp.* Bajo ninguna circunstancia, definitivamente no está permitido. *Ej.* "No way, José, don't even think about dating my sister."

NOGGIN: *s.* La cabeza de una persona, gen. el cerebro. *Ej.* "He got hit in the noggin with a fast ball."

NOHOW: *adv.* De ninguna manera, bajo ninguna circunstancia. *Ej.* "You ain't getting' one cent off of me nohow."

NOISE: *s.* 1) Una queja. *Ej.* "The workers are making a lot of noise about their working conditions." 2) Conversación sin sentido que uno ignora. *Ej.* "My boss makes a lot of noise, which I just pretend I'm listening to."

NOODLE: *s.* 1) La cabeza de una persona, gen. el cerebro. *Ej.* "Why don't you try using your noodle for once!" 2) Una persona débil, tonta, y/o estúpida. *Ej.* "That noodle couldn't play football. He's as skinny as a rail!" VER TAMBIEN *wet noodle*.

NOOKY: *s.* Forma graciosa para referirse al acto sexual. *Ej.* "He was so desperate for some nooky, he was practically drooling on her."

NOPE: (sin. *naw*) *adv.* No. *Ej.* "Nope, I ain't going."

NOSE: VER *brown nose; poke one's nose in; skin off my nose/back/no!; stick one's nose in; turn one's nose up at others*.

NOSY: *adj.* Describe a una persona que se entromete en los asuntos de otros. *Ej.* "My grandma is so nosy she'll tell you to be quiet so she can listen to other people's conversations."

NOT: *adv.* Forma sarcástica para decir "de ninguna manera", "imposible", o "jamás". *Ej.* "Sure you could be a beauty queen - not!"

NOT ALL THERE: (sin. not playing with a full deck, screw loose /a/) *exp.* Un poco loco o senil, no completamente sano mentalmente. *Ej.* "I'm afraid that age has gotten the better of my grandfather and he's not all there anymore."

NOT EVEN: *exp.* Se dice al no importarle o no interesarle alguien o algo. *Ej.* "Not even man, just mind your own business."

NOT IN A LAUGHING MOOD: *exp.* No estar de humor para chistes o bromas o asuntos poco serios. *Ej.* "Stop joking around! I'm giving birth damn it, I'm not in a laughing mood."

NOT TOO SHABBY: *exp.* Forma sarcástica y graciosa para decir "muy bien", "bien hecho" o "excelente". *Ej.* "Making a hundred grand at your age is not too shabby, Paul."

NOT TOO SWIFT: *exp.* Forma graciosa para referirse a una persona que no es muy inteligente o que hace algo poco astuto. *Ej.* "That wasn't too swift to forget your wife's birthday." Or "It wasn't too swift of him to put his finger in the electric socket."

NOTHING BUT THE SHIRT ON ONE'S BACK: *exp.* Quedar sin nada. *Ej.* "The poor man, he's got nothing but the shirt on his back."

NOTHING TO SET THE WORLD ON FIRE: *exp.* Una respuesta a "¿qué tal es algo (ej. un libro, una película, una persona)?" que en la opinión de uno es regular, ni bueno ni malo. *Ej.* "There was some good acting, but in general the play was nothing to set the world on fire."

NOTHING TO SNEEZE AT: *exp.* Algo que debe valorizarse, tomarse en serio o tratarse con respeto. *Ej.* "Being class President is nothing to sneeze at."

NOTHING TO WRITE HOME ABOUT: *exp.* Una opinión indiferente sobre algo. *Ej.* "How was the movie? Oh, nothing to write home about."

NOWHERE: *adj.* Extremadamente

NUKe

aburrido, inútil o menos que inferior. Ej. "You are so nowhere since you got that dumb job."

NUKE: 1) s. Un artefacto nuclear o un arma. Ej. "It's time to get rid of all the nukes." 2) v. Atacar con armas nucleares. Ej. "Mess with the US and we'll nuke you!" 3) v. Calentar en el horno microondas. Ej. "This coffee is cold, would you nuke it for me?"

NUMBER: s. 1) Discurso, argumento, o acción que se repite con frecuencia y a menudo es engañoso, destinado a lograr un objetivo deseado. Ej. "My kids always give me this number about how they should have Nintendo because all the other kids have it." 2) Una mujer sensual. Ej. "Have a look at the number Paul's dating." VER TAMBIEN a-number one (1); do a number on; hot number; look out for number one (1); someone's number to be up;

NUMBER CRUNCHER: s. Una computadora o persona capaz de realizar cálculos largos y complejos que dejarían aturdido a cualquiera. Ej. "Ask my sister about math, she's the number cruncher in the family."

NUMBER ONE (1): 1) exp. Forma diplomática de decir que uno tiene que orinar. Ej. "I'll admit that it's a little odd how he approaches strangers on the street and tells them he has to go number one." 2) s. Uno mismo, esp. los intereses propios y gen. egoístas. Ej. "You're always looking out for number one and someday it will catch up with you."

NUMBER TWO: exp. Forma diplomática de decir que uno tiene que defecar. Ej. "Mommy, I did number two in my pants."

NUT CASE: (sin. nut) s. Una persona demente o excéntrica. Ej. "He's become a nut case since he started sniffing glue."

NUT: s. 1) (sin. nut case) Una persona demente o excéntrica. Ej. "Don't tease the nut, he might bite you." 2) Un entusiasta, un hincha o fanático. Ej. "My daughter's a nut about basketball." 3) La cabeza de una persona, gen. el cerebro. Ej. "God gave you a nut, try using it!" 4) La cantidad mínima de dinero que uno necesita para pagar sus gastos semanales

OFF SOMEONE'S CASE

o mensuales. Ej. "I need a base salary that will cover my nut, and then we can talk about working on commission." VER TAMBIEN *off one's nut*.

NUT HOUSE: s. Asilo para dementes (manicomio) o en lenguaje PC, un "establecimiento de salud mental". Ej. "They should send him to a nut house before he hurts someone."

NUTS: 1) *adj.* Loco, demente. Ej. "You must be nuts to play with fire." VER *bats*. 2) *s.pl.* [Vul.] Los testículos. Ej. "She kicked him in the nuts and ran away."

NUTTY: *adj.* 1) Loco, demente. Ej. "She's getting nutty in her old age." Ver *bats*. 2) Tonto o idiota. Ej. "What nutty ideas she has!"

NYMPHO: *abr.* Nymphomaniac = Ninfomaníaca. Ej. "That chick is a nympho. She'll do the horizontal mambo all day!"

O

.T.T.: VER *over the top*.

OBIT: *abr.* Obituary = Obituario. Ej. "What kind of a nut case reads the obits everyday?"

OD: 1) s. Dosis excesiva de una droga, una substancia o cosa. Ej. "He died of an OD." 2) *v.* Ingerir una dosis excesiva. Ej. "When I diet, I have to fight the urge to OD on junk food."

ODD MAN/WOMAN OUT: (sin. *third wheel*) *exp.* Ser la tercera persona con una pareja o estar sin pareja cuando todos los demás están acompañados. Ej. "I need a date, I hate being the odd man out."

OFF: 1) *adj.* Bordeando la demencia, o simplemente muy, muy excéntrico. Ej. "I wouldn't say he's nuts, I'd say he's a little off." 2) *v.* Matar, asesinar. Ej. "They offed him with a .38 special." VER *waste*.

OFF ONE'S GOURD: VER *out of one's gourd*.

OFF ONE'S NUT: (sin. *off one's rocker*) *exp.* Loco, demente. Ej. "She must be off her nut to date a convicted murder."

OFF ONE'S ROCKER: VER *off one's nut*.

OFF SOMEONE'S BACK: VER *off someone's case*.

OFF SOMEONE'S CASE: (sin. *off someone's tail/back*) *exp.* Dejar de

OFF tHE CuFF

presionar o criticar a alguien, dejar de molestar a alguien. *Ej.* "I finally got him off my back by giving him a C-note." Or "I wish she'd get off Tim's back and just leave him be."

OFF THE CUFF: *exp.* Hacer algo de manera improvisada, esp. cuando hay poco tiempo para prepararlo. *Ej.* "There's no time to prepare for the lecture, you'll just have to do it off the cuff."

OFF THE WAGON /BE/: *exp-vi.* Luego de un período de abstinencia, volver a tomar bebidas alcohólicas. *Ej.* "She's off the wagon again and causing trouble at home."

OFF THE WALL: *exp.* 1) Excesivamente excéntrico o poco convencional. *Ej.* "Maybe he is a bit off the wall to wear his wife's clothes, but he only does it at home." 2) Ridículo o extremadamente poco probable. *Ej.* "What an off the wall accusation to say I poisoned my own dog."

OJ: *abr.* Orange juice = Jugo de naranja. *Ej.* "I'd like a glass of OJ, please."

OKEY - DOKEY: *int.* Modo humorístico de decir okay. *Ej.* "When he asked me if I wanted to go to the movies, I said 'okey-dokey'."

OLD LADY: *s.* 1) Madre. *Ej.* "I love my old lady." 2) Esposa. *Ej.* "I'm taking the old lady out to dinner."

BE OFF THE WaGON

ON THE EDGE

3) Novia. *Ej.* "Yeah, I'm pretty lucky my old lady is so cool."

OLD MAN: s. 1) Padre. *Ej.* "The old man is on my case again to get a job." 2) Esposo. *Ej.* "My old man loves me dearly." 3) Novio. *Ej.* "I love my old man, but I don't know if he's the marrying kind."

ON A ROLL: *exp.* En medio de la buena suerte o de hechos fortuitos. *Ej.* "He's on a roll playing craps."

ON ONE'S TOES /BE/: (sin. on the lookout /be/) *exp-vi.* Estar listo para actuar. Estar atento a que suceda algo. *Ej.* "Be on your toes. We've got trouble coming."

ON SOMEONE'S CASE: (sin. on someone's tail/back/ass) *exp.* Presionando, criticando o molestando a alguien, esp. recordándole constantemente a alguien que debe hacer algo. *Ej.* "I can't go fishing this weekend. My wife's been on my case to paint the house all summer." Or "The boss is on my case to reduce costs."

ON SOMEONE'S DIME: *exp.* El uso del tiempo o dinero de otro, cuando uno debe gastar su propio tiempo o dinero. *Ej.* "If you want my help doing the translation, no problem, but don't expect me to call you. It should be on your dime, not mine."

ON SOMEONE'S TAIL/BACK/ASS: VER on someone's case.

ON THE BALL: *exp.* Alerta, despierto, muy competente. *Ej.* "Listen, Fred's on the ball, you should heed his advice."

ON THE BLINK: (sin. on the fritz) *exp.* Algo que no está funcionando bien o está a punto de dejar de funcionar del todo, gen. referente a objetos mecánicos. *Ej.* "The fridge is on the blink again, it's time we got a new one."

ON THE DOUBLE: (sin. chop-chop) *exp.* Hacer algo en forma muy rápida y/o inmediata. *Ej.* "When I tell you to do something, you'd better do it on the double."

ON THE EDGE: *exp.* 1) En un estado de excitación, esp. estar a punto de un colapso nervioso. *Ej.* "I'm worried about all the stress on Sam. He seems on the edge." 2) En una posición precaria, esp. peligrosa o arriesgada. *Ej.* "That

ON THE FRITZ

dude lives his life on the edge. He's always bungee jumping or parachuting or doing other crazy stunts."

ON THE FRITZ: VER *on the blink.*

ON THE LAM: *exp.* A escondidas de la policía. *Ej.* "They've been on the lam for over a year."

ON THE LOOKOUT /BE/: VER *on one's toes /be/.*

ON THE MAKE: *exp.* Desesperadamente resuelto a seducir. *Ej.* "Phil gets rather pathetic when he's on the make."

ON THE RAG: [Vul.] *exp.* Estar menstruando, ciclo menstrual de la mujer. *Ej.* "Jane can get real bitchy when she's on the rag."

ON THE ROCKS: *exp.* 1) En una situación o condición precaria, esp. cuando hay posibilidades de un fracaso o tropiezo. *Ej.* "Unfortunately, Mary and I have been on the rocks for the past month." 2) Servido con cubos de hielo, gen. si se trata de alcohol fuerte. *Ej.* "I'll have a whiskey on the rocks."

ON THE SAME PAGE: *exp.* Totalmente de acuerdo y en armonía con alguien. *Ej.* "Are we on the same page on this deal?"

ON THE SAME WAVELENGTH: *exp.* Tener un entendimiento profundo con otra persona. *Ej.* "Ever since we both started doing yoga, we've been on the same wavelength."

ON THE TAKE: *exp.* Aceptando coimas o ingresos ilegales. *Ej.* "Are all public officials on the take?"

ON THE TIP OF ONE'S TONGUE: *exp.* Saber algo, gen. un nombre o palabra, pero ser incapaz de recordarlo en un momento dado. *Ej.* "I know his name, it's...darn, it's on the tip of my tongue, but I can't remember it."

ON THE WAGON /BE/: *exp-vi.* Abstenerse de hábitos insalubres, gen. alcohol. *Ej.* "Sarah's been on the wagon ever since she got wasted and puked all over her dog."

ON THE WARPATH: *exp.* Muy enojado, estar de humor para discutir, pelear, o, metafóricamente, listo para cortarle la cabeza a alguien. *Ej.* "Dad's on the warpath. Someone broke his favorite beer glass."

ON THE WAY OUT: *exp.* Decayendo o empeorando. *Ej.* "Don't mind him.

ONE (1)-NIGHT STAND

He's just frustrated because he's on the way out of the company."

ON THE WRONG TRACK /BE/: *exp-vi.* Avanzando en dirección equivocada, ya sea físicamente o en el desarrollo de ideas. *Ej.* "No, you're on the wrong track. You need to think of another solution."

ONCE AND FOR ALL: *exp.* Hacer algo inmediatamente y de principio a fin. *Ej.* "Enough stopping and starting, let's just get this over with once and for all."

ONCE OVER: (sin. touch up) *s.* Superficialmente mejorar el aspecto de algo o alguien. *Ej.* "You'll get a higher price for the car if you give it a once over before you try to sell it."

ONE (1) GOOD TURN DESERVES ANOTHER: *exp.* La buena obra se paga con otra buena obra. *Ej.* "You helped me, so I'll help you. Hey, one good turn deserves another."

ONE WHO LAUGHS LAST, LAUGHS LONGEST: VER get the last laugh.

ONE WHO SNOOZES, LOSES: (sin. if you snooze, you lose) *exp.* El que no está atento pierde. *Ej.* "He who snoozes, loses pal. You left your seat."

ONE'S (OWN) THING: *exp.* Refiriéndose a algo que es del gusto de uno, gen. en cuanto a estilo de vida o actividad favorita. *Ej.* "Hey, if it's his thing to play on the computer all day, leave him to it." Or "It's her own thing to still suck her thumb."

ONE'S EYES ARE BIGGER THAN ONE'S STOMACH: *exp.* Al pedir o servirse más comida de lo que se es capaz de consumir. *Ej.* "Look at all the food that's left over. Once again your eyes were bigger than your stomach."

ONE'S MAIN SQUEEZE: *exp.* La pareja de uno, esp. permanente. *Ej.* "Don't mess with her, she's Joey's main squeeze."

ONE'S TAIL OFF: *exp.* Hacer algo con el máximo nivel de esfuerzo posible. *Ej.* "He worked his tail off to finish on time."

ONE (1)-NIGHT STAND: *exp.* Relación sexual de una o pocas noches. *Ej.* "It's not a serious relationship, they just had a one-night stand."

OOMPH

OOMPH: s. Entusiasmo fogoso, gran energía o vigor. *Ej.* "To finish this project we'll need a lot of oomph."

OOPS: (sin. shucks!) *int.* Expresión de arrepentimiento, gen. después de un pequeño accidente o algún comentario o gesto inapropiado. *Ej.* "Oops, I didn't mean to spoil the surprise!"

OPEN (SOMETHING) UP: *exp-v.* 1) Hablar sin tapujos, gen. acerca de un asunto personal o de un problema. *Ej.* "It's great that she feels comfortable enough to open up with you." 2) (sin. pedal to the metal) Acelerar, tratar de alcanzar máxima velocidad. Se usa en relación con vehículos motorizados. *Ej.* "Let's open this baby up and see what she'll do!"

OPEN SEASON: *exp.* Momento para cazar y matar, y por lo tanto, un tiempo peligroso. (etim. La estación del año impuesta por el gobierno para cazar.) *Ej.* "With the turf war going on, it's open season out on the streets."

ORDINARY JOE: *exp.* Un hombre común o ciudadano cualquiera. *Ej.* "Hey pal, I don't want any trouble. I'm just an ordinary Joe trying to make an honest buck."

OTHER SIDE OF THE COIN: *exp.* El otro lado de un argumento o situación. *Ej.* "I understand your argument, but the other side of the coin is that nuclear weapons bring peace."

OUNCE OF PREVENTION IS WORTH A POUND OF CURE /AN/: VER *a stitch in time saves nine.*

OUT: *v.* Divulgar o revelar al público la homosexualidad de alguien, gen. contra la voluntad de esa persona. *Ej.* "Much to his chagrin, the gay rights group outed the actor."

OUT LIKE A LIGHT: *exp.* Dormirse de inmediato quedarse dormido rápidamente. *Ej.* "The dear boy was so tired he went out like a light."

OUT OF DODGE: *exp.* Fuera del pueblo o ciudad. Gen. se dice ordenando la salida de alguien de alguna parte. (etim. Dodge City, un antiguo pueblo del oeste famoso por sus pistoleros.) *Ej.* "You best get out of Dodge, or there are going to be problems."

OUT OF IT: *exp.* 1) Ajeno a lo que

OUT OF WHACK

está pasando a nuestro alrededor, esp. porque uno está cansado. Ej. "I'm feeling really out of it today." 2) No estar al día con la(s) última(s) tendencia(s) o moda. Ej. "My dad is so out of it he doesn't even know how to use a computer!"

OUT OF ONE'S GOURD: (sin. off one's gourd) *exp.* Emocionalmente volátil, esp. enojado o irracional. Ej. "He went out of his gourd when they told him his teenage daughter was pregnant."

OUT OF ONE'S SKULL: *exp-v.* Absolutamente loco, demente o irracional. Persona que está fuera de sus cabales. Ej. "You must be out of your skull to single-handedly care for thirty six-year-olds."

OUT OF PLACE: *exp.* Un lugar o momento inapropiado para algo o alguien. Ej. "I felt out of place surrounded by transvestites." Or "She was way out of place to give the finger to the priest."

OUT OF SIGHT: *exp.* Increíble, fantástico. Ej. "You should go see the play, it's outta sight!"

OUT OF SOMEONE'S FACE: *exp.* Haber dejado de presionar o molestar a alguien. Ej. "You'd better get out of my face or I'm gonna smack you!"

OUT OF THE BLUE: *exp.* Inesperado. Ej. "We were on a coffee break when the CEO showed up out of the blue."

OUT OF THE CLOSET: *exp-vi.* Públicamente reconocer la condición homosexual de uno. Ej. "It's about time George Michael came out of the closet."

OUT OF WHACK: *exp.* Funcionando mal, desequilibrado o actuando en forma irregular. Ej. "Don't mind

OUT OF THE CLOSET

OUT ON ONE'S ASS

Theo, he's been out of whack ever since his pet turtle died. He really loved it." Or "Don't put your money in that machine, it's out of whack."

OUT ON ONE'S ASS: [Vul.] *exp.* Rechazado, despedido. Ej. "The boss put him out on his ass for loafing on the job." Or "The landlord threw him out on his ass for having ten cats in his house."

OUT ON ONE'S BUTT: *exp.* La forma más educada de *out on one's ass*.

OUT TO LUNCH: *adj.* Se dice de alguien mentalmente inestable o que es incapaz de razonar en forma lógica. Ej. "The guy is out to lunch. He walks around the city in his bathrobe."

OUTDO ONESELF: *exp-vi.* Hacer un gran esfuerzo por otros. Ej. "You outdid yourself with the preparations for the party!"

OUTIE: *s.* Ombligo que sobresale. Ej. "The good thing about an outie is that lint doesn't get caught in it."

OUTTA: *abr.* Out of = No tener algo o echar a alguien. Ej. "Sorry pal, we're outta tomatoes today." Or "You're outta here!"

OVER MY DEAD BODY: *exp.* Expresión que indica que bajo ninguna circunstancia se permitirá algo. Ej. "Over my dead body you'll get a tattoo!"

OVER THE BARREL: *exp.* Encontrarse en una situación muy difícil de la cual cuesta salir. Ej. "With his fingerprints on the gun, I'd say that the prosecution has us over the barrel."

OVER THE HILL: *exp.* Viejo, que ya no sirve. Ej. "In professional sports, most athletes are over the hill at 30."

OVER THE TOP: *exp.* Exceso de personalidad y/o estilo, algo totalmente exagerado. Ej. "George, it is most definitely over the top wearing a fur coat, gold chains and lavender colored cowboy boots."

P

.D.Q.: *abr.* Pretty Damn Quick. = Bastante rápido. Ej. "You'd better start cleaning up this mess P.D.Q."

P.J.'s: *abr.* Pajama = Pijama. Ej. "Put your P.J.'s on and then I'll read you a bed-time story."

P.O'D.: *abr.* Pissed off = Muy molesto. *Ej.* "I was P.O'd. with my brother for telling mom I had my boyfriend over."

PACK: *v.* Transportar una pistola u otra arma consigo para estar listo para usarla. *Ej.* "Watch your back with that guy, I think he's packing heat." VER TAMBIEN *jam packed; rat pack; send someone packing.*

PACK IT IN: *exp-v.* Parar una actividad o dejar un lugar. *Ej.* "Come on guys, it's twelve o'clock, time to pack it in."

PAD: (sin. crib) *s.* El departamento, dormitorio, habitaciones de uno. *Ej.* "I'm having a party at my new pad."

PAD THE BILL: *exp-v.* Agregar gastos que no corresponden a la cuenta de un cliente. *Ej.* "I don't eat at that restaurant after I caught them padding the bill with a charge for a $25 bottle of wine."

PADDLE: VER *up a creek without a paddle /be/; up shit creek without a paddle /be/.*

PAGE: VER *on the same page.*

PAIN IN THE ASS: (Vul) *exp.* Persona o situación desagradable o molestosa. *Ej.* "It's been a pain in the ass getting my car fixed."

PAIN IN THE BUTT: (sin. pain in the neck) *exp.* Persona o situación desagradable o molestosa. La forma más educada de *pain in the ass*. *Ej.* "Restoring our old house has been a pain in the butt."

PAIN IN THE NECK: VER *pain in the butt.*

PAINT THE TOWN RED: *exp-v.* Pasarlo bien en plan de fiesta prolongada. *Ej.* "You kids have a good time tonight. Go paint the town red."

PAIR: (sin. set) *s.* Los senos de una mujer, gen. bonitos y voluminosos. *Ej.* "He only dates women with a big pair."

PAL: (sin. sport) *s.* Amigo, buen amigo. *Ej.* "Tim and I are good pals. We hang together a lot."

PALEFACE: *s.* Persona de raza blanca. (Desp.) *Ej.* "He started the fight by calling me paleface."

PAN: *v.* Criticar duramente, esp. algo artístico. *Ej.* "The critics panned the new show."

PAN OUT: *v.* Tener éxito, resultar

PANSY

tal como uno quería. *Ej.* "I hope this job interview pans out."

PANSY: s. 1) Hombre que se considera afeminado. *Ej.* "You look like a pansy in those tight shorts." 2) Hombre homosexual. (Desp.) *Ej.* "It's a pansy parade."

PANTS: VER *ants in one's pants; catch someone with one's pants down; get into someone's pants; hot pants; shit one's pants.*

PAPER PUSHER: exp. Una persona que sólo trabaja con papeles sin gran importancia y cuyo trabajo es muy aburrido. Trabajo de escritorio. *Ej.* "Henry is just a paper pusher, he doesn't have any pull in the office."

PARADE: VER *rain on the/ someone's parade.*

PARTNER IN CRIME: s. Mejor amigo o amigo cercano, gen. con quien uno se mete en enredos o sencillamente lo pasa muy bien. *Ej.* "Phil is my partner in crime. We always have a real good time together."

PARTY ANIMAL: s. Persona a quien le encantan las fiestas y generalmente es la primera en llegar y la última en irse. *Ej.* "Steve is some party animal. Did you see him doing the mambo on the table?"

PARTY CRASHER: s. Persona que llega a una fiesta sin ser invitado. *Ej.* "Those guys weren't invited, they're party crashers."

PARTY GIRL: s. Una mujer que ha tenido muchas experiencias, gen. con actividades de tipo festivas. *Ej.* "Just because she's a party girl doesn't mean she's not a virgin."

PARTY-POOPER: s. Persona que se niega a participar en las actividades, esp. entretenidas, de un grupo. *Ej.* "Don't be a party-pooper, come to the disco with us."

PASS THE BUCK: exp-v. Pasarle la responsabilidad o una tarea a otro, esp. algo desagradable. *Ej.* "Don't try and pass the buck, just deal with the problem."

PATCH THINGS UP: exp-v. Corregir, hacer las paces. *Ej.* "The kids are fighting again. I don't know how to patch things up between them."

PATIENCE OF A SAINT: exp. Tener mucha paciencia. *Ej.* "She must have the patience of a saint to handle those three hyperactive kids."

PEACH FUZZ

PATSY: s. 1) Persona a quien embaucan o se aprovechan de ella fácilmente. Ej. "The world is full of patsies, who'll fall for any scam that promises to make them rich." 2) Un chivo expiatorio, una persona que asume la culpa por los demás. Ej. "We need to find a patsy so the boss doesn't go to jail."

PAVEMENT: VER *pound the pavement*.

PAY BACK TIME: *exp.* Venganza. Ej. "Come pay back time, the gang will be looking to spill someone's blood."

PAY LIP SERVICE: *exp-vi.* 1) Hacer promesas sin intención de cumplirlas. Ej. "Sometimes it's better to pay lip service to one's parents than just say, 'No'." 2) Hacer cumplidos no sinceros. Ej. "If you want to get in good with the boss, pay lip service to his toy car collection. He's a bit insecure about it."

PAY (SOMEONE) OFF: *exp-vi.* Sobornar (a alguien). Ej. "I got paid off to not interfere in their affairs." Or "Pay me off or I'll rat you out."

PAY THE PRICE: *exp-vi.* Asumir las consecuencias de las acciones de uno. Ej. "You stayed out past your curfew, now you have to pay the price."

PC: *abr.* Politically correct = Políticamente correcto. Un movimiento y filosofía que comenzó en la década de los ochenta, destinado a dar un nuevo nombre a términos que eran considerados ofensivos o despectivos, convirtiéndolos en términos más positivos y engrandecedores (por ej. indio americano autóctono, retardado o mentalmente discapacitado, etc.). Asimismo, a fin de cambiar el comportamiento y terminar con las tendencias sexistas o racistas y ser más sensibles a las necesidades e inseguridades de otros. Por ejemplo: Casa de Orates (Manicomio) a Establecimiento de Salud Mental, etc. Ej. "It's not PC to go to a striptease bar."

PEA SOUP: (sin. *soup*) s. Neblina espesa. Ej. "I wouldn't drive, it's pea soup out there."

PEACH FUZZ: s. Vello facial suave que generalmente aparece en la cara de los adolescentes. Ej. "You

PEANUT GALLERY

call that peach fuzz a mustache?"

PEANUT GALLERY: s. 1) Los asientos - de un cine/teatro - más baratos, generalmente los de más arriba donde casi no se puede respirar y los actores se ven en miniatura. ¡Disfruta el espectáculo! Ej. "The show was sold out except for a few seats in the peanut gallery." 2) Persona o grupo de personas tonta(s), estúpida(s). Ej. "That's enough from the peanut gallery. You all keep quiet."

PEANUTS: s.pl. 1) (sin. chicken feed) Una cantidad insignificante de dinero, en relación con el ingreso que uno gana. Ej. "I paid peanuts for the house. It only cost a hundred grand." 2) adj. Insignificante, de poca o ninguna importancia. Ej. "Your opinion is worth peanuts here."

PEARLY WHITES: s. Los dientes, esp. limpios y muy blancos. Ej. "Let's see those pearly whites!"

PECK: s. Beso. Ej. "We didn't make out, I just gave him a peck on the lips."

PECKER: s. El pene. Ej. "Look at the size of his pecker!" VER jimmy.

PEDAL TO THE METAL/PUT THE/: exp. Acelerar, aumentar velocidad. Ej. "We'll never get there on time unless you put the pedal to the medal and your foot on the floor!"

PEE: (sin. piss, whiz*) 1) s. Orina. Ej. "Damn, I got pee on my pants!" 2) v. Orinar. Ej. "She was laughing so hard she peed in her pants."

PEEK: VER sneak a peek.

PEEL OUT: v. Marcharse rápidamente en un vehículo motorizado, esp. acelerar rápidamente. Ej. "Let's peel out and lay some rubber."

PEEPERS: s.pl. Ojos. Ej. "Keep your peepers open and maybe you'll see a dolphin."

PEEPING TOM: s. Una persona que mira a escondidas, esp. a gente y esp. a mujeres desnudas. Ej. "They found a peeping Tom looking in the girls locker room."

PEN: s. Prisión, cárcel. Ej. "He's in the pen doing time for auto theft." VER clink /the/.

PENCIL PUSHER: (sin. desk jockey) s. Oficinista, esp. aquel que pasa el día entero en su escrito-

PET pEEVe

PEEpiNG toM

rio. *Ej.* "They think I'm just a pencil pusher, but I'm more than that!"

PENNY: VER *pretty penny.*

PEOPLE IN HIGH PLACES: *exp-vi.* Contactos con personas importantes, esp. aquellas que le pueden conseguir trabajo a alguien. *Ej.* "If you want to get ahead, it helps to know people in high places."

PEP TALK: s. Discurso a un equipo o grupo de personas cuyo propósito es infundir entusiasmo o mejorar el estado de ánimo. *Ej.* "The boss always gives us a pep talk right before crunch time."

PEPPER-UPPER: (sin. picker-upper) s. Algo que despierta o estimula, gen. un producto con cafeína. *Ej.* "I need a pepper-upper to get me through the afternoon."

PERIOD: (sin. that time of the month, on the rag*) s. Ciclo menstrual de la mujer. *Ej.* "She doesn't seem much bothered by her period."

PET: s. El favorito/la favorita, la persona preferida, esp. una a quien se le mima. *Ej.* "You know he just loves being the teacher's pet."

PET PEEVE: s. Molestia o disgusto en particular, esp. con respecto a una persona contra la cual a menudo se reclama. *Ej.* "My pet peeve is people saying, 'I told you so.'" or "Once he starts talking about his pet peeve — traffic jams — he doesn't shut up."

PHAt

PHAT: *adj.* Tremendo, maravilloso, espectacular. *Ej.* "Yo, that's a phat ride!"

PHILLY: *abr.* Philadelphia = Filadelfia. *Ej.* "She lives in Philly."

PICK ON SOMEONE: *exp-v.* Molestar, intimidar a alguien. *Ej.* "Leave her alone! Why don't you pick on someone your own size." Or "The kids tend to pick on the weaklings in their class."

PICK UP THE (BROKEN) PIECES: *exp-v.* 1) Asumir la responsabilidad por algo que uno cometió o que otro cometió. *Ej.* "Typical, you make all the trouble and leave me to pick up the broken pieces." 2) Volver a comenzar después de una serie de eventos desastrosos. *Ej.* "When the business went bust, we had to pick up the pieces and start something new."

PICK UP THE TAB: *exp-v.* Pagar la cuenta de todos, gen. en un restaurante. *Ej.* "I'm glad men are no longer expected to always pick up the tab."

PICKER-UPPER: VER *pepper-upper*.

PICK-ME-UP: *s.* Algo que se usa para despertar o darse energía cuando se está cansado. *Ej.* "I need a pick-me-up. Pour me some coffee."

PICK-UP LINE: *exp.* Una frase o cuento que se usa para seducir a alguien o por lo menos despertar su interés por desarrollar una relación romántica. *Ej.* "If he didn't have such hurtin' pick-up lines, he might get a date occasionally."

PICK-UP: 1) *v.* Conocer a alguien, gen. en un lugar público, para pasar una noche de pasión. *Ej.* "I picked-up the hottest chick last night." 2) *v.* Pasar a buscar a alguien. *Ej.* "I can't go, I have to pick-up my daughter at school." 3) *exp.* Equipos escogidos al azar. *Ej.* "I'm going to the park for a pick-up game of basketball."

PICKY: *adj.* Una persona difícil de agradar, esp. muy selectiva en cuanto a comida. *Ej.* "She's so picky, her idea of an ethnic restaurant is a pizza parlor."

PIE IN THE SKY: *exp.* Una ilusión, algo inaccesible. *Ej.* "That's a pie in the sky dream if you think she's coming back to you."

PIECE: *s.* Pistola, revólver. *Ej.* "The

PILL

robber pulled out a piece and shot him." VER TAMBIEN *pick up the (broken) pieces*.

PIECE OF ASS: [Vul.] *exp*. Persona, gen. una mujer, que se considera como un objeto sexual y nada más. *Ej*. "I need to get me a piece of ass tonight."

PIECE OF CAKE: *exp*. Algo fácil de hacer o conseguir. *Ej*. "The robbery was a piece of cake. No cops, no alarms and a cool million in ice."

PIECE OF CHANGE: *exp*. Forma sarcástica para describir algo que vale mucho dinero. *Ej*. "I bet that Ferrari cost you a piece of change."

PIECE OF CRAP: [Vul.] VER *piece of shit*.

PIECE OF SHIT: [Vul.] (sin. piece of crap) *exp*. Sin ningún valor, esp. se dice referente a una persona despreciable. *Ej*. "You know George, you truly are a piece of shit. I wish you'd just take a long walk off a short pier."

PIECE OF THE ACTION: *exp*. 1) Una parte de la ganancia o ingreso. *Ej*. "The cop wants a piece of the action or he's going to bust us." 2) Participación en un negocio financiero. *Ej*. "How much do I have to invest in the deal to get a piece of the action?"

PIER: VER *take a long walk off a short pier*.

PIG: *s*. 1) Un funcionario policial. (Desp.) *Ej*. "The protestors threw stones at the pigs." 2) Una persona racista o sexista. *Ej*. "She ought to slap that pig for what he said to her!" VER TAMBIEN *in a pig's eye; scream like a stuck pig; sweat like a pig*.

PIG HEADED: *s*. Persona sumamente porfiada. *Ej*. "If you weren't so damn pig headed, you might learn something new."

PIG-OUT: *v*. Comer vorazmente y en forma excesiva, gen. más allá de la capacidad normal que uno tiene. *Ej*. "I pigged out at the bar-b-que."

PILL: *s*. 1) Una persona insípida, aburrida o desagradable. (nota del ed.: Piense en una píldora que no desea tomarse; así es esa persona.) *Ej*. "I got stuck talking to this pill at the conference." 2) *the pill*: Anticonceptivo oral. *Ej*. "It's safe, I'm on the pill."

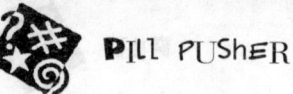

PILL PUSHER

PILL PUSHER: s. Doctor - médico. Ej. "He's nothing more than a pill pusher who drives a fancy car."

PIMP MOBILE: s. Auto grande y ostentoso que parece adecuado para un *pimp* = alcahuete, cafiche. Ej. "You're gonna get hassled by the cops for driving around in that pimpmobile."

PINCH: v. 1) Robar, hurtar, gen. algo de poco valor. Ej. "She pinched a candy bar from the store." Ver swipe. 2) Arrestar. Ej. "The Feds pinched him with the drugs in his pocket."

PINCH OF SALT: (sin. grain of salt) exp. Un grado de escepticismo o sana desconfianza. Ej. "He's a little over optimistic, so take everything he says with a pinch of salt."

PINHEAD: s. Una persona considerada estúpida, o en realidad, una persona estúpida. Ej. "Get that pinhead away from the computer."

PINK SLIP: (sin. walking papers) s. Aviso de despido. Ej. "They sent pink slips to all the strikers."

PINKO: s. Persona que tiene opiniones políticas de izquierda y que, por lo tanto, se le acusa de ser comunista o partidaria del comunismo. Ej. "They're all pinkos at that liberal school!"

PINT: s. Cerveza. VER brew.

PIPE: VER *put that in your pipe and smoke it.*

PIPE DOWN: v. Dejar de hablar o hablar en voz más baja. Ej. "Pipe down in there, I can't hear the Radio."

PIPE DREAM: exp. Sueño imposible o quijotesco. (etim. de la pipa usada para fumar drogas alucinógenas.) Ej. "You, President!? That's a pipe dream if I ever heard one."

PIPE UP: v. Hablar en alta voz o alzar la voz a fin de ser escuchado más claramente. Ej. "I wish he'd pipe up, I can't hear a word he's saying."

PISS: (sin. pee, whiz*) 1) v. Orinar. Ej. "I need to piss." 2) s. Orina, pipí. Ej. "You got piss on your pants!"

PISS AND VINEGAR /FULL OF/: exp. Lleno de energía, vivaz, esp. en un sentido picarón. Ej. "Her kids are a handful. They're always full of piss and vinegar."

PIT STOP

PISS LIKE A RACEHORSE: *exp-v.* Orinar con urgencia y voluminosamente, casi como abrir una represa. *Ej.* "After the long car ride, I had to piss like a racehorse."

PISS ON: [Vul.] *int.* Sin el mínimo de respeto por alguien; total aversión, antipatía. *Ej.* "The bastard's been pulling my chain for weeks, but now he wants a favor from me! Well, I say piss on him!"

PISS OUT OF SOMEONE /THE/: [Vul.] *exp.* Algo extremadamente fastidioso, molesto o miedoso. *Ej.* "It bothers the piss out of me how my girlfriend flirts with everyone." Or "She really knows what to say to take the piss out of someone." Or "You scared the piss out of me!"

PISS (SOMEONE) OFF: [Vul.] *exp-v.* 1) Molestar o irritar a alguien enormemente. *Ej.* "She really pissed me off when she told me she preferred her dog to me." 2) *v.* Hacer enojarse o enojarse uno mismo. *Ej.* "I got pissed off when he insulted my mother." 3) *int.* Decirle a alguien que se largue. *Ej.* "Piss off asshole!"

PISSANT: *s.* Una persona despreciable e insignificante, y a veces también inflexible en detalles menores. *Ej.* "I wish we could get rid of that pissant auditor."

PISSED: [Vul.] *adj.* 1) Muy borracho. *Ej.* "We got pissed Friday night." (Ing.) VER *plastered.* 2) (sin. pissed off) Muy enojado. *Ej.* "I don't want to speak with you, I'm still pissed about you ruining my painting."

PISSER: *s.* 1) Una persona realmente notable y gen. divertida. *Ej.* "My cousin is a real pisser. He has a great sense of humor and is always traveling to exotic places." 2) Una labor difícil y poco grata. *Ej.* "Moving the piano five floors was a pisser."

PISS-POOR: [Vul.] *adj.* Vilmente malo, se dice referente a la calidad o recursos financieros. *Ej.* "That was a piss-poor performance." Or "She's piss-poor after losing all her money in the stock crash."

PIT STOP: *s.* Una parada corta para descansar, ir al baño y/o tomarse un refresco, gen. durante un viaje largo en auto, motocicleta o bus. *Ej.* "Let's make a pit stop. I

PITCH IN

need to stretch my legs and take a leak."

PITCH IN: (sin. kick in) *exp-v.* Compartir los gastos de algo. Ej. "Are you going to pitch in for the boss's gift?"

PITS /THE/: *adj.* Sin gracia, último, algo muy malo. Ej. "Working on Xmas is the pits!"

PIZZA-FACE: *s.* Rostro cubierto por espinillas o acné. Ej. "That pizza-face won't get a date until his skin clears up."

PIZZAZZ: *s.* Estilo, resplandor, extravagancia. Ej. "I wouldn't say she's o.t.t., I'd just say she has a lot of pizzazz."

PLACE: VER *between a rock and a hard place; forget one's place; out of place; people in high places.*

PLAGUE: VER *avoid someone/something like the plague.*

PLAIN CLOTHES: *s.* Oficiales de policía sin uniforme. Ej. "Be careful what you smoke, there's a plain clothes hanging around."

PLANT: *v.* 1) Ocultar, esconder o enterrar, esp. de manera que sea encontrado más tarde como evidencia acusadora. Ej. "The Feds planted evidence on the drug dealer." 2) Dar o colocar un puñetazo o golpear. Ej. "She planted a hard right in the kisser." 3) Besar. Ej. "Plant one on me big boy!" 4) Espía. Ej. "She was the plant the Feds used to break up the pawn shop."

PLASTERED: (sin. hammered, blind drunk, blotto, smashed, three sheets to the wind, pissed*, trashed*, loaded*, shitfaced, tanked) *adj.* Muy borracho. Ej. "The way you look, I'd say you got plastered last night."

PLAY BALL: *exp-v.* Estar listo para actuar, esp. unirse a otros como equipo en una actividad. A menudo se usa la expresión en el sentido de presionar a alguien para que forme parte del equipo. Ej. "If you're not willing to play ball, and go along with the plan, you should quit."

PLAY DIRTY: *exp-v.* Jugar o actuar sin respetar las reglas. Ej. "That guy plays dirty. I wouldn't do business with him."

PLAY DUMB: *exp-v.* Hacer como que no ve o no entiende lo que está ocurriendo. Ej. "When the cops get here, just play dumb."

PLAY ROUGH

PLAY FOOTSIE WITH: *exp-v.* Coquetear, gen. topando pies por debajo de la mesa y secretamente. *Ej.* "12 years old and you're already playing footsie with boys?"

PLAY GAMES: *exp-v.* Expresar un deseo con evasivas, no ser sincero con respecto a las verdaderas intenciones, a tal punto de hacer sentir inseguro de su afecto a otra persona. *Ej.* "I'm sick of playing games with you. Do you or don't you love me?"

PLAY HOOKY: (sin. skip school) *exp-v.* No ir al colegio. *Ej.* "If I catch you playing hooky again, you'll be grounded for a month."

PLAY INTO ONE'S HANDS: *exp-v.* Actuar inconscientemente como al adversario le gustaría que uno actuara. *Ej.* "You're just playing into his hands if you get into a bidding war with him."

PLAY IT BY EAR: *exp-v.* Actuar según el momento sin planificar actividades de antemano. *Ej.* "I'm not sure what I'm going to do. I'm just going to play it by ear."

PLAY IT COOL: *exp-v.* Actuar en forma controlada y calmada, esp. para no mostrar las verdaderas intenciones. *Ej.* "I know you're excited about the offer, but you need to play it cool or they'll pay you less than you deserve."

PLAY IT SAFE: *exp-v.* Optar por actuar en forma segura y no arriesgada. *Ej.* "Ted thinks we should play it safe and not invest in anything until the recession ends."

PLAY ONE'S CARDS CLOSE TO ONE'S CHEST: VER *keep one's cards close to one's chest.*

PLAY ONE'S CARDS RIGHT: *exp-v.* Actuar cuidadosamente y a menudo con tal habilidad que se consigue el resultado deseado, que era difícil de lograr en la mayoría de los casos. *Ej.* "If you play your cards right, you can get the house and the car in the settlement."

PLAY POSSUM: *exp-v.* Fingir estar muerto o dormido. *Ej.* "Give him a kick to see if he's just playing possum."

PLAY ROUGH: *exp-v.* Actuar en forma agresiva o recurrir a la fuerza física; esp. valerse de medios extremos e injustos para asegu-

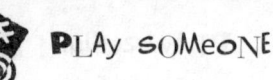

PLAY SOMEONE

rarse la victoria. *Ej.* "If they want to play rough and bring in a ringer, we'll do the same."

PLAY SOMEONE: *exp-v.* Engañar o manipular a alguien. *Ej.* "Stop playing me man, I wasn't born yesterday, so don't expect me to be the lookout in your robbery."

PLAY THE FIELD: *exp-v.* No comprometerse a una sola persona como compañero romántico sino buscar tantas experiencias románticas como sea posible. *Ej.* "One day I'll stop playing the field and settle down."

PLAY THE GAME: *exp-v.* Ajustarse al comportamiento aceptado, actuar de acuerdo con las costumbres o normas establecidas. *Ej.* "If you want to get ahead in the corporation, you need to play the game and not rock the boat."

PLAY UP TO: *exp-v.* Buscar congraciarse con alguien por razones ulteriores, gen. egoístas. A menudo, ello implica recurrir a halagos poco sinceros. *Ej.* "He makes me sick watching him play up to the boss!"

PLAY WITH FIRE: *exp-v.* Participar en una actividad peligrosa, correr riesgos o confiar en la suerte. *Ej.* "You know that if you play with fire, someday you'll get burned."

PLAY WITH ONESELF: [Vul.] *exp-v.* 1) Masturbarse. *Ej.* "Where's Teddy?" "Oh, he's playing with himself in the bathroom." 2) Ser flojo e improductivo, gen. no estar haciendo absolutamente nada. *Ej.* "Stop playing with yourself and come help me move this furniture."

PLAYED: (sin. spent) *adj.* 1) Algo que ha sido usado hasta sus reservas. *Ej.* "The keg's played, someone needs to make a beer run." 2) Un ser sin energía, gen. como consecuencia de agotamiento. *Ej.* "I'm played, there's no way I can go dancing tonight."

PLAYING WITH A FULL DECK /NOT/: *exp.* Totalmente loco o demente. *Ej.* "Stay away from that gal, she's not playing with a full deck." VER *not all there*.

PLUG: 1) *s.* Una mención pública favorable de algo o de alguien con fines comerciales. *Ej.* "I'd appreciate it if you gave the play

POOnTANg

a plug on your TV show." 2) v. Hacer publicidad favorable, gen. de un producto o de un político, mencionándolo en un discurso público o en una emisión radial o televisa. Ej. "He's a genius at plugging products." 3) v. Disparar con una pistola. Ej. "She plugged him as he was coming up the stairs." VER TAMBIEN *pull the plug (on)*.

PLUG AWAY: *exp-v.* Trabajar con perseverancia para terminar algo. Ej. "He's no rocket scientist, but at least he plugs away at his work."

PLUMBING: s. Tracto intestinal. Ej. "Eating beans always gives me trouble with my plumbing."

PLUNGE: VER *take the plunge*.

POINT: VER *get to the point; win bonus points*.

POKE: 1) v. Dar un puñetazo, golpear. Ej. "He poked him right in the kisser." 2) s. Puñetazo, golpe. Ej. "She gave him a poke right between the eyes." 3) [Vul.]) s. Una relación sexual. Ej. "They went for a poke out in the barn."

POKE ONE'S NOSE IN: *exp-v.* Meterse en los asuntos de otros. Ej. "Don't poke your nose in my affairs, or I'll poke you in the nose!"

POLACK: s. Polaco, persona nacida en Polonia o descendiente de polaco. (Desp.) Ej. "Do you want to hear another Polack joke?"

POND: s. Océano Atlántico. Ej. "I've got to fly across the pond tomorrow." (Ing.)

POO: (sin. doo-doo, poop*, shit*, turd*, crap*) s. Excremento. Ej. "Gross, you've got poo on your shoe."

POOCH: s. Un perro. Ej. "That's a nice looking pooch you've got there."

POOH: *diminutive*. Terminación humorística y pueril para un sustantivo al cual se le ha agregado una 'y'. Ej. "Would you like a drinky-pooh?" Or "I need a snacky-pooh."

POOL: v. Juntar algo, gen. dinero, desde varias fuentes. Ej. "If we pool our money, we can buy something better."

POONTANG: [Vul.] (sin. pussy*, fanny*, cunt*, twat*) s. Vagina, pero, aunque sea de muy mal gusto, se usa para referirse a una mujer. ¡El colmo! Ej. "Let's go to the

Poop

disco and get some poontang."

POOP: s. 1) Información confidencial. Ej. "I've got the poop on Steve and Linda's affair." 2) Excremento. VER *poo*.

POOP OUT: exp-v. Agotarse, abandonar lo que uno está haciendo por sentirse fatigado. Ej. "I'm pooped out. I can't walk any further."

POOR THING: int. Expresión de conmiseración por un mal resultado. Ej. "Poor thing, I hope she'll be all right now that she's by herself."

POP: 1) v. Consumir drogas, esp. pastillas. Ej. "You'd better stop popping those things before they kill you." 2) s. Un trago de alcohol. Ej. "Let's go to the corner for a pop." 3) s. Padre. Ej. "Hi pop, can I have some money?" 4) s. Bebida gaseosa. Ej. "It's hot out, would you like a pop?" 5) v. Disparar con una pistola. Ej. "The thief popped the cop." 6) *a pop*: adv. Cada uno, por cada uno. Ej. "The records are ten bucks a pop." VER *throw /a/*.

POP FOR: VER *spring for*.

POP SOMEONE'S CHERRY: [Vul.] exp-v. Tener sexo con una virgen. Ej. "I never popped her cherry. She's still a virgin."

POP THE QUESTION: exp-v. Proponer matrimonio (a). Ej. "She began to wonder if he would ever pop the question."

PORK BARREL: s. Un proyecto o asignación de fondos emprendido por el gobierno que constituye un derroche y cuya razón de ser radica en motivos políticos más que prácticos. Ej. "The politicians talk of getting the pork barrel out of the budget, but they all have projects they want to protect."

PORN: (sin. porno) abr. Pornografía. Ej. "Let's check out a porn flick tonight."

PORNO: (sin. porn) abr. Pornografía. Ej. "I dumped him when he said he was into porno flicks with animals."

PORRIDGE: VER *do porridge*.

POSSE: s. Grupo de buenos amigos, esp. miembros de una pandilla. Ej. "Those guys are my posse. They're here to cover my back."

POSSUM: VER *play possum*.

POT: s. 1) Marihuana. Ej. "Let's get

PRAYER

some pot for the party." 2) *the pot:* El baño. *Ej.* "It's strange, but sometimes when I have a hit of pot, it makes me want to hit the pot. Go figure?"

POTHEAD: (sin. stoner) *s.* Persona que fuma marihuana en forma habitual. *Ej.* "With his clean-cut looks you'd never think that he's a pothead."

POTLUCK: *s.* Fiesta donde todos aportan comida y/o trago. *Ej.* "We thought the best idea was to have a big potluck, that way we don't have to buy everything."

POUND: *v.* Beber mucho alcohol durante una fiesta o una tomatera, cuyo efecto es una resaca al día siguiente. *Ej.* "I feel horrible. I was pounding beers last night." Ver *hit it hard*.

POUND THE PAVEMENT: *exp-v.* Recorrer las calles, gen. ya sea en busca de trabajo o para cumplir una tarea. *Ej.* "I found the job by pounding the pavement."

POWDER: VER *take a powder*.

POWER TRIP: *s.* Imposición desenfrenada de poder o autoridad, esp. a raíz de haberlo obtenido recientemente. *Ej.* "That jerk Tom is on a total power trip since he was made manager. He loves telling us what to do."

PRAISE: VER *sing one's own praise(s)*.

PRAY TO THE PORCELAIN GODDESS: *exp-v.* Forma graciosa de decir "vomitar". VER *chuck up*.

PRAYER: VER *wing and a prayer*.

PRAY TO THE PORCELAIN GODDESS

PREGGY

PREGGY: *adj.* Embarazada. *Ej.* "If she's not preggy, she'd better go on a serious diet."

PREPPY: *s.* Persona elitista, de mentalidad conservadora. También un estilo de vestir que se encuentra en su forma más pura en el catálogo de la compañía L.L. Bean. *Ej.* "She's such a preppy that she wears matching pink monogramed shirts and skirts."

PRETTY PENNY: *exp.* Muy caro, de alto valor. *Ej.* "Yeah, the boat cost me a pretty penny."

PRICE: VER bargain basement price; pay the price.

PRICK: [Vul.] *s.* 1) Pene. *Ej.* "Your problem is that you only think with your prick!" 2) Persona muy desagradable y antipática. *Ej.* "That guy is a prick. He tried to steal my notebook so I wouldn't be able to study for the exam."

PRICK UP ONE'S EARS: *exp-v.* Escuchar atentamente o poner atención. *Ej.* "When I heard her mention my name, I pricked up my ears."

PRIME: *adj.* Lo mejor, lo máximo. *Ej.* "I found us a prime location to camp."

PRIMO: *adj.* De primera categoría, el mejor, excepcional. *Ej.* "This is some primo grass you scored!"

PROPS: *s.* Respeto logrado a través de una posesión o de una acción. Esto viene de aquellas comunidades donde el respeto se logra, a menudo, a través de acciones mal vistas o poco éticas desde el punto de vista de la sociedad en general (i.e. matanza, golpiza, etc.) *Ej.* "If you don't get your props, everyone on the street is going to be messing with you."

PSYCHE: *int.* Como broma, extender la mano o algo y luego retractarla al extender la otra persona la suya. *Ej.* "Do you want some of my ice cream – psyche!"

PSYCHE SOMEONE OUT: *exp-v.* Hacer que alguien se sienta mentalmente inseguro o que pierda la confianza. *Ej.* "Staring Joe in the eyes will psyche him out."

PSYCHE UP: *exp-v.* Alentar, animar, entusiasmar, esp. prepararse mentalmente para un esfuerzo. *Ej.* "You need to get psyched up for

PULL SOMEONE'S CHAIN

the big match or you'll lose."

PSYCHED: *adj.* Entusiasmado, animado. *Ej.* "I'm psyched for summer vacation."

PSYCHO: (sin. wacko) 1) *s.* Un psicópata. *Ej.* "He's got the look of a psycho." 2) *adj.* Loco, demente. *Ej.* "I'll go psycho on you if you mess with my family!"

PUBES: *s.* Pelo púbico. *Ej.* "Gross, you left your pubes on the soap bar!"

PUDDLE-JUMPER: *s.* Avión que realiza vuelos cortos. *Ej.* "I'm going to take the afternoon puddle-jumper from Miami to Orlando."

PUKE: [Vul.] 1) *v.* Vomitar. *Ej.* "He puked on my shoes!" VER *chuck up*. 2) (sin. barf*) *s.* Vómito. *Ej.* "How did this puke get here?" 3) Persona despreciable. *Ej.* "I hate that puke, he always insults people."

PULL: *s.* Influencia que se usa en negociaciones para obtener ciertos resultados. Gen. se refiere a la política. *Ej.* "She's got a lot of pull with the board of trustees."

PULL (SOME) STRINGS: *exp-vi.* Usar la influencia o contactos de uno para sobrepasar cualquier obstáculo o trámite burocrático con tal de conseguir una meta o alcanzar un fin. *Ej.* "It'll be hard to get tickets, but I think I can pull some strings." Or "Pull strings, call in debts, do whatever it takes, but get me on the anniversary cruise of the Loveboat!"

PULL A U-Y: (sin. make a U-y) *exp-v.* Hacer un viraje en U. *Ej.* "You passed the store. Pull a U-y at the corner."

PULL AN ALL-NIGHTER: *exp-vi.* Pasar la noche en vela, esp. para completar una tarea o para una fiesta. *Ej.* "I pulled an all-nighter to finish my thesis."

PULL DOWN: *exp-v.* Lo que uno gana por su sueldo (pero se ocupa como un verbo). *Ej.* "How much are you pulling down at your new job?"

PULL ONE OVER ON SOMEONE: (sin. pull the wool over someone's eyes, take someone for a ride) *exp-v.* Engañar a otro haciéndole creer algo que es falso. *Ej.* "They really pulled one over on George. He was convinced the police were looking for him when they weren't."

PULL SOMEONE'S CHAIN: *exp-v.* 1)

PULL SOMEONE'S LEG

Molestar, fastidiar, hasta un punto realmente desagradable. *Ej.* "Okay, enough is enough. You've been pulling my chain about my girlfriend for an hour now." 2) Engañar, mentir. *Ej.* "Stop pulling my chain and tell me the truth."

PULL SOMEONE'S LEG: *exp-v.* Hacerle una broma, un engaño a alguien. *Ej.* "Stop pulling my leg. I know they don't rent rooms at the White House." Or "We were pulling your leg when we told you you'd been fired."

PULL THE PLUG (ON): *exp-v.* 1) Retirar un apoyo, respaldo. *Ej.* "Better start packing the boxes, they've pulled the plug on the project." 2) Dejar que alguien finalmente muera desconectándolo de una máquina. *Ej.* "He's been in intensive care for years. I think it's time we pulled the plug."

PULL THE RUG OUT FROM UNDER: *exp-v.* Retirar el apoyo y/o la ayuda en algún cometido, esp. hacerlo inesperadamente. *Ej.* "When the sponsor pulled the rug out from under us, we had to scramble to find financing."

PULL THE WOOL OVER SOMEONE'S EYES: (sin. pull one over on someone, take someone for a ride) *exp-v.* Engañar alguien. *Ej.* "You have to stop pulling the wool over his eyes and be honest with him. I'm sure he won't care that you're actually a stripper and not a nurse."

PUMPKIN: VER *honey*.

PUNCH: VER *roll with the punches*.

PUNK: *s.* 1) Una persona joven, molesta con los valores sociales convencionales y en busca de anarquía. A menudo, esta persona se caracteriza por usar ropa negra, raída, un corte de pelo extraño y le gusta escuchar música iracunda a todo volumen. *Ej.* "What will I do if my daughter dates a punk?" 2) Una persona joven ruda, detestable, agresiva y muchas veces, también precoz. ¡Un gusto tenerla cerca! *Ej.* "Tell that punk to get off my car before I smack him!"

PURSE SNATCHER: *s.* Ladrón, esp. el que roba y se arranca. *Ej.* "She caught up with the purse snatcher and, much to his surprise, threw

PUSSYFOOT

him to the ground."

PUSH: *v.* 1) Promover o vender. *Ej.* "I can't believe George is pushing <u>Amway</u> on all his friends!" 2) Vender narcóticos. *Ej.* "You try pushing drugs around here and you won't live long."

PUSH IT: *exp-v.* 1) Acercarse peligrosamente a un comportamiento en que se falta el respeto o se aprovecha de otros. *Ej.* "You know, you're really pushing it with all the favors you've been asking." 2) Romper con las normas sociales de consideración por otros. *Ej.* "First you wanted a bicycle and now you want a car; you're pushing it son."

PUSH ONE'S LUCK: *exp-v.* Poner en peligro una racha de buena suerte al intentar repetir lo mismo. *Ej.* "You've already won twice. Don't push your luck."

PUSH (SOMEONE'S) BUTTONS: *exp-v.* Enemistar, provocar, esp. hablar de las debilidades de alguien para causar vergüenza o enojo. *Ej.* "I hate her, she's always pushing people's buttons." Or "He knows how to push buttons to make people feel lousy about themselves."

PUSHER: *s.* Persona que vende drogas ilegales. *Ej.* "The pusher was caught selling to kids."

PUSHING UP DAISIES: *exp.* Forma sarcástica para referirse a la muerte o decir "muerto", "enterrado". *Ej.* "If you don't pay me back, you'll be pushing up daisies sooner than you'd like."

PUSS: *s.* La cara. *Ej.* "What an ugly puss she has!"

PUSSY: [Vul.] *s.* 1) Vagina. VER *poontang*. 2) Una mujer, esp. considerándola como un objeto sexual. *Ej.* "Let's see what pussy is at the party." 3) Relación sexual con una mujer. *Ej.* "I need to get me some pussy tonight!" 4) Hombre tímido o cobarde. *Ej.* "Don't be a pussy, it won't hurt you to jump." VER *yellow-belly*.

PUSSYFOOT: [Vul.] *v.* Actuar o proceder muy cautelosamente a fin de evitar comprometerse u ofender al otro. *Ej.* "You can't pussyfoot around the subject forever. You have to confront him about it."

PUSSY-WHIPPED

PUSSY-WHIPPED: [Vul.] adj. Totalmente controlado por la pareja o esposa. Ej. "He's so pussy-whipped he never goes anywhere without her permission."

PUT A CONTRACT OUT ON: exp-vi. Dar la orden de asesinar a alguien. Ej. "The mob put a contract out on him for ratting out the boss."

PUT A CORK IN IT: exp-vi. Orden/pedido para dejar de hablar. Ej. "Put a cork in it Hal, we've heard enough of your complaining."

PUT A LID ON IT: int. ¡Cállate!, ¡Deja de hablar! Ej. "You kids had better put a lid on it when I'm talking."

PUT A SOCK IN IT: (sin. put a lid on it, put a cork in it, stifle it) int. Quedarse tranquilo, dejar de hablar. Ej. "That's enough of your whining, now put a sock in it!"

PUT ALL ONE'S EGGS IN ONE BASKET: exp.- vi. Se dice en sentido contrario como una recomendación para distribuir los bienes o las posibilidades en diferentes lugares y así mantener varias opciones. Ej. "I think you should apply to several places instead of putting all your eggs in one basket."

PUT IT TO SOMEONE: exp-vi. 1) Tratar injustamente, en forma irrespetuosa, o actuar sin tener consideración por el otro. Ej. "The boss really put it to him making him work overtime on Xmas." 2) [Vul.] Tener sexo con una mujer. Ej. "He said he put it to her, but I don't believe him."

PUT MONEY IN THE POT: exp-vi. Juntar dinero para una fiesta o en forma colectiva para comprar algo, gen. comida o trago. Ej. "If everyone puts money in the pot, we can have a really great party."

PUT ONE'S BEST FOOT FORWARD: exp-vi. Hacer el mejor esfuerzo o dar la mejor impresión para lograr algo. Ej. "I wanted to put my best foot forward on the new job, but I was so nervous that I broke three things."

PUT ONE'S FOOT DOWN: exp-vi. No aguantarle más algo a alguien. Ej. "That's it, I'm putting my foot down — no more slacking off or you're fired!"

PUT ONE'S FOOT IN ONE'S

PUT UP OR SHUT UP

MOUTH: *exp-vi.* Hacer un comentario desatinado o estúpido que provoca una situación embarazosa. *Ej.* "He put his foot in his mouth big time by talking about the football game when he'd said he had been at the office."

PUT ONE'S MONEY WHERE ONE'S MOUTH IS: *exp-vi.* Esto se dice de alguien después que ha dicho lo bien que hace algo, pero nunca se le ha visto hacerlo. *Ej.* "Enough talk, it's time to put your money where your mouth is. Meet me on the basketball court tomorrow at noon."

PUT ONESELF OUT: *exp-vi.* Esforzarse, llegar a extremos por hacer algo para uno mismo o para otro. *Ej.* "She put herself out to find a job for him, so he's taking her out to dinner to thank her."

PUT OUT /BE/: *exp-vi.* Estar enojado o irritado con alguien o haber recibido una falta de consideración por parte de alguien. *Ej.* "The boss is really put out with you for being late again." Or "I was put out when they didn't call to cancel dinner."

PUT OUT: [Vul.] *exp-vi.* Desear tener una relación sexual, se usa refiriéndose a niñas. Terminología típica de los adolescentes. *Ej.* "So, does she put out?"

PUT THAT IN YOUR PIPE AND SMOKE IT: *exp-vi.* Señalar hechos irrefutables y sobre los cuales jamás se podrá llegar a un acuerdo. *Ej.* "You want to take over my company? Ha! Not only is it not for sale, but I'm going to put you out of business. So put that in your pipe and smoke it!"

PUT THE BITE ON: (sin. put the squeeze on, hit someone up, touch) *exp-vi.* Pedirle dinero a un amigo o conocido. *Ej.* "I stay away from Larry. He's always putting the bite on his friends."

PUT THE MAKE ON: *exp-vi.* Intentar seducir a alguien. *Ej.* "He tried to put the make on her, but she would have none of it."

PUT THE SQUEEZE ON: VER put the bite on.

PUT UP OR SHUT UP: *exp-vi.* Probar o demostrar lo que se ha supuesto o terminar con las suposiciones. *Ej.* "You've talked

PUTDOWN

and talked. Now it's time to put up or shut up."

PUTDOWN: s. Crítica dura, humillante y degradante. Ej. "I won't tolerate any more putdowns from him."

PUT-ON: s. Simulación, una broma que pretende engañar al otro. Ej. "He never realized that the whole story was a put-on."

PUTZ: 1) s. Persona tonta. Ej. "My boss is such a putz it drives me up the wall having to take orders from him." 2) v. Hacer algo sin ánimo; dejar pasar el tiempo sin hacer nada. Ej. "Are you going to work or just putz about all day?"

Q

QUARTERBACK: v. Dirigir, mandar. Ej. "Who's quarterbacking this operation?"

QUEER: 1) adj. Marica, homosexual, muy afeminado. (Desp.) Ej. "He acts kind of queer, but he's straight." 2) s. Una persona homosexual, gen. hombre. (Desp.) Ej. "He's a queer and proud of it." VER fag.

QUESTION: VER *pop the question*.

QUICKIE: s. 1) Algo que se realiza rápidamente. Ej. "I need to take a shower before we go, but don't worry, I'll make it a quickie." 2) Relación sexual rápida. Ej. "How about a quickie before work?"

QUIET AS A MOUSE: exp. Estar muy callado, hacer ningún o poco ruido. Ej. "I never hear my husband get up in the morning, he's as quiet as a mouse."

R

RACK UP: exp-v. 1) Acumular, juntar puntos o dinero. Ej. "He'll rack up a fortune playing profesional basketball." 2) Chocar, estrellar, hacer pedazos, esp. un auto. Ej. "He racked up my new car!"

RACKET: s. Un negocio u ocupación. Ej. "I'm in the laundry racket."

RACY: (sin. saucy) adj. Sexualmente provocativo, es-cabroso. Ej. "Don't you think that skirt is a little racy? I can see the lace on your underwear."

RAD: abr. Radical, maravilloso, extraordinario. Ej. "He can do some rad moves on a surfboard!"

RAG: 1) s. Diario o revista, por lo

RAISE HELL

general, malo y escandaloso. Ej. "I cannot believe you read that rag!" 2) (sin. threads) Ropa, a menudo, aunque no siempre, raída, demasiado gastada. Ej. "Oh, this old rag, I bought it at a second hand clothing store." Or "Check out my new rags." VER TAMBIEN *on the rag; wet rag.*

RAG ON: (sin. rank on) *v.* Tomar el pelo, burlarse o criticar, esp. criticar duramente. Ej. "I'd appreciate it if you wouldn't rag on my brother."

RAGE: *v.* Celebrar o festejar con mucho entusiasmo y soltura. ¡Prepárate para divertirte! Ej. "When I get together with my college buddies, we really rage."

RAIN: VER *save (something) for a rainy day; when it rains, it pours.*

RAIN CATS AND DOGS: *exp.* Llover muchísimo. Ej. "I'm soaking wet! It's raining cats and dogs today."

RAIN ON THE/SOMEONE'S PARADE: *exp-v.* 1) No tener voluntad para participar con los demás y, en consecuencia, arruinar la diversión de los demás. Ej. "Come on, don't rain on the parade, we need one more person to have even teams." 2) Ser muy desagradable, o estar deprimido o pesimista cuando los demás están en buen humor. Ej. "I don't want to invite him to the picnic because he always rains on everyone's parade."

RAINMAKER: *s.* Persona que atrae muchos clientes convenientes o lucrativos a una empresa. Ej. "He may be a slimeball, but he's the rainmaker in this firm."

RAISE A STINK: (sin. make a stink) *exp-v.* Crear un escándalo, quejarse ruidosamente o crear un gran alboroto. Ej. "Boy, did she raise a stink about the new non-smoking policy in the office."

RAISE CAIN: *exp-v.* Comportarse de manera desordenada o camorrera. Ej. "Every time he drinks whiskey, he starts raising Cain."

RAISE HELL: *exp-v.* Armar un boche, un alboroto, una conmoción. Ej. "My mom raised hell at the restaurant when she found a roach in her food." Or "He'll raise hell if he doesn't get the promotion."

RAKE SOMEONE OVER THE COALS

RAKE SOMEONE OVER THE COALS: exp-v. Someter a alguien a una fuerte crítica o amonestación que llega a dar la sensación de haber pasado sobre las brasas. Ej. "The teacher raked me over the coals for not preparing for my class presentation."

RALPH: v. Vomitar. Ej. "Someone ralphed in the john." Ver chuck up.

RANK ON: VER rag on.

RAP: 1) s. Una acusación o condena criminal. Ej. "He got the chair on a murder rap." 2) s. Una supuesta característica negativa en una persona. Ej. "She has this rap of being a bad teacher, but it's not true." 3) s. Una conversación, una discusión. Ej. "I finally had a good rap with my mom about my fiancé." 4) s. Un tipo de música inventada por grupos de jóvenes latinos y de color de los sectores urbanos y densamente poblados en los Estados Unidos en el cual la lírica que rima es hablada rápidamente al son de un acompañamiento rítmico. Ej. "With two turntables and a microphone, these city kids invented rap." 5) Onda, cuento, de que se trata. Ej. "What's his rap? What's he do for a living?" VER TAMBIEN bad rap; beat the rap; bum rap; take the rap.

RAP SHEET: s. Registro policial de arrestos y condenas anteriores. Ej. "The girl has a rap sheet as long as my arm."

RASPBERRY: s. 1) Leve moretón, gen. como resultado de contacto fuerte y rápido de la piel con una superficie raspante. Ej. "He got a raspberry when he scraped his knee on the sidewalk." 2) Sonido de

RAKE SOMEONE OVER THE COALS

RAZZLE-DAZZLE

desprecio producido por la vibración de la lengua entre los labios. *Ej.* "The audience gave the play a big raspberry."

RAT: *s.* Persona que delata a los demás, esp. a los amigos o asociados. *Ej.* "It's hard to believe that she could be a rat."

RAT ON: (sin. sing, squeal, squeak, snitch*) *exp-v.* Confesar o delatar a otros, esp. a los amigos o asociados a las autoridades, esp. la policía. *Ej.* "They found the guy who ratted on them."

RAT PACK: *s.* Un grupo de íntimos amigos a quienes los une una actividad en común. *Ej.* "Hollywood has been invaded by a new rat pack of young stars."

RAT RACE: *s.* Una actividad o ambiente competitivo y agotador gen. en la ciudad. *Ej.* "I need to get out of this rat race before it kills me."

RATFINK: *s.* Una persona despreciable y aborrecible, y a menudo también traidora. *Ej.* "You're a real ratfink to have stolen my girlfriend"

RAUNCHY: *adj.* 1) Obsceno, libidinoso, sexualmente explícito. *Ej.* "I saw this raunchy movie on cable TV." 2) Mugriento, asqueroso, desaseado. *Ej.* "The kitchen is looking pretty raunchy dude, I don't want to cook in there."

RAVE: *adj.* Aprobación total y entusiasta. *Ej.* "The play received a rave review from the press."

RAVE PARTY: *s.* Agrupación de muchas personas, la mayoría de las cuales ha ingerido "éxtasis" (o sea "X": narcótico que provoca una sensación de éxtasis) que los hace bailar durante horas al son de la música "tecno". *Ej.* "The police broke up the rave party just when it had begun."

RAYS: *s.pl.* Rayos de sol. Gen. se expresa como *catch some rays. Ej.* "Let's go to the beach and catch some rays."

RAZZ: *v.* Tomar el pelo, burlarse, reírse de. *Ej.* "Don't razz the other team. They feel bad enough after losing by 30 points."

RAZZLE-DAZZLE: *s.* Despliegue deslumbrante, llamativo. *Ej.* "He's a crowd favorite with his razzle-dazzle moves."

READ SOMEONE THE RIOT ACT

READ SOMEONE THE RIOT ACT: (sin. read the riot act to someone) exp-vi. Decirle a alguien en términos sumamente claros la verdad de una situación, esp. en cuanto al comportamiento de uno o lo que se espera de uno. Ej. "My mom read me the riot act when I failed math again." Or "I'm going to have to read the riot act to these punks if they don't clean up their act."

READ THE RIOT ACT TO SOMEONE: VER read someone the riot act.

READY TO SPRING: exp. Listo para actuar. Estar atento a que ocurra algo esperado. Ej. "Everyone get ready to spring, this could go down at any moment."

REAL: adv. Muy, sumamente. Se usa antes de un sustantivo o adjetivo para describir un valor superlativo. Ej. "Hey, I'm real glad to meet you." Or "John has a real good body." VER TAMBIEN for real.

REAL CHARACTER: s. Una persona de personalidad original, muy divertida y simpática. Ej. "Oh, Ted is a real character. You'd have fun speaking with him."

REAL McKOY: exp. El artículo auténtico y original. Ej. "This ain't no cheap imitation, this diamond is the Real McKoy."

REAM: v. Tratar en forma extremadamente injusta y horrible; cometer un acto en extremo injusto. Ej. "The company reamed him when they fired him one week before he was eligible for a pension."

REAR /ONE'S/: s. Uno mismo. Forma educada de decir one's ass. Ej. "I need to get my rear going if I'm going to arrive on time."

RED: VER catch someone red handed; paint the town red; see red.

RED CENT /NOT HAVE A/: VER not have a red cent.

RED COAT: s. Traidor. (etim. De la Guerra de Independencia Estadounidense; los ingleses, el enemigo, usaban uniforme rojo.) Ej. "You red coat, how could you switch to the other team?"

RED LETTER DAY: exp. Un día muy improbable en un futuro imaginario, o una fecha memorable de algún acontecimiento alegre o es-

RINGER

pecial. *Ej.* "It was a red letter day yesterday. Mr. Never-step-foot-in-the-kitchen actually cooked dinner for me."

RED NECK: *s.* Persona de raza blanca, no educada, que proviene de zonas rurales, esp. del sur de los EE.UU. con ideas retrógradas esp. sobre racismo y machismo. Se supone que tienen el cuello rojo por trabajar al sol. *Ej.* "Be careful not to exceed the speed limit down here. We're northerners in red neck country."

REDEYE: *s.* Vuelo de noche, como ésos en que uno aterriza a la mañana siguiente con los ojos hinchados por no haber dormido, por lo tanto, con los ojos rojos. *Ej.* "He's taking the redeye from LA to New York so he can attend the morning meeting."

REEFER: *s.* Marihuana. *Ej.* "It smells like they're smoking reefer." VER *grass*.

RENT-A-COP: *s.* Guardia de seguridad. *Ej.* "It should be a piece of cake. There's only two rent-a-cops guarding the joint."

RETARD: *s.* Una persona mentalmente retardada. (Desp.) *Ej.* "Are you a retard or something? Don't you understand English?"

RICH: VER *strike it rich*.

RIDE: (sin. *wheels, set of wheels*) *s.* Un auto, camión o motocicleta. *Ej.* "Nice ride Sam, when did you buy it?" VER TAMBIEN *take someone for a ride; thumb a ride*.

RIFLE THROUGH: *exp-v.* Buscar algo en una pila de cosas. *Ej.* "Stop rifling through my things."

RIGHT ON: *int.* Conforme. *Ej.* "Right on, bro, I'm game for a beer."

RIGHTEOUS: *adj.* Excelente, fantástico. *Ej.* "That was one righteous party last night." VER *awesome*.

RIGHTO: *adj.* Absolutamente correcto. *Ej.* "Righto! Ready for the next question?"

RINGER: *s.* Una persona que participa en una competencia, que posee una habilidad superior y que en general, se le incorpora ilegalmente a la competencia. *Ej.* "There is no way we can beat them. They have two ringers on their team." VER TAMBIEN *dead ringer*.

RINKY-DINK

RINKY-DINK: (sin. two-bit) *adj.* Insignificante, barato, inferior o sin importancia. *Ej.* "I hate these rinky-dink productions. They're lacking in both plot and scenery" Or "He works for a rinky-dink law firm."

RIOT /A/: *s.* Una persona o cosa muy divertida. *Ej.* "He's a riot." Or "The show was a riot." VER TAMBIEN *read someone the riot act.*

RIP INTO: *exp-v.* Atacar física o verbalmente. *Ej.* "My girlfriend ripped into me for flirting with another girl." Or "First the thugs stole his money, and then they ripped into him with bats."

RIP-OFF: 1) *exp-v.* Estafar a alguien o ser engañado, gen. con respecto a dinero. *Ej.* "He got ripped-off on the car. The engine went kaput within a week." 2) *s.* Un precio/valor injusto por algo. *Ej.* "What a rip-off! Ten bucks for a little, lousy hamburger."

RIP-OFF ARTIST: (sin. con man) *s.* Persona que intenta quitarle dinero a otros por medios ilegales como estafas financieras. *Ej.* "That's what happens when you do business with a rip-off artist; you lose all your money."

RITZY: *adj.* Elegante, lujoso, de primera categoría y gen. ¡sumamente caro! *Ej.* "This is some ritzy place. You must be paying a fortune to stay here."

ROACH: *s.* El extremo o colilla de un cigarrillo de marihuana. *Ej.* "Save the roach, I'll smoke it later."

ROAD: VER *don't go down that road.*

ROAD TRIP: *s.* Un viaje largo en automóvil con fines recreativos. *Ej.* "Let's go on a road trip to Florida."

ROB THE CRADLE: *exp-v.* Buscar y/o tener una relación sexual con alguien mucho más joven que uno. Por lo general, en este caso existe un problema que sólo con terapia se podría resolver. *Ej.* "Let's see, he's 40 and she's 16. Yeah, that's robbing the cradle all right."

ROCK: 1) *v.* Ser/estar maravilloso, fantástico, excelente. *Ej.* "The Figments rock. They're an awesome band!" Or "I rocked my job interview." 2) *s.* Un diamante o, menos frecuentemente, cualquier piedra preciosa. *Ej.* "Check out the rock on her finger!" 3) *s.* Cocaína para

ROUGH

fumar. *Ej.* "They were smoking the rock before they drove off the bridge."

ROCK THE BOAT: *exp-v.* Trastornar y/o perturbar el equilibrio en una situación o relación. *Ej.* "Everything was going smoothly till he showed up and started rocking the boat."

ROCKER: VER *off one's rocker.*

ROCKET SCIENTIST: *s.* Persona excepcionalmente inteligente; sin embargo, casi siempre se usa con una negación para referirse a una persona que no lo es. *Ej.* "He's a nice enough guy, but he's no rocket scientist."

ROCKS: VER *on the rocks; get one's rocks off.*

ROLL: 1) *v.* Robar, esp. robarle a alguien que no es capaz de defenderse gen. un borracho. *Ej.* "They rolled the poor bastard coming out of the bar." 2) *s.* Dinero, esp. un fajo grande y gordo de billetes. *Ej.* "He's either happy to see me or he's got a roll in his pocket." VER TAMBIEN *on a roll.*

ROLL IN THE HAY: *exp.* Forma humorística de describir una relación sexual. *Ej.* "It felt so good to have a roll in the hay after being at sea for two months."

ROLL WITH THE PUNCHES: *exp-v.* Enfrentar la adversidad, esp. adaptándose a los crueles caprichos del destino y la fortuna. *Ej.* "He can handle the worst situations because he just rolls with the punches."

ROME: VER *all roads lead to Rome; when in Rome, do as the Romans do.*

ROMP: *v.* Derrotar en forma decisiva (a alguien) en un deporte o competencia. *Ej.* "It was great! We romped all over the other team."

ROOTING-TOOTING: *adj.* Revoltoso y estrepitoso (ruidoso), gen. en forma positiva, festiva. *Ej.* "You kids go out and have a rootin'-tootin' good time, you hear!?"

ROSE TINTED GLASSES/SPECTACLES: *exp.* Que ve la vida de una forma engañosa o que no es real. *Ej.* "She goes around wearing rose tinted spectacles, and therefore she's very happy with her life."

ROUGH: *adj.* Muy difícil o

ROUTINE

desagradable. Ej. "It's rough to lose after playing so well." VER TAMBIEN *diamond in the rough; play rough*

ROUTINE: (sin. shtick) s. Una rutina característica, ya sea hablada o actuada, que se usa para divertir. Ej. "Her routine about preppy girls is a scream."

ROYAL /A/: s. Algo que supera, excede a todo el resto, en sentido negativo. Ej. "Fixing my car has been a royal pain."

ROYALLY: adv. Extremadamente, completamente, en sentido negativo. Ej. "I got royally screwed on that deal."

RUB ELBOWS WITH: exp-v. Entablar contactos sociales esp. con personas importantes o influyentes. Ej. "Susan was rubbing elbows with the head honchos at the party."

RUB OUT: exp-v. Asesinar. Ej. "Let's rub him out before he squeals to the Feds."

RUBBER: s. Un condón. Ej. "I won't do it unless we use a rubber." VER TAMBIEN *lay rubber.*

RUBBER CHECK: (sin. bounced check) s. Cheque sin fondos. Ej. "That hurts: a $10,000 rubber check."

RUBBERNECK: v. Girar el cuello lo más posible al ir conduciendo, a fin de mirar o fijar la vista en algo, que casi siempre es un accidente. Es esto - la fascinación humana por la abominación – lo que tan a menudo produce en nuestras carreteras esos atochamientos de vehículos que son una pesadilla. Ej. "Everyone was rubbernecking at the accident, and

there wasn't even any blood!"

RUG: s. Un postizo pequeño. Ej. "The rug business is hurting since they started doing hair transplants." VER TAMBIEN *pull the rug out from under; cut a rug.*

RUG RAT: s. Niños pequeños, esp. con carácter malvado o irritante y generalmente antes de que comiencen a caminar. Ej. "I have to go pick-up my brother's rug rats from the baby-sitter's house."

RUMBLE: s. 1) Una pelea pandillera. Ej. "The two gangs had a big rumble in the schoolyard." 2) Expresión generalizada de insatisfacción o desaprobación. Ej. "There's an unhealthy rumble going on in the factory. I think they might go on strike soon."

RUMMY: s. Un borracho, un alcohólico. Ej. "I got drunk just smelling that rummy!"

RUN A TIGHT SHIP: exp-vi. Mantener un orden estricto, no permitir que puedan haber divergencias. Ej. "The key for a business to survive a recession is to run a tight ship."

RUN AROUND: exp. El hecho de pasar a través de muchos obstáculos o ir a muchos lugares para hacer una sola cosa. Esp. se usa para describir la interacción con la burocracia. Ej. "What a run around I had with City Planning to get my building permits."

RUN OF THE MILL: exp. Común y corriente. Ej. "He's just an ordinary Joe from a run of the mill kind of town."

RUN OFF AT THE MOUTH: exp-vi. Hablar innecesariamente y a menudo sin un propósito o idea claro. Ej. "I cannot stand Janet because she's always running off at the mouth."

RUN OUT OF GAS: exp-vi. Quedar sin energía. Ej. "The party was hopping, but I ran out of gas at around 3 am and went home."

RUN WITH: exp-vi. Estar asociado con algo o alguien por un período largo de tiempo. Ej. "She runs with a loose group of friends."

RUNS /THE/: (sin. trots /the/) s.pl. Tener diarrea. Ej. "He's been on the throne for an hour. He must have the runs."

RUSH: s. Sensación de emoción o

RUSSKI

placer cuando la adrenalina sube rápidamente y de improviso. Ej. "It was a rush speaking in front of a crowd."

RUSSKI: s. Ruso. (Desp.) Ej. "Is she a Russki? She doesn't talk like one."

RUSTLE UP SOME GRUB: exp-v. Cocinar, preparar la comida. Ej. "Let's say you get in that there kitchen and rustle up some grub for us."

Sack

SACK: 1) s. Despido del trabajo o empleo. Ej. "If you get the sack from this job, you'd better not even come home." 2) s. Una cama o colchón. Ej. "Come on kids, it's eight o'clock, time to hit the sack." 3) v. Despedir, echar del trabajo. Ej. "They sacked you after only one day?!!" VER TAMBIEN sad sack.

SACK OUT: exp-v. Dormir, quedarse dormido. Ej. "I'm so tired I just want to sack out."

SACK TIME: s. Hora de ir a la cama. Ej. "Okay kids, no more TV, it's sack time."

SAD SACK: s. Una persona patética, esp. una considerada sumamente inepta. Ej. "He turned into a sad sack after his girlfriend dumped him."

SALT: VER pinch of salt.

SALT AWAY: exp-v. Poner a un lado, ahorrar dinero. Ej. "She's salting away for a new fur coat."

SANDBAG: v. Intimidar, reprimir, esp. obligar a alguien a hacer algo contra su voluntad. Ej. "They tried to sandbag me with their thugs, but I'm not giving in."

SAP: s. Una víctima de engaño, persona tonta, crédula. Ej. "That sap will fall for any gag."

SAPPY: adj. 1) Emoción fácil, empalagoso, muy sentimental. Ej. "That soap opera is so sappy I can't bear to watch it." 2) Tonto, ridículo. Ej. "You have such sappy ideas."

SAUCE: (sin. booze, drink) s. Bebida alcohólica. Ej. "Go easy on the sauce, it's only 10 am."

SAUCY: (sin. racy) adj. Sexualmente provocativo, escabroso. Ej. "What a dish! Now that's what I call saucy!"

SAVE IT: int. Dejar de hablar, esp. dejar de dar excusas inútiles. Ej.

SCARF UP/DOWN

"You've given me this malarkey before Dave, just save it."

SAVE SOMEONE'S BACON: *exp-v.* Sacar a alguien de un problema. Ej. "I've saved your bacon twice now, any more mess ups and you're history."

SAVE (SOMETHING) FOR A RAINY DAY: *exp-v.* Una recomendación para guardar el dinero o alguna cosa como reserva para tiempos difíciles en el futuro. Ej. "Don't spend all of it, save some for a rainy day." Or "I don't touch 10% of my salary because I'm saving for a rainy day."

SAVVY: *adj.* 1) Bien informado, astuto, conocedor o sabio. Ej. "Listen to her advice, she's a savvy investor." 2) Conocimiento práctico o entendimiento de, astucia. Ej. "You'd better be street savvy if you're going to survive in the Big Apple."

SAY UNCLE: (sin. throw in the towel) *exp-vi.* Desistir, darse por vencido. Ej. "Say uncle or I won't let you up." Or "After twisting his arm, he finally said uncle."

SCALP: *v.* Comprar algo (gen. una entrada) y revenderla a un precio más alto que el inicial. Ej. "They arrested him for scalping tickets."

SCALPER: *s.* Persona que hace una ganancia rápida comprando y revendiendo algo, gen. entradas. Ej. "Scalpers are predators on the unorganized; I'm a regular customer."

SCAM: 1) *s.* Una estafa; un negocio fraudulento. Ej. "What a scam the lottery is." 2) *v.* Engañar, estafar. Ej. "He tried to scam me on the tickets, but I didn't fall for it." VER burn.

SCARDY CAT: *s.* Un cobarde, en el lenguaje de los niños y desde su punto de vista. Ej. "Don't be a scardy cat. Go ahead and climb the tree."

SCARE THE LIVING DAYLIGHTS OUT OF: *exp-v.* Espantar o asustar a un grado extremo. Ej. "It scared the living daylights out of me. I thought I was all alone and then Ted appeared in the kitchen."

SCARF UP/DOWN: (sin. wolf down) *exp-v.* Devorar, comer o tomar vorazmente. Ej. "Did you see how quickly he scarfed up that pizza?"

SCENE

Or "Just give me a sec to scarf down my sandwhich."

SCENE: s. Situación, cicunstancia. Ej. "It was an ugly scene when the fight erupted."

SCHIZO: s. Persona esquizofrénica. Ej. "Why are you so paranoid? Are you a schizo or something?"

SCHLEP: v. Acarrear, llevar algo, esp. algo grande y difícil de llevar. Ej. "I'm always schleping around too much stuff."

SCHMEAR: VER *the whole schmear*.

SCHMO: s. Una persona tonta o irritante, a menudo con la gracia añadida de ser crédula. Ej. "Another rip-off scheme targeting the schmos of this world."

SCHMOOZE: v. 1) Conversar, charlar casualmente. Ej. "I was hanging out and schmoozing with some friends yesterday." 2) Hablar en lenguaje amable y engañador para conseguir un objetivo. Ej. "That guy is so smooth he could schmooze a statue."

SCHMUCK: s. Persona antipática, generalmente desatinada, tonta y/o estúpida, frecuentemente se compara a un *loser*. Ej. "Don't be a schmuck, come with us to the lake."

SCHNOZ: s. Nariz. Ej. "Check out the schnoz on her face!" VER *beak*.

SCHOOL: v. 1) Enseñarle a alguien cómo hacer algo, esp. de una manera condescendiente. Ej. "You're talking big now, but when we get on the court I'm gonna school you boy." 2) Perder decisivamente, a menudo en forma humillante. Ej. "I had to hang my head low after getting schooled by Freddie in hoops." VER TAMBIEN *skip school*.

SCHWANK: v. Desempeñarse pobremente, esp. ser derrotado con decisión. Ej. "After playing well all week, he schwanked it in the finals and got blown out."

SCOFF: v. Comer con muchas ganas, casi con avaricia. Ej. "Did you see how he scoffed all the cake?"

SCOOP /THE/: s. VERsión sobre un acontecimiento de persona informada, la información que no es pública. Ej. "Ask the secretary what's the scoop on the Senator and that lady."

SCREW AROUND WITH

SCOPE OUT: *exp-v.* Examinar o investigar, en forma cuidadosa y detallada. *Ej.* "We need to scope out a good place for the class reunion."

SCORE: 1) *v.* Estar contento con una elección. *Ej.* "We scored coming to this place. The food's great and really cheap." 2) *v.* Tener éxito en un intento. *Ej.* "I scored big getting this job." 3) *v.* Comprar algo, gen. drogas. *Ej.* "Let's go downtown to score some pot." 4) *v.* Hacer una conquista sexual. *Ej.* "I scored last night with Gina." 5) *s.* El botín de un robo. *Ej.* "They took a nice score from that last bank job." 6) *score /the/:* (sin. lowdown /the/) *s.* Toda la verdad; información esencial y más importante. *Ej.* "What's the score here? What do we need to know about this competitor?"

SCOUT'S HONOR: *s.* Declaración solemne en la que uno promete que está diciendo absolutamente la verdad. *Ej.* "Scout's honor, I didn't throw your model airplane out the window."

SCRAM: VER *beat it.*

SCRAPING BY /BE/: *exp-vi.* Tener poco dinero, justo lo necesario para sobrevivir. *Ej.* "That family will never be able to save for a house. They're just scraping by as it is."

SCRATCH: *s.* Dinero. *Ej.* "I've got to get me some scratch for the weekend." VER *dough.* VER TAMBIEN *you scratch my back and I scratch yours.*

SCREAM: *s.* Persona o cosa (ej. película, obra teatral, etc.) que es muy pero muy divertida. *Ej.* "She's such a scream, I bet she could be a professional comedian."

SCREAM BLOODY MURDER: (sin. *scream like a stuck pig*) *exp-v.* Gritar muy fuerte. *Ej.* "My hemorrhoids are so bad that every time I go to the john, I scream bloody murder."

SCREAM LIKE A STUCK PIG: VER *scream bloody murder.*

SCREW: [Vul.] 1) (sin. *lay*) *s.* Acto sexual. *Ej.* "They went for a screw in the woods." 2) *v.* Tener relación sexual con alguien. *Ej.* "I screwed him last night." 3) *v.* Engañar, estafar, aprovecharse de. *Ej.* "A casino will screw you out of your money everytime." VER *burn.*

SCREW AROUND WITH: *exp-v.* 1)

SCREW AROUND

Tratar sin respeto o sin cuidado apropiado. Ej. "Stop screwing around with my camera!" 2) Ser sexualmente promiscuo. Ej. "He's so unparticular, he'd screw around with practically anyone."

SCREW AROUND: exp-v. Actuar sin producir, pasar el tiempo sin objetivo para lograr nada. Ej. "Instead of screwing around, why don't you do something with your life."

SCREW LOOSE /A/: exp. Inestable, loco, mentalmente insano. Ej. "He must have a screw loose to show up at 4 am asking if he can cut the grass." VER not all there.

SCREW OFF: [Vul.] Hacer algo sin ánimo; dejar pasar el tiempo sin hacer nada. Ej. "Stop screwing off and get to work!"

SCREW ONE/IT: [Vul.] (sin. fuck one/it) exp. Para expresar el gran disgusto que le provoca alguien o algo. ¡Insulto mayor! Ej. "Screw it, I'm not going to class." Or "Screw him, he's owed me money for over a year."

SCREW OVER: [Vul.] exp-v. Tratar a alguien en forma excepcionalmente injusta, castigar. Ej. "I got screwed over in the lawsuit."

SCREW (SOMEONE) OUT OF: [Vul.] exp-v. Engañar a alguien en relación a algo, o evitar que alguien obtenga algo que se merece. Ej. "She screwed me out of the job by telling the boss I moonlighted as a stripper."

SCREW UP: [Vul.] exp-v. 1) Hacer algo en forma deficiente o incorrecta. Ej. "If I screw up this test, I'm screwed!" 2) Hacer algo de la cual uno se arrepiente. Ej. "I screwed up at work when I told my boss to fuck off." 3) Herir, lastimar, dañar. Ej. "I screwed up my knee skiing." 4) Hacer neurótico/a, traumatizar o crearle gran ansiedad a alguien. Ej. "She got screwed up by her crazy parents."

SCREW WITH (SOMEONE): [Vul.] exp. Faltarles el respeto o maltratar a los demás. Ej. "Tim is such a jerk, he's always screwing with smaller kids."

SCREWBALL: 1) s. Una persona excéntrica, loca o irracional. Ej. "That guy is a screwball!" 2) (sin. screwy) adj. Excéntrico, impro-

SCUZZY

bable, irracional. Ej. "It's a screwball idea, Dave, thinking you could recycle rubbers."

SCREWED: [Vul.] adj. 1) Estar en una situación problemática. Ej. "I'm screwed if I don't get the money for the loan shark!" 2) Loco, improbable, excéntrico. Ej. "His ideas about marriage are screwed."

SCREWUP: VER fuckup.

SCREWY: adj. 1) Excéntrico, loco. Ej. "There's something screwy about his having 55 pictures of his mother on the wall." VER bats. 2) Improbable, no apropiado, absurdo. Ej. "She always comes up with these screwy inventions."

SCROUNGE AROUND: exp-v. Buscar algo entre muchas cosas. Ej. "I'll break your hands if I catch you scrounging around in my things."

SCROUNGE UP: exp-v. Conseguir, obtener o juntar algo deseado con gran esfuerzo, esp. al no encontrarse a mano o localizarse difícilmente lo que se desea. Ej. "I need to scrounge up some money for train fare."

SCROUNGY: adj. Sucio, destartalado o roñoso. Ej. "I won't eat in that scroungy looking joint."

SCRUB: v. Cancelar o abandonar, esp. debido a una dificultad imprevista. Ej. "Scrub the plans for the weekend, I've got to work."

SCUMBAG: [Vul.] s. Una persona despreciable, inmunda, inmoral, o al menos una a quien se le considera de esta manera. Ej. "What's that scumbag doing at my wedding?"

SCUMMY: adj. Sumamente desagradable, ofensivo, poco atractivo. Ej. "I don't like him, he's scummy."

SCUTTLEBUTT: s. Copucha, rumor o información confidencial. Ej. "What's the scuttlebutt about the merger?"

SCUZZ: s. 1) Persona de mala fama, repulsiva y/o desaseada. Ej. "I won't do business with that scuzz. Aside from having bad hygiene, he's also a thief." 2) Mugre, tizne. Ej. "Look at that scuzz in the water!"

SCUZZY: adj. Sucio, mugriento, repulsivo. Ej. "What a scuzzy bath-

SECOND BANANA

room! Don't you ever clean it?"

SECOND BANANA: s. Subordinado o persona secundaria que se distingue del *top banana* o persona más importante. Ej. "I may be the second banana now, but some day I'll be the manager of this Dairy Queen!"

SECOND BASE: exp. Acariciar los senos de una mujer. Ej. "Her bra was such a hassle, that they skipped second base and went right to third." VER etimología de *first base*.

SECURITY BLANKET: s. Frazada con que duerme un bebé, o metafóricamente algo que reconforta y tranquiliza. Ej. "The stuffed bear is her security blanket."

SEE RED: exp-vi. Sentirse resentido y enojado, y querer vengarse, o simplemente perder el auto control al extremo de perder totalmente el control. Ej. "I saw red when some stranger smacked my son."

SEE THE LIGHT: exp-vi. Una revelación; darse cuenta de golpe de una verdad sobre alguien o algo. Esp. VER la real naturaleza de alguien o algo. Ej. "It took a long time before I saw the light and realized the cult leader was a fraud."

SEE YA': int. Adiós. Ej. "See ya' dude, maybe we'll catch up with each other at the movies tonight."

SELL LIKE HOT CAKES: exp-vi. Vender mucho de algo rápido. Ej. "It was awesome, my book sold like hot cakes."

SELL SOMEONE SHORT: exp-vi. Predecir equivocadamente la habilidad de alguien. Ej. "Don't sell him short. You'd be surprised by what lurks behind that meek exterior."

SEND SOMEONE PACKING: exp-vi. Echar o despedir a alguien. Ej. "Hey, what happened with your boyfriend?" "Oh, he was a creep. I sent him packing last week."

SEND UP: (sin. *get sent away, get locked up*) exp-vi. Ir a la cárcel. Ej. "She got sent up for hooking."

SERIOUS: adj. Muy importante y significativo, considerable o impresionante. Ej. "I've got a serious problem with my in-laws." Or "The cop gave her a serious speed-

SHAKE DOWN

ing ticket - $200!"

SERVE TIME: *exp-v.* Estar preso. *Ej.* "He's serving time for dealing drugs."

SET: (sin. pair) *s.* Los senos de una mujer, gen. bonitos y voluminosos. *Ej.* "Most Hollywood actresses have quite a set on them."

SET OF WHEELS: (sin. ride, wheels) *s.* Un auto, camión o motocicleta. *Ej.* "Fancy set of wheels you've got there."

SET ONE'S SIGHTS HIGH: *exp-vi.* Tener altas expectativas o metas muy ambiciosas. *Ej.* "She set her sights too high and never realized her dream."

SET ONE'S SIGHTS LOW: *exp-vi.* Tener bajas expectativas o metas muy modestas. *Ej.* "It kills me how my son sets his sights low. He's got zilch for ambition."

SET (SOMEONE) UP: *exp-vi.* 1) Planificar acontecimientos para atrapar a alguien. *Ej.* "They set him up to take a big fall." 2) Planificar un encuentro romántico entre dos personas, gen. personas que no se conocen. *Ej.* "I set up my sister with a good friend."

SHABBY: VER *not too shabby*.

SHACK UP: *exp-v.* 1) Vivir juntos gozando la intimidad sexual sin estar casados. *Ej.* "Married? Hell no, we're just shacking up." 2) Vivir o quedarse en alguna parte que no es la casa de uno. *Ej.* "MaryAnn is shacking up at her in-laws' house."

SHADES: *s.pl.* Anteojos de sol. *Ej.* "This sun is so strong I can't see without my shades."

SHAFT: 1) *v.* Victimizar, maltratar. *Ej.* "He shafted me on the deal." 2) *the shaft: s.* Tratamiento duro, injusto o victimizante. *Ej.* "I'm getting the shaft, I have to work every weekend."

SHAKE: *s.* 1) Una ganga o buen negocio. *Ej.* "You got a good shake on that used car." 2) *shakes /the/:* Estremecimiento descontrolado debido a miedo, frío o la necesidad de alcohol o drogas. *Ej.* "I need a drink so bad that I've actually got the shakes." VER TAMBIEN *no great shakes*.

SHAKE DOWN: *exp-vi.* 1) Chantajear o extorsionar por dinero. *Ej.* "The thugs are trying to shake

SHAKEDOWN

down all the local store owners." 2) Registrar minuciosamente a una persona o a un lugar. Ej. "The cops are shaking down all the local dealers."

SHAKEDOWN: s. 1) Extorsión de dinero, chantaje. Ej. "We caught him with three gees of shakedown money." 2) Una inspección minuciosa, de un lugar o de una persona. Ej. "The principal is doing a shakedown of all the gym lockers for possible drugs and weapons."

SHARK: s. Una persona muy hábil o experta en una actividad. Hay una implicación de peligro acerca de esta persona, esp. en cuanto un shark explota a los demás. Ej. "Play that guy for money? Are you crazy, he's a pool shark." VER TAMBIEN *loan shark*.

SHEBANG: VER *whole shebang /the/*

SHEEPSKIN: s. Un diploma, esp. de una universidad. Ej. "He's got his sheepskin from Harvard on the wall."

SHEET: VER *crib sheet; rap sheet; three sheets to the wind*.

SHELLACK: v. 1) Golpear o pegar severamente. Ej. "The fighter got shellacked in the last round." VER *beat someone up*. 2) Derrotar total y despiadadamente. Ej. "We're gonna shellack you guys in the championship!" VER *smear*.

SHINDIG: (sin. *bash**) s. Fiesta o celebración. Ej. "You've gotta come to the shindig were having at Tom's pad. It's gonna be a blast!"

SHINER: s. Un ojo en tinta. Ej. "You need to put some ice on that shiner."

SHINOLA: VER *not know shit from shinola*.

SHIP: VER *run a tight ship*.

SHIRT: VER *nothing but the shirt on one's back; keep one's shirt on; lose one's shirt*.

SHIRT OFF ONE'S BACK /THE/: exp. Todo: dispuesto a darlo todo, a ser totalmente generoso. Ej. "She'd give the shirt off her back to help a friend out."

SHIT: [Vul.] 1) int. Expresión de gran disgusto. Ej. "Shit, I broke another nail!" 2) s. Excremento. Ej. "Ew, there's shit on your dress!" 3) vi. Cagar. Ej. "I need to shit before we leave." 4) s. Cosa(s) u

SHITFACED

objeto(s), a menudo de uno mismo, o cosas sin valor. Ej. "How am I ever going to clean up all this shit?" 5) s. Una persona muy desagradable. Ej. "He's a shit." 6) s. Una droga ilegal, gen. marihuana o heroína. Ej. "Yo, this dope is good shit!" 7) s. Trato malo o indeseable, esp. tratamiento que parece injusto. Ej. "They are giving me a lot of shit at work." 8) s. Mentira o exageración. Ej. "Don't give me that shit, I know you're lying." 9) s. Trabajo o demandas irritantes o aburridos/as. Ej. "It's the little shit that makes this work a drag." 10) vi. Enojarse o perturbarse mucho. Ej. "He'll shit if he sees you touching his stuff." 11) vi. Mentir o exagerar mucho. Ej. "Don't shit me, just tell me the truth." 12) s. Nada, absolutamente nada. Ej. "I don't give a shit what you think." 13) adj. Mal, horrible, o terriblemente. Ej. "I feel like shit today." 14) the shit: exp. Algo excelente. Ej. "This is the shit." VER TAMBIEN *beat the shit out of; catch shit from; chicken shit; crock of shit; full of shit; get one's shit together; give a shit; go ape shit; holy shit; deep shit /in/; jack shit; no shit; know shit from shinola; piece of shit; shit a brick; shoot the shit; shovel the shit; sick of someone's shit; tough shit; up shit creek without a paddle; when the shit hits the fan*.

SHIT A BRICK: [Vul.] *exp-vi*. Enojarse o perturbarse mucho. Ej. "I shat a brick when she told me about her affair with another woman!"

SHIT ON: [Vul.] *exp-vi*. Maltratar, tratar sin respeto. Ej. "Talk about getting shat on, first she dumps me, and then she tells everyone I'm a lousy lover!"

SHIT ONE'S PANTS: [Vul.] *exp-vi*. 1) Enojarse o perturbarse mucho. Ej. "My mom is gonna shit her pants when she finds out I had a party this weekend." 2) Sentir gran susto o temor. Ej. "I nearly shit my pants when he jumped me from behind."

SHIT OUT OF LUCK: [Vul.] *exp*. Sin ninguna suerte. Ej. "You're shit out of luck Sam, we already gave the last beer away."

SHITFACED: [Vul.] *adj*. Intoxicado,

SHItHEAd

borracho. *Ej.* "You were shitfaced last night."

SHITHEAD: [Vul.] *s.* Una persona detestable y despreciable. *Ej.* "I don't ever want to see that shithead again!"

SHITLIST: *s.* Una lista de personas despreciadas e indeseables. Gen. se dice que se está on someone's shitlist que significa ser el objeto del enojo o disgusto de alguien. *Ej.* "He's on my shitlist after ridiculing me in public."

SHITS /THE/: [Vul.] *s.pl.* 1) Diarrea. *Ej.* "Get me some TP, I've got the shits." 2) Cosa o hecho molestoso, desagradable o problemático. *Ej.* "Having to work on Sunday is the shits."

SHITTER: [Vul.] (sin. crapper) *s.* Excusado. *Ej.* "Give me a few moments, I've got to use the shitter."

SHITTY: [Vul.] *adj.* Mal, malo. *Ej.* "I feel shitty." Or "What a shitty movie!"

SHITWORK: [Vul.] *s.* Trabajo o quehacer desagradable y tedioso. *Ej.* "Why do they always give me the shitwork?"

SHOESTRING: *s.* Un presupuesto muy apretado (implica vivir con muy poco dinero). *Ej.* "I'm tired of being poor and living on a shoestring all the time." Or "We'll have to travel on a shoestring if we want to make it across Europe."

SHOO-IN: *s.* Alguien de quien se espera que gane o que está asegurado/a de ser nominado o elegido. *Ej.* "With her qualifications, she's a shoo-in to get the job."

SHOOK-UP: *adj.* Emocionalmente turbado, gen. demasiado nervioso o asustado. *Ej.* "I was very shook-up after the robbery."

SHOOT BLANKS: *vi.* Tener semen infértil. *Ej.* "He was shooting blanks for years before he went to a doctor. Now his wife's got a bun in the oven."

SHOOT FOR THE STARS: *exp-vi.* Apuntar a lo más alto; fijarse la meta más alta. *Ej.* "It's better to shoot for the stars than settle for second best."

SHOOT FROM THE HIP: *exp-vi.* Decir descaradamente lo que uno piensa, esp. sin avergonzarse de expresar un comentario inapropiado o impopular. *Ej.* "The way

SHORT FUSE

he shoots from the hip, at least you know he's honest."

SHOOT ONE'S MOUTH OFF: *exp-vi.* Hablar indiscretamente o indistintamente. Ej. "He ruined the surprise party by shooting his mouth off and telling the birthday boy."

SHOOT ONESELF IN THE FOOT: *exp-vi.* Perjudicarse, o hacerse daño al hacer o decir algo estúpido, erróneo o inadecuado en frente de los demás. Ej. "Poor Joey, he's always shooting himself in the foot by saying the wrong thing to the wrong person."

SHOOT THE BULL: *exp-vi.* Conversar dentro de un contexto social esp. sobre cosas triviales para matar/dejar pasar el tiempo. Ej. "I spent the whole morning shooting the bull down at the gym."

SHOOT THE SHIT: *exp-vi.* Conversar con alguien sobre cualquier cosa en forma relajada y amistosa. Ej. "John and I shot the shit for a while before we did business."

SHOOT THE WORKS: *exp-vi.* Gastar todas las energías o recursos o jugárselo todo. Ej. "I shot the works on the housing project and it paid off big later on."

SHOOT UP: *exp-vi.* 1) Acribillar a balazos. Ej. "The bandits shot up the town." 2) Inyectar una droga a la vena. Ej. "Don't be stupid and shoot up drugs, especially not with dirty needles."

SHOOTER: *s.* Un trago, un vasito de alcohol fuerte. Ej. "Sally got drunk slamming shooters last night." VER TAMBIEN *straight shooter.*

SHOP LIFT: *exp-v.* Robar, escamotear, hurtar de una tienda. Ej. "It is so easy to shop lift from that store; the owner is blind."

SHORT: VER *sell someone short; take a long walk off a short pier.*

SHORT END OF THE STICK: *exp.* Recibir el peor trato en una situación dada. Ej. "She always gets the short end of the stick in her family, having to watch the house while they go on vacation."

SHORT FUSE: *s.* Enojo que se enciende fácilmente. Ej. "Mary has

SHOt

had a real short fuse ever since she started the grapefruit diet."

SHOT: 1) s. Un golpe, una bofetada. Ej. "That was some shot he took." 2) a shot: adv. Cada uno. Ej. "The pants are ten bucks a shot." Ver throw /a/. VER TAMBIEN big shot; give it one's best shot; mug shot; call the shots.

SHOT IN THE ARM: exp. Una expresión poco lógica si se considera que shot se refiere tanto a una inyección como a un puñete (entre otras cosas), que significa una fuerte dosis de entusiasmo o energía. Ej. "Getting that phone call from the producer was a real shot in the arm. Now I feel encouraged to continue writing."

SHOT IN THE DARK /A/: exp. Un intento para lograr algo de lo cual hay poca probablilidad de éxito. Ej. "It's a shot in the dark, but maybe Tom has that special camera lens you need."

SHOTGUN WEDDING: s. Casarse después de encontrarse embarazada la mujer. Esp. sentir presión para casarse de parte del padre armado de la novia. Ej. "When her father found out that she was pregnant, he forced them into a shotgun wedding."

SHOULDER: VER chip on one's shoulder; weight off one's shoul-

SHOtGUN WEDDiNG

SHUT ONE'S FACE

der.

SHOVE: v. Deshacerse de algo desagradable o no deseado; también, poner, llevar(se). Ej. "It felt great to tell my boss he could take this lousy job and shove it."

SHOVE OFF: v. Irse, marcharse. Ej. "Well it's getting late, I think we should shove off."

SHOVEL THE SHIT: [Vul.] exp-v. Ser el "rey" de los mentirosos, de los que dicen mentiras ingeniosas o exageraciones realmente imaginativas. Ej. "You should listen to her shovel the shit when she wants something from her dad."

SHOW: VER steal the show.

SHOW ONE SOMETHING: exp-v. Probar el valor de uno, esp. en cuanto a valentía, frente a otros. Ej. "Yeah, you talk about being a boxer, so how about you showing me something? Put up your dukes!"

SHOW ONE'S TRUE COLORS: exp-v. Revelar los puntos débiles o mostrar la verdad del espíritu de una persona. Ej. "He really showed his true colors when I asked him for a favor and he said he couldn't be bothered."

SHOW-OFF: s. Persona que le gusta exhibir, sin que le pidan, sus talentos frente a los demás. Ej. "Don't be such a show-off, we already know you're a great skier."

SHRIMP: s. Una persona pequeña. Ej. "That shrimp is good at basketball?"

SHRINK: s. Un psiquiatra. Ej. "You go to a shrink? You seem so normal!"

SHTICK: (sin. routine) s. Una rutina característica, ya sea hablada o actuada, que se usa para divertir. Ej. "You have to see Martin's shtick about people obsessed with their dogs. It's a scream!"

SHUCKS: (sin. damn) int. Expresión de descontento, conmiseración o lamentación por algún acontecimiento negativo. Ej. "Shucks, I'd like to go, but I can't."

SHUT: VER put up or shut up.

SHUT ONE'S FACE: int. Dejar de hablar en forma inmediata, esp. dejar de hacer comentarios desagradables y maleducados. Ej. "Just shut your face, I'm sick and tired of your nonsense."

SHUTEYE

SHUTEYE: VER catch a few winks.

SHYSTER: s. Una persona inmoral, inescrupulosa. Ej. "Do business with that shyster and you'll lose your shirt."

SICK OF SOMEONE'S SHIT: [Vul.] exp. Absolutamente cansado y sin intenciones de seguir soportando las groserías o el comportamiento desagradable de otra persona. Ej. "I am so sick of my boyfriend's shit that I don't ever want to see him again!"

SICKO: s. Persona mental o emocionalmente desequilibrada, o trastornada o pervertida. En todo caso, ¡evítela! Ej. "What kind of sicko runs around poking people with a needle?"

SIDEKICK: s. Mejor amigo, compañero/a constante. Ej. "Yeah, Tom's my sidekick, we go everywhere together."

SIGHT: VER out of sight; set one's sights high; set one's sights low.

SIGNIFICANT OTHER: s. El compañero especial y largamente establecido, gen. un amante o esposo. Ej. "It would be great if my significant other could meet your significant other. Let's do lunch someday."

SING: VER rat on.

SING ONE'S OWN PRAISE(S): exp-vi. Fanfarronear, cachetonearse. Ej. "He's such a bore. He always sings his own praises."

SIS: abr. Sister = Hermana. Ej. "I get along really well with my sis."

SIX OF ONE, HALF-A-DOZEN OF THE OTHER: exp. Expresión que significa que no hay una diferencia o preferencia entre dos opciones o dos cosas. Ej. "It doesn't matter to me which one you want. They're both basically the same so it's really six of one, half-a-dozen of the other."

SIXTY-NINE: s. Sexo oral simultáneo entre dos personas. Ej. "They showed a couple doing a sixty-nine in the porn movie."

SKANKY: (sin. grody, icky) adj. Baboso, asqueroso, sumamente poco atractivo. Ej. "I don't know why she's dating that skanky guy."

SKELETONS IN THE/ONE'S CLOSET: exp. Secretos poco halagadores, acriminadores que se intentan olvidar y nunca darse

SKIRT

a conocer en público. *Ej.* "We've all got our skeletons in the closet." Or "He was truly afraid that someone might discover the skeletons in his closet."

SKETCHY: *adj.* 1) Muy inseguro, muy dudoso, esp. en cuanto a calidad o a la honestidad y rectitud de una persona o situación dada. *Ej.* "I wouldn't put my life in that doctor's hands, he seems a little sketchy to me." 2) Peligroso, inseguro. *Ej.* "Dude, the waves are looking gnarly today. I think surfing would be pretty sketchy."

SKIDS: *s.* Encaminado hacia, o en el proceso de, la ruina o fracaso. Gen. *on the skids* o *hit the skids*. *Ej.* "From chief corporate executive to garbage collector, Bob had truly hit the skids."

SKIM (OFF): *v.* No declarar o quitar parte del ingreso o ganancias para evitar pagar impuestos o tomar un beneficio mayor para uno. *Ej.* "If you skim a little off the books, who's to know?"

SKIN: 1) *v.* Estafar, engañar. *Ej.* "He skinned that couple for a few hundred bucks." Ver *burn*. 2) *adj.* Desnudez, gen. se refiere a pornografía. *Ej.* "Hey, it wouldn't be a bachelor party without a skin flick!" VER TAMBIEN *by the skin of one's teeth; tough skinned; under one's skin.*

SKIN OFF MY NOSE/BACK /NO/: *exp.* No hay problema, no me molesta ni me preocupa. *Ej.* "Hey, it's no skin off my back if you want to take his car for the day."

SKIP OUT (ON): *exp-v.* Abandonar, dejar apresuradamente o desertar. *Ej.* "My partner skipped out on me after emptying our bank account and stealing my wife."

SKIP SCHOOL: (sin. *play hooky*) *exp-v.* No ir al colegio. *Ej.* "I'm a bad boy. I skipped school today."

SKIP TOWN: *exp-v.* Dejar apresuradamente un lugar, gen. un pueblo, para evitar algo desagradable como tener que pagar una cuenta, afrontar una acusación criminal, etc. *Ej.* "You boys better skip town if you know what's good for ya."

SKIRT: *s.* Mujer, tipa. *Ej.* "Hey, check out the skirt crossing the

SKIRT-CHASER

street." VER gal.

SKIRT-CHASER: s. Persona que acosa agresiva y constantemente a las mujeres, mujeriego. Ej. "Get real sweetheart, you'll never find a good man at a meat market like Bill's Pub. They're all skirt-chasers there."

SKULL: VER out of one's skull.

SKY: VER pie in the sky.

SLACKER: s. Persona que no se esfuerza en nada, excepto en evadir el trabajo y/o responsabilidad. En esto se destaca. Ej. "The problem with this country is today's youth are all a bunch of slackers."

SLAM: v. Criticar severamente, insultar. Ej. "I read that it is a really bad movie. The critics slammed it."

SLAMMER: s. La cárcel. VER clink /the/.

SLAUGHTER: v. 1) Golpear o pegar severamente. Ej. "The fighter got slaughtered in the last round." VER beat someone up. 2) Derrotar total y despiadadamente. Ej. "We're gonna slaughter you guys in the championship!" VER smear.

SLAY: v. 1) Causarle gran diversión a alguien, esp. riéndose. Ej. "That comedian slays me." 2) Sorprender, afligir terriblemente. Ej. "The news of Mary's death slayed me."

SLEAZE: s. Persona despreciable o censurable. Ej. "She's a sleaze and I don't want anything to do with her."

SLEAZEBAG: (sin. slimeball, slimbag) s. Persona inmoral y despreciable; persona que pertenece a un tipo de subespecie del género humano. Ej. "What kind of sleazebag sells drugs to kids?"

SLEEPER: s. Moco del ojo, gen. que se acumula en el rincón del ojo después de haber dormido. Ej. "Wipe your eyes, you've got sleepers in them."

SLICK: adj. 1) Atrayente, atractivo, que llama la atención. Ej. "That's a slick tie you've got on." Or "You can tell by the way he walks and talks that he thinks he's pretty slick." 2) Inteligente, brillante, astuto e innovador. Ej. "It was a slick move hiring your competitor's accountant."

SMArT-ASs

SLIME: 1) s. Persona inmoral y despreciable. Ej. "She's a slime for flirting with your boyfriend." 2) adj. Característica de una persona de este tipo. Ej. "Stay away from him, he's slime."

SLIMEBAG: VER sleazebag.

SLIMEBALL: VER sleazebag.

SLOUCH: s. Persona inepta, incapaz y a menudo perezosa además. No obstante, gen. se usa slouch en el sentido contrario. Ej. "She ain't no slouch at chess, in fact, she's thinking about turning pro."

SLUG: s. Persona floja y/o increíblemente inactiva. Ej. "You've been watching TV. all day. Get off your rear you slug!"

SLUM: v. Intentar gastar lo mínimo o intentar gastar lo menos posible, esp. a través de aprovecharse de la generosidad de los demás. Ej. "Those backpackers have been slumming around South America for six months."

SMACK: (sin. horse, junk, smack) s. Heroína. Ej. "Who's got the smack?"

SMACK-DAB: adv. De frente, directamente, derecho, gen. refiriéndose a un impacto físico o choque. Ej. "His car skidded on the gravel and went smack-dab into a tree."

SMACKER: s. Un dólar. Ej. "I'll give you five smackers for it." Ver buck.

SMACKEROO: s. Un dólar. Ej. "Here, you'll need a few smackeroos for the weekend." Ver buck.

SMALL TALK: s. Conversación liviana a la cual se recurre generalmente al conocer recién a alguien o entre amistades. Ej. "Did you have any interesting conversations, or was it all small talk?"

SMART DRUGS: exp. Compuesto/mezcla de vitaminas y minerales que supuestamente mejora la inteligencia y/o memoria. Ej. "Smart drugs are the new rage in California. Even my father is taking them."

SMARTALECK: (sin. wise guy*) s. Una persona arrogante, irritantemente presumida. Creído, farsante. Ej. "Okay smartaleck, you come up here and teach the class."

SMART-ASS: [Vul.] (sin. wise ass)

SMArTS

s. Una persona desagradablemente asertiva y segura de sí misma. Ej. "Don't be such a smart-ass or you'll never have any friends."

SMARTS: s.pl. Inteligencia. Ej. "Your kid's got smarts. He'll go far in this world."

SMASHED: adj. Muy borracho. VER plastered.

SMEAR: (sin. spank*, clobber*, cream*, kick ass*, kick some ass*, massacre*, murder*, shellac*, slaughter*) v. Derrotar en forma decisiva. Ej. "The Dolphins smeared the Cowboys 42-10."

SMELL A RAT: exp-vi. Sospechar traición o engaño o que algo anda mal. Ej. "I smell a rat Bugsy, and there's only one thing to do with a rat...get rid of it!!"

SMOKE: 1) v. Avanzar o actuar con gran velocidad y brillo. Ej. "He was smoking in the race and won easily." 2) v. Actuar bien, tener éxito. Ej. "I think I smoked that test." 3) s. Cigarrillo. Ej. "Who's got a smoke?" VER cig.

SMOKE LIKE A CHIMNEY: exp-v. Fumar muchos cigarillos con frecuencia. Ej. "I'm not surprised he got the big C. The guy smoked like a chimney for twenty years."

SMOKE SOMEONE: exp-v. Matar a alguien. Ej. "Yo, bad news, your main man got smoked by some junkie with a .45." VER waste.

SMOKER: [Vul.] (sin. blow job, B.J., head*) s. Felonía. Ej. "You paid a whore to give you a smoker? You're a desperate man."

SMOKEY: s. Un oficial de policía de carretera. Ej. "Slow down, there's a Smokey up ahead."

SMOKING: adj. Excelente, increíble. Ej. "We had a smokin' good time last night."

SMOKING GUN: s. Algo que constituye evidencia irrefutable o prueba de un crimen. Ej. "The blood stained glove was the smoking gun the cops had been looking for."

SMOOCH: v. Besar. Ej. "They were smooching in the rain."

SMOOTH AS GLASS: exp. Una extensión de agua (ej. un lago, el océano, etc.) que está en calma. Ej. "What a super day for water skiing. The lake's as smooth as glass."

SNOg

SMOOTH TALK: *exp-v.* Hablar en lenguaje amable y engañador para conseguir un objetivo. Gen. se refiere a la conquista sexual del hombre a la mujer. *Ej.* "It's almost comical, listening to that lounge lizard try and smooth talk my girlfriend."

SMOOTHIE: *s.* Persona con la habilidad para smooth talk. *Ej.* "Listen to that smoothie. He's got a velvet tongue."

SNAFU: *s.* 1) Una situación confusa o caótica. *Ej.* "There was a tremendous snafu down at the office when the computers crashed." 2) Un problema inesperado o error que detiene el desarrollo de un proyecto o plan. *Ej.* "One more snafu and we'll never get this project finished!"

SNAG: *v.* 1) Robar, a menudo robar algo rápidamente. *Ej.* "Damn, someone snagged my book." VER swipe. 2) Hacer algo rápidamente. *Ej.* "Give me a sec to snag a bite to eat."

SNAP: VER *ah snap*.

SNAZZ UP: *v.* Arreglar para quedar más de moda, elegante o llamativo. *Ej.* "She did a great job snazzing up that old restaurant."

SNAZZY: *adj.* De moda, elegante o llamativo. *Ej.* "Hey, that's a snazzy new jacket."

SNEAK A PEEK: *exp-vi.* Echar un vistazo a escondidas. Mirar furtivamente. *Ej.* "The boy sneaked a peak at her while she was changing her clothes."

SNEAK IN: *exp-vi.* 1) Entrar sin pagar a un recinto público. *Ej.* "Let's try and sneak in." 2) Entrar desadvertido. *Ej.* "He tried to sneak into class without the teacher noticing, but the teacher busted him."

SNEEZE: VER *nothing to sneeze at*.

SNITCH: 1) *s.* Un informante, el que delata información a las autoridades. *Ej.* "Find out who the snitch is!" 2) *v.* Delatar a otros. *Ej.* "His own mother snitched on him. She felt guilty about hiding the stolen money and called the police." VER *rat on*. 3) Robar. *Ej.* "Someone snitched my bag." VER *swipe*.

SNOG: *v.* Besuquearse. *Ej.* "They were snogging in the back seat of

SNOOKER

the car." Or "I snogged a girl last night." (Ing.)

SNOOKER: v. Engañar, embaucar, atrapar o estafar. Ej. "They tried to snooker me, but I caught the shysters." VER burn.

SNOOT: s. 1) Nariz. Ej. "He got hit in the snoot." Ver beak. 2) Esnob. Ej. "Those private school girls are a bunch of real snoots."

SNOOTY: adj. Esnob, presuntuoso. Ej. "That's a very snooty golf club."

SNOOZE: VER one who snoozes, loses.

SNORT: 1) s. Un trago o vasito de licor. Ej. "Let's go have a snort at the bar." 2) v. Ingerir una droga, gen. cocaína y recientemente heroína también, inhalando por la nariz. Ej. "He snorted a gram of flake and died of a heart attack."

SNOT: s. 1) (sin. bugger) Moco nasal seco. Ej. "You've got some snot on your shirt." 2) Una persona irritante y arrogante. Ej. "He's a snot man, it's such a drag to be his partner."

SNOW: 1) v. Abrumar con adulación para convencer o engañar. Ej. "Instead of being honest he tried to snow me." 2) s. Cocaína. VER coke.

SNOW JOB: s. Un esfuerzo por engañar, embaucar o convencer con adulación o manipulación. Ej. "This jerk tried to give me this snow job about how I could be a model, but I knew what he was after - my body!"

SNUFF: v. Matar a alguien. Ej. "He got snuffed walking out of the bar." VER waste.

SOAK: v. Cobrar demasiado, cobrar más de lo que vale algo. Ej. "I got soaked at the resort hotel. They charged an arm and a leg for everything."

SOAP: s. Una teleserie, una telenovela. Ej. "My daughter is obsessed with a soap. She cries when she can't watch it"

SOB: [Vul.] abr. Son of a bitch = Hijo de puta. Ej. "I don't ever want to see that SOB around here again!"

SOB STORY: exp. Una historia o cuento triste. Ej. "She gave the cop a tremendous sob story about why she was speeding, but he didn't buy it."

SOCIAL CLIMBER: s. Persona que

SOUP

trata de escalar socialmente. Ej. "Jane is such a social climber that even though she can't really afford it, she attends all the fashionable events to schmooze with the rich and famous"

SOCK: Ver *put a sock in it.*

SOCK IT TO (SOMEONE): *exp-v.* Emplear gran fuerza y resolución para conquistar o impresionar a otro. Ej. "Son, go out there and sock it to them!"

SOFT IN THE HEAD: *exp.* Poco pillo, falto de inteligencia. Una persona de escasa inteligencia que posiblemente se cayó de cabeza en la infancia. Ej. "She's got to be a bit soft in the head. There's no other explanation for sticking her hand in the blender."

SOMEONE'S NUMBER TO BE UP: *exp.* Momento en que uno debe morir, expirar, o cuando se arruina. Ej. "When your number is up, there ain't no fighting it."

SOMETHING FIERCE: *adv.* Con gran urgencia, fuerza, deseo. Ej. "You need psychological help something fierce."

SON OF A BITCH: [Vul.] 1) *s.* Una persona despreciable, vil o desagradable. Un tremendo insulto. Ej. "That son of a bitch hit my car!" 2) *int.* Expresión de molestia, enojo o frustración. Ej. "Son of a bitch, I forgot my briefcase at home!" 3) *s.* Una tarea muy molesta o difícil. Ej. "It's been one son of a bitch trying to fix my car."

SONG: (sin. *steal*) *s.* Por muy poco dinero, muy barato en cuanto al valor de algo. Ej. "Talk about buying something for a song, I only paid five gees for the car and it's practically new."

SONG AND DANCE: *exp.* Un cuento, exageración o mentira larga y intrincada cuya intención es decepcionar a alguien. Ej. "Instead of just saying, 'No, I don't want to go out with you', she gave me this song and dance about her grandmother needing a kidney transplant."

SOUND: *s.* Música, esp. el ritmo o melodía de una canción. Ej. "Nirvana had a great sound. I knew they'd go far in the music world."

SOUP: (sin. *pea soup*) *s.* Neblina espesa. Ej. "I can't see a thing, it's

Soup Up

like soup out here."

SOUP UP: *v.* Modificar un motor para aumentar su velocidad, poder o capacidad. *Ej.* "That shop specializes in souping up race cars."

SOUR GRAPES: *adj.* Malhumorado, generalmente porque otro ha logrado lo que uno no pudo. *Ej.* "Don't be sour grapes, Mary! Diane also deserved that promotion."

SOUTHPAW: *s.* Persona zurda. *Ej.* "It's tough to fight a southpaw."

SPACE: 1) *v.* Trancarse mentalmente al pensar o hablar de algo. *Ej.* "I totally spaced, what were you saying?" 2) *v.* Tener muchos pensamientos y estar mentalmente distante del cuerpo. *Ej.* "You look spaced. What are you thinking about?" 3) Olvidar. *Ej.* "Oh damn, I spaced my dentist appointment!" 4) *s.* Persona que siempre olvida su deber y/o tiene muchos pensamientos y esto hace que esté mentalmente distante del cuerpo. *Ej.* "I'm such a space today, I keep forgetting what I'm doing." VER TAMBIEN *lost in space; waste of space*.

SPACE CADET: *s.* Persona distraída, fácilmente confundida, desorientada. Alguien que parece siempre tener la cabeza en las nubes. *Ej.* "Are you a space cadet or just really stupid?"

SPACED-OUT: *adj.* Estar tan ensimismado que pareciera que la persona anda en el espacio sideral. *Ej.* "I was so spaced-out, I couldn't remember where I parked my car."

SPACE CADET

SPACEY: *adj.* Distraído, fácilmente confundido, de-sorientado. Mentalidad de alguien que siempre parece tener la cabeza en las nubes. *Ej.* "She's so spacey that often times she'll be looking for her glasses and they'll be on her head."

SPIKE

SPACING OUT /BE/: exp-vi. Estar tan ensimismado que pareciera que la persona anda en el espacio sideral. Ej. "Look at John, he's spacing out as always."

SPADE: s. Un afroamericano, una persona negra. (Desp.). Ej. "He punched the guy for calling him a spade." Ver darky.

SPANK: v. 1) Derrotar total y despiadadamente. Ej. "It was an embarrassment. Our team got spanked." Or "We're gonna spank you guys this weekend." VER smear. 2) Masturbarse. Ej. "Locked up in prison, he spent a lot of time spanking it."

SPARK STILL BURNS: VER there still burns a spark.

SPASTIC: adj. Raro, excéntrico, y gen. descoordinado, refiriéndose a una persona. Ej. "Tim's too spastic to play tennis, he always hits the ball out of the court."

SPAZ: s. Una persona hiperactiva, gen. un niño. (etim. spastic = espástico) Ej. "Check out that spaz trying to play golf. He can't even hit the ball!"

SPAZ OUT: exp-v. Reaccionar en forma exagerada, esp. con rabia. Ej. "Bill spazzed out when I told him I had trashed his car."

SPEAK OF THE DEVIL: exp. Al aparecer la persona de quien se habla. Ej. "Speak of the devil, I was just telling Teddy about your crazy adventure in Panama."

SPEED: s. Una anfetamina, un estimulante. Ej. "If you're feeling tired, take some speed."

SPENT: (sin. played) adj. 1) Algo que ha sido usado hasta sus reservas. Ej. "The keg is spent, man. Someone needs to make a beer run." 2) Persona sin energía, gen. como consecuencia de agotamiento. Ej. "We were spent after a long day of football."

SPIC: s. Un hispanoamericano. (Desp.) Ej. "There's a spic parade this weekend."

SPIFF UP: v. Hacer algo atractivo, elegante, o moderno. Ej. "They did a great job spiffing up their house."

SPIFFY: adj. Atractivo, a la moda, elegante. Ej. "That's a spiffy car you've got there Hal."

SPIKE: v. Agregar alcohol a algo, esp. cuando no se debe incluir el

SPILL ONE'S GUTS

alcohol. Ej. "The teacher busted the kids trying to spike the punch."

SPILL ONE'S GUTS: exp-vi. Revelar secretos o intimidades, confesarlo o divulgarlo todo. Ej. "Give her two drinks and she'll spill her guts."

SPILL THE BEANS: (sin. let the cat out of the bag) exp-vi. Contar un secreto o cometer una indiscreción. Ej. "We can't do the prank. Alfred spilled the beans so the teacher knows about it."

SPIN: s. La modificación del tono, significado o mensaje de una comunicación verbal para conveniencia propia. Ej. "She put a spin on what I said and completely changed my meaning." Or "Well, that's your spin on what happened."

SPIN A YARN: exp-v. Mentir de forma complicada y creativa. Ej. "I don't believe a word he says, but he sure does spin a good yarn."

SPIN-DOCTOR: s. Persona experta en cambiar el sentido de cierta información de tal manera que la presenta distorsionada. Ej. "Behind every successful politician you're sure to find a spin doctor."

SPLASH: s. Una cantidad muy pequeña de líquido. Ej. "Do you want some whiskey?" "Sure, but just a splash."

SPLIT: (sin. cut out, take off*) vi. Irse, partir desde alguna parte. Ej. "Hey, we better split if we want to get there on time."

SPLIT HAIRS: exp-vi. Complicarse más la vida, esp. encontrando imperfectos de que quejarse o discutir. Ej. "Except for you, everybody is fine with the food and wine. You however, have to split hairs over the slightest detail."

SPLIT ONE'S SIDES: exp-v. Reírse hasta el punto en que uno queda adolorido; morirse de la risa. Ej. "I practically split my sides when he imitated the teacher."

SPLIT UP: exp-vi. 1) Terminar una relación romántica. Ej. "Sally and I split up last week." 2) Partir cada uno por su lado. Ej. "Let's split up; you go right and I'll go left."

SPONGE: (sin. mooch*, freeload) v. Tener la costumbre de pedirles cosas a los amigos (ej. cigarrillos, bebidas, comida, etc.). Ej. "Stop sponging dude! Go buy your own

SQUEAKY WHEEL GETS THE GREASE

ice cream!"

SPOOK: s. Un afroamericano, una persona negra. (Desp.) VER darky.

SPOON: v. El acto de dormir acurrucados en forma de cuchara. Ej. "On a cold night, I just love to spoon with my wife."

SPORT: (sin. pal) s. Amigo, amigote. Ej. "Hey sport, you wanna go fishing?"

SPORTING WOOD: exp. Teniendo una erección. Ej. "I went through puberty sportin' wood every time the darn wind changed direction." VER woody.

SPOT: v. Prestar dinero. Ej. "Hey Ted, can you spot me a fiver?"

SPREAD ONESELF TOO THIN: exp-vi. Intentar hacer demasiado a la vez, con el resultado que nada sale bien. Ej. "Don't spread yourself too thin. You should focus your attention more."

SPRING: vi. 1) Pagar, pagar los gastos de otro. Ej. "Don't worry, I'll spring for dinner." 2) Liberar de la cárcel. Ej. "Even if you lock me up, my lawyer will spring me within two hours." VER TAMBIEN ready to spring.

SPRING CHICKEN: s. Una persona, esp. una persona de edad que se comporta más joven que para su edad. Ej. "He may be sixty, but he's a spring chicken."

SPUD: s. Patata, papa. Ej. "I don't want spuds, I want rice!"

SPUR OF THE MOMENT: exp. Un acto espontáneo o no planificado. Ej. "I decided to go to the movies on the spur of the moment."

SQUARE: s. Una persona demasiado rígida, demasiado convencional y atrasada en la moda. Ej. "That guy is such a square. He uses a pen liner in his shirt pocket."

SQUAT: VER diddly.

SQUEAK: VER squeal.

SQUEAKER: s. Algo, gen. un juego o elección, que es muy peleado y se decide por un margen estrecho. Ej. "The game was a squeaker. It was decided in the last ten seconds."

SQUEAKY WHEEL GETS THE GREASE: exp. Un proverbio que significa que la persona que hace el mayor ruido, gen. en forma de una queja, recibirá lo que se quiere.

SQUEAL

Ej. "Joe was complaining and you weren't. You know, the squeaky wheel gets the grease, I gave it to him."

SQUEAL: *v.* Delatar o traicionar a otros. *Ej.* "If you squeal on us you'll be sorry." VER *rat on*.

SQUEEZE: VER *one's main squeeze; put the squeeze on*.

STACKED: *adj.* Figura sexy y atractiva, gen. incluyendo generosos senos. Por lo tanto refiriéndose a una mujer. *Ej.* "Demi sure is stacked!"

STAGE FRIGHT! *exp.* La inhabilidad de orinar frente a otros. *Ej.* "I hate going to concerts because the bathrooms are so crowded and I always get stage fright."

STALLION: VER *stud*.

STAND: VER *stand someone up; one-night stand; cannot stand someone*.

STAND SOMEONE UP: *exp-vi.* No cumplir con una cita con otra persona. *Ej.* "I'm through with him! He's stood me up for the last time."

STARS: VER *shoot for the stars*.

STARS IN ONE'S EYES: *exp.* 1) Una sensación irreal como resultado de una feliz noticia, o una sorpresa muy agradable, o al estar enamorado. *Ej.* "They had stars in their eyes during the wedding." 2) Pensamiento de uno que espera ser famoso. *Ej.* "My daughter has stars in her eyes. She wants to be like Madona."

STASH: 1) *v.* Esconder o guardar en un lugar secreto. *Ej.* "We'd better stash the guns before the cops get here." 2) *s.* La provisión de uno de drogas ilegales. *Ej.* "I keep a little stash just in case I

STArs IN oNE'S eYES

Stick It to (Some)One

get the urge to smoke."

STATIC: s. Oposición, réplica insolente, objeción. Ej. "I'm not going to change my opinion, so don't bother giving me any static."

STAY REAL: exp. Una variante de despedida, deseándole buena suerte y salud a la persona. Ej. "Stay real bro, I'll catch you later."

STEAL: (sin. song) s. Por muy poco dinero, muy barato en cuanto al valor de algo. Ej. "I had to buy the car. At two grand, it was a steal."

STEAL THE SHOW: exp-vi. Cuando una persona que no es el supuesto centro de atención en una película, conferencia, etc. es tan buena que atrae la mayor parte de la atención y elogios. Ej. "Even though it was a supporting role, her performance stole the show."

STEAM: v. Enojarse, enfurecerse. Ej. "I was steaming when she called me a schmo." VER TAMBIEN let off steam; blow off steam.

STEAMED UP: adj. Enojado, muy enfadado, como el personaje de una tira cómica al que le sale humo por las orejas. Ej. "The judge got steamed up when the lawyer accused him of being corrupt."

STEAMY: adj. Erótico, sexy, tan caliente que produce vapor. No se usa para una persona, solo para una cosa o acción. Ej. "It was such a steamy love scene in the movie, that my boyfriend started getting a woody."

STICK: vi. Engañar, estafar, esp. para cobrar de más. Ej. "The taxi driver tried to stick me because he thought I was a foreigner." VER burn. VER TAMBIEN cancer stick; get on the stick; night stick; short end of the stick.

STICK IT IN ONE'S EAR: int. Expresión de rabia o frustración. Ej. "After he insulted me I told him to go stick it in his ear!"

STICK IT OUT: exp-vi. Aguantarlo. Ej. "I know you don't like geometry, but you have to stick it out and finish the semester."

STICK IT TO (SOME)ONE: exp-vi. Cometer una injusticia con alguien, esp. obligar a esa persona a pagar un alto precio por algo, ya sea

STICK ONE'S NOSE IN

monetariamente o de otra manera. Ej. "I hate taking a taxi in a foreign city. The drivers are always trying to stick it to you."

STICK ONE'S NOSE IN: exp-vi. Inmiscuirse en asuntos ajenos. Ej. "Can you believe the way she's always sticking her nose in other people's affairs?"

STICK TO ONE'S GUNS: exp-vi. Mantenerse firme en una posición aunque sea criticada. Ej. "If you believe in your idea, you should stick to your guns and hang in there."

STICK TO/AT SOMETHING: exp-vi. Demostrar pujanza al intentar cumplir con una tarea, ya sea de larga o corta duración. Ej. "I know calculus is difficult son, but you just have to stick to it." Or "I know if you stick at it, you'll be able to figure it out."

STICK-IN-THE-MUD: s. Persona sin imaginación ni entusiasmo, esp. alguien que se niega a experimentar con nuevas actividades o cosas. Ej. "Don't invite that stick-in-the-mud, he's no fun at all."

STICKS /THE/: s.pl. Un área remota o rural. Ej. "Aren't you afraid to live in the sticks all by yourself?"

STICKUP: s. Un robo, gen. bajo el blanco de un arma de fuego. Ej. "Okay folks, this is a stickup! Put your money on the floor and no one will get hurt."

STIFF: s. 1) Cadáver. Ej. "They found a stiff in his basement." 2) Alguien que no paga o no puede pagar sus deudas. Ej. "With the number of stiffs in this business, it's hard to make a buck." 3) Una persona considerada forzada, pedante, o demasiado formal. Ej. "He's such a stiff that he wears a coat and tie to the beach." 4) Una persona. Ej. The lucky stiff won a free trip to Hawaii." 5) Alguien que da poca propina. Ej. "The worst thing about this restaurant is the number of stiffs who come in here."

STIFLE IT: int. Dejar de hablar, quedarse callado. Ej. "I was sick of listening to his B.S. so I told him to stifle it." VER put a sock in it.

STING: s. Embaucamiento complicado y fraudulento, esp. una trampa puesta por oficiales de la policía secreta para detener a criminales. Ej. "They set up a sting at the local pawn shop to catch the jewel thieves."

STINK: vi. Ser tan malo o de tan mala calidad que se llega a ser lamentable. Ej. "That movie Waterworld really stunk. I left before it even finished." VER TAMBIEN raise a stink.

STINKING: 1) adj. Maldito, despreciable. Ej. "She's a no-good, stinking person." 2) adv. Se usa para expresar extremos o excesos. Ej. "That family is stinking rich." Or "He got stinking drunk on Tequila."

STIR THINGS UP: exp-v. Animar una situación. Ej. "This party is so boring I think I'll stir things up a bit."

STIR-CRAZY: adj. Intranquilo, agitado o bordeando en la locura debido a un largo encierro o inmovilidad. Ej. "I'm going stir-crazy waiting for the cable company to come and fix the TV."

STITCH IN TIME SAVES NINE /A/: (sin. an ounce of prevention is worth a pound of cure) exp. Un poco de prevención antes que se agrave un problema evita muchas molestias más adelante. Ej. "Hey, a stitch in time saves nine. If you do the job correctly the first time, you won't have problems later on."

STOKED: adj. Excelente, fantástico. Ej. "I'm stoked for the road trip. I've been psyched to go for weeks." VER awesome.

STOMACH: VER one's eyes are bigger than one's stomach.

STOMP: VER shellac.

STOMPING GROUND: s. Un lugar habitual o favorito para encontrarse o visitar. Ej. "Bar Central is my stomping ground."

STONED: (sin. wasted, baked) adj. Efecto después de fumar marihuana. Gen. indica ganas de no hacer nada, salvo ver tele y/o comer y eludir a las figuras autoritarias. Ej. "I'm too stoned to do anything except sit here."

STONER: (sin. pot head) s. Persona que fuma marihuana en forma habitual. Ej. "She's a stoner, but she's also a brilliant mathematician."

STRaIGHt

STRAIGHT: 1) s. Heterosexual. *Ej.* "Just because he has a lisp doesn't mean he's not straight." 2) adj. No estar sufriendo los efectos de alcohol o drogas. *Ej.* "I'm not worried about taking a blood test because I'm straight." 3) s. Alguien que ha dejado de ser criminal o involucrado en actividades ilegales. *Ej.* "I'm straight. I learned my lesson in the big house." 4) *go straight:* exp-vi. Ponerse honesto y observante de la ley. *Ej.* "After twenty years of crime, he decided to go straight."

STRAIGHT ARROW: s. Una persona honesta y rígidamente convencional. *Ej.* "He won't speed on the highway, he's too much of a straight arrow."

STRAIGHT SHOOTER: s. Persona honesta, justa y directa, esp. en cuanto a tratos de negocios. *Ej.* "You can trust her, she's a straight shooter."

STRAIGHT UP: (sin. word up) exp. La verdad. *Ej.* "Straight up man, tell it like it is."

STRAW THAT BROKE THE CAMEL'S BACK: exp. El incidente o palabra(s) que colma(n) una situación que se desequilibra o conduce a desbarajuste. *Ej.* "I could deal with the lack of affection, but when he started talking about me behind my back, it was the straw that broke the camel's back."

STREAK: v. Correr desnudo en un espacio público. Gen. se hace como una travesura, aunque uno se pregunta sobre el estado de sanidad mental de una persona que accede a este tipo de comportamiento. *Ej.* "I'll give you five bucks if you streak through the girls locker room."

STREAKER: s. Persona que corre desnuda en un lugar público. *Ej.* "They forced him to get psychological counseling after he repeatedly appeared naked at little league baseball games."

STREET KID: s. Un niño que se pasa en la calle, y que a menudo se mete en líos. *Ej.* "Delinquency has increased with the added number of street kids."

STRESSED OUT /BE/: exp-vi. Sentir mucho apremio, temor y/o tensión.

Ej. "I'm so stressed out trying to finish my thesis that I'm about ready to lose it."

STRETCH ONE'S LEGS: *exp-v.* Levantarse y caminar un rato después de haber estado sentado durante mucho tiempo. *Ej.* "By the third act of the opera, I really needed to stretch my legs."

STRIKE IT RICH: *exp-vi.* Repentinamente ganar mucho dinero. *Ej.* "I struck it rich in the stock market."

STRIKE OUT: *exp-vi.* Fracasar, no tener éxito en un esfuerzo o no lograr el fin deseado. *Ej.* "I struck out with everyone I asked to the prom."

STRING: VER *pull (some) strings*.

STRING BEAN: *s.* Alguien alto, delgado. *Ej.* "Hey string bean, don't your mommy feed you?"

STRING SOMEONE OUT TO DRY: VER *hang someone out to dry*

STRIPPER: *s.* Alguien que hace striptease (i.e. se quita toda la ropa). *Ej.* "Old George has a thing for strippers."

STROKE: *v.* Inflar el ego, adular. *Ej.* "That lounge lizard sure is good at strokin' the lady folks."

STRUNG-OUT: *adj.* Inquieto, nervioso, estar mal de salud por el uso prolongado de drogas. *Ej.* "She's been strung out for over a year."

STRUT ONE'S STUFF: *exp-v.* Desempeñarse al máximo, lo mejor posible, ante los demás para hacer gala del talento o físico de uno. *Ej.* "He's unabashed to go out and strut his stuff to the audience." Or "Look at her strutting her stuff while she walks down the beach."

STUBBORN AS A MULE: *exp.* Una persona muy porfiada o desobediente. *Ej.* "Don't even bother trying to convince him. Once he's decided something he's as stubborn as a mule."

STUCK UP: *exp.* Una persona que adopta una actitud superior con otros, esp. basada en clase social o en supuesto nivel de sofisticación. *Ej.* "She's so stuck up she won't date anyone unless his family belongs to the same country club."

STUD: (sin. *stallion*) *s.* 1) Un

 STUFF

hombre considerado viril y sexualmente activo. Hombre sexy. Ej. "When did you start dating that stud? He looks like a model!" 2) Persona con habilidad o talento sobresaliente en un campo dado. Ej. "If you have a computer question, go ask Michael, he's a stud with computers."

STUFF: s. Drogas ilegales. Ej. "You guys want to smoke some great stuff?" VER TAMBIEN green stuff; hard stuff; hot stuff; strut one's stuff.

STUFF IT: int. 1) ¡Qué me importa! Ej. "Stuff it! I'm going to the party whether he wants me to or not." 2) Enviar a alguien a un lugar desagradable. Ej. "If you don't like the work I've done, you can stuff it." (Ing.)

STUFF ONE'S FACE: exp-v. Comer grandes cantidades de comida en forma grosera. Ej. "It's a great restaurant 'cause you can stuff your face for five bucks."

STUFFED /BE/: exp-vi. Tener el estómago muy lleno de comida. Ej. "I'm stuffed, if I eat anymore I'll puke."

STYLING: adj. A todo lujo, esp. haber gastado mucho dinero para hacer algo de alta categoría. Ej. "Wow, this place is stylin', it must be expensive."

SUCK: v. ¡Ser desagradable, muy malo, ofensivo, lamentable, antipático - en fin, si es negativo, es apropiado para este verbo demasiado común y descriptivo! Ej. "He sucks at baseball." Or "You suck for ratting on me." Or "The movie sucked." Or "Let's go, this place sucks."

SUCK DOWN: v. Beber o comer. Ej. "I was so thirsty I sucked down a whole bottle of water."

SUCK FACE: exp-v. ¡Besarse, muy apasionadamente, con harta saliva y movimiento de lengua! Ej. "It was so romantic the first time we sucked face."

SUCK IN: exp-v. Estafar, engañar, embaucar. Ej. "You got sucked in to that land scheme? You are a loser!" Ver burn.

SUCK IT UP: exp-v. Aguantar dolor y sufrimiento para poder terminar algo difícil. No ceder al cansancio y terminar fuerte. Ej.

SUPER-DUPER

"Suck it up man, we've only got a few more miles to go."

SUCK UP TO: *exp-v.* Comportarse en forma zalamera, lisonjeramente, para obtener un favor. Ej. "She's pathetic how she always tries to suck up to her boss."

SUCKER: 1) *s.* Persona fácilmente engañada o embaucada. Alguien indistintamente atraída a algo. Ej. "I'm a sucker for stray dogs, I always take them home." Or "There's a sucker born every minute just waiting to be ripped-off." 2) *s.* Una cosa no especificada y a menudo problemática. Ej. "I can't get this sucker to work." 3) *v.* Engañar, estafar o embaucar, esp. manipular para hacer algo desagradable o imprudente. Ej. "He suckered me into cutting class when he knew I'd get in trouble."

SUCKY: *adj.* Malo/a, horrible, muy desagradable. Ej. "I had a sucky time at the party." Or "What a sucky movie! It was boring and dumb."

SUGAR: (sin. honey, pumpkin) *int.* Expresión afectuosa para tratarse en pareja. Ej. "Hey sugar, how was work today?"

SUGAR DADDY: *s.* Un hombre adinerado y mayor que le da regalos caros y/o dinero a una persona joven a cambio de favores sexuales o compañía. Ej. "Look at that babe all over that old guy. He must be her sugar daddy."

SUIT: *s.* Hombre que viste de terno. Ej. "That suit has a real attitude problem."

SUN: VER *where the sun doesn't/don't shine.*

SUNDAY: VER *wear one's Sunday's best.*

SUNDAY DRIVER: *s.* Persona que conduce muy lento, esp. dícese de una persona que conduce sin rumbo fijo, sólo por diversión o para relajarse. Ej. "These Sunday drivers are so slow they drive me up the wall!"

SUPER: *adv.* Sumamente, muy. Ej. "I had a super time last night." Or "That was super fun."

SUPER-DUPER: *adj.* Fantástico, excelente, maravilloso. Ej. "That was a super-duper play."

SURF THE NET

SURF THE NET: *exp-v.* Conectarse a la red/Internet y trasladarse de de sitio en sitio para explorar las infinitas posibilidades de la red. *Ej.* "My kid says he's surfing the net for news items, but I bet he's checking out those porno pages."

-SVILLE: *sufijo.* Que está lleno, repleto con algo. *Ej.* "I love camp, it's funsville." Or "Let's go. This place is dullsville."

SWALLOW: *v.* Creer una mentira o tragarse un cuento. Ser ingenuo. *Ej.* "I can't believe he swallowed that line about your dog eating your homework."

SWEAT: *v.* 1) Preocuparse de, inquietarse por. *Ej.* "Hey, don't sweat it, you can pay me back anytime." 2) Extraer información de alguien bajo coacción. *Ej.* "The cops sweated the suspected drug dealer for hours." VER TAMBIEN *no sweat.*

SWEAT BLOOD: *exp-v.* Preocuparse terriblemente, crear gran ansiedad. *Ej.* "She was sweating blood trying to finish her thesis in time."

SWEAT BULLETS: *exp-v.* Sudar profusamente debido a miedo. *Ej.* "I was sweating bullets waiting for the verdict."

SWEAT LIKE A PIG: *exp-v.* Sudar profusamente. *Ej.* "He was sweating like a pig in the sauna."

SWEET: *adj.* Excelente, fantástico. *Ej.* "Sweet play by Jordan." VER *awesome.*

SWEET TALK: *exp-v.* Usar un lenguaje seductor. *Ej.* "Even though I knew he was full of it, it was nice to hear him try and sweet talk me."

SWIFT: *adj.* Ingenioso, con recursos o inteligente. *Ej.* "It was a swift idea getting your wife to call in sick for you." Or "Oh, he's a swift one, you'd better watch yourself!" VER TAMBIEN *not too swift.*

SWIM ON: *v.* Cuando una prenda de ropa le queda nadando, le queda grande. *Ej.* "It's a nice coat, but it swims on you."

SWING: *vi.* 1) Ser ahorcado. *Ej.* "You're gonna swing from the highest branch for your crime." 2) Organizar con éxito o cumplir una meta según un plan. *Ej.* "I don't know how I'm going to swing these

SWITCHEROO

different obligations." 3) Tener relaciones sexuales en forma promiscua. Ej. "People who swing in the age of AIDS are simply crazy." 4) Intercambiar parejas para relaciones sexuales. Se usa específicamente con parejas casadas. Ej. "Some couple approached my wife and I at a party, and asked us if we'd like to swing."

SWING BOTH WAYS: exp. Bisexual. Ej. "He swings both ways to increase his chances of getting lucky." VER *double gated*.

SWINGER: s. 1) Alguien que tiene relaciones sexuales con muchas personas. Ej. "I hear that Leonardo guy is a real swinger."

2) Alguien dentro de una pareja, especialmente un matrimonio, que intercambia pareja sexual. Ej. "It's not so easy any more to find a couple of other swingers for a good old-fashioned orgy."

SWINGING: adj. Festivo, divertido, animado, lleno de emoción. Ej. "The band was swinging last night."

SWIPE: (sin. five finger something, snag*, boost, clip*, nick, lift*, snitch*, pinch*) v. Robar, sacar sin permiso. Ej. "Okay, who swiped my pen?" VER TAMBIEN *take a swipe at*.

SWITCH HITTER: s. Bisexual. Ej. "Tom's a switch hitter, he goes both ways." VER *double gated*.

SWITCH OFF: exp-v. Dejar de prestar atención, perder interés o abstraerse.

SWING BOTH WAYS

Ej. "I just switch off when he launches into his traumatic childhood stories."

SWITCHEROO: s. Un reverso inesperado o un intercambio de

SYSTEM

objetos inesperado. Ej. "I thought I had received the envelope with the money in it, but they had done a switcheroo on me. There was nothing but paper in it."

SYSTEM /THE/: s. El orden establecido percibido o aquello que se percibe como tal. Ej. "You need smarts to beat the system."

T

AND A: [Vul.] exp. Tits and ass = Tetas y culo; normalmente se usa en relación a pornografía o striptease. Ej. "Let's check out a T and A show tonight."

T.P.: 1) abr. Toilet paper = Papel higiénico. Ej. "Hey, there's no t.p. in here!" 2) v. Tapar, tapizar o incluso llenar un lugar/recinto con papel higiénico. Ej. "It was so fun when we t.p.'ed the science building."

TAB: s. Una cuenta en un restaurante o bar. Ej. "I'll pay for the drinks. I have a tab with the club."

TABLE: VER drink someone under the table; under the table.

TABLE-HOP: v. Irse de mesa en mesa para saludar a amigos y conocer a gente nueva. Ej. "She can never sit still in a restaurant, she's always table-hopping."

TACKY: adj. 1) De mal gusto, sin estilo. Ej. "What a tacky house." 2) Grosero, de mal gusto, ofensivo. Ej. "When he gets drunk, he starts making the tackiest comments."

TAIL: 1) s. Alguien que sigue y observa las acciones de otro. Ej. "Am I paranoid or do we have a tail following us?" 2) s. Las nalgas. Ej. "You need to lose a few pounds off your tail, darling." 3) [Vul.] s. Relación sexual o la mujer/niña con quien se tuvo una relación sexual. Ej. "I got me some tail last night!" 4) v. Seguir y mantener bajo vigilancia. Ej. "I want you to tail that crook. Don't let him out of your sight." 5) one's tail: Uno mismo, a menudo usado en forma peyorativa. Ej. "Get your tail over here right now!" Or "I've been working my tail off." VER TAMBIEN on someone's tail; off someone's tail; one's tail off; with one's tail between one's legs; get the cat by the tail.

TAILGATE: v. Seguir otro vehículo

demasiado cerca. *Ej.* "They crashed their cars because Julie was tailgating."

TAKE: VER *on the take*.

TAKE A BREAK: *exp-vi.* Tomarse un recreo de manejar, trabajar, estudiar, etc. *Ej.* "If you want to take a break, I'll drive for a while."

TAKE A DIVE: *exp-vi.* Fallar o perder intencionalmente, esp. ser derrotado en boxeo luego de un acuerdo predeterminado. *Ej.* "The boxer must have taken a dive to lose against that weakling."

TAKE A DUMP: [Vul.] (sin. pinch a loaf) *exp-vi.* Manera muy coloquial de referirse al acto de defecar. *Ej.* "Wait a sec, I need to take a dump before we go."

TAKE A HIKE: *int.* Para expresar disgusto con alguien y el deseo de que esa persona se aleje de la presencia de uno. *Ej.* "Take a hike, you don't belong here!"

TAKE A LEAK: *exp-vi.* Manera muy coloquial de referirse al acto de orinar. *Ej.* "Where's the can? I need to take a leak."

TAKE A LOAD OFF: *int.* Sentarse y tomar un descanso. *Ej.* "Take a load off, you make me nervous standing there."

TAKE A LONG WALK OFF A SHORT PIER: *exp-vi.* Desaparecer para siempre, nunca más volver. Gen. esto se dice en broma. *Ej.* "I've got a better idea, why don't you take a long walk off a short pier."

TAKE A POWDER: (syn cut out, make tracks) *exp-vi.* Moverse o hacer abandono rápidamente, esp. arrancar. *Ej.* "If you know what's good for you, you'll take a powder before the sheriff gets back."

TAKE A SWIPE AT: *exp-vi.* Dar puñetazos. *Ej.* "He took a swipe at my head, but I ducked just in time."

TAKE A WALK: *int.* ¡Lárgate! *Ej.* "Take a walk, you loser!"

TAKE A WHACK AT: (sin. have a whack at) *exp-vi.* Probar, hacer un intento. *Ej.* "It looks difficult, but I'll take a whack at it."

TAKE FIVE: *exp-vi.* Tomarse un breve descanso, generalmente de unos 5 minutos. *Ej.* "Okay folks, take five and then we'll start from the top."

TAKE IT EASY: *int.* Una orden para

TAKE IT ON THE CHIN

relajarse. *Ej.* "Take it easy, we'll get to the airport in time."

TAKE IT ON THE CHIN: *exp-vi.* Aguantar o sufrir una derrota o castigo. *Ej.* "He really took it on the chin when his girlfriend dumped him."

TAKE IT THERE: *exp.* Interpretar algo, gen. un insulto en forma personal. *Ej.* "No man, don't take it there, I ain't trying to dog you."

TAKE OFF: *exp-vi.* 1) (sin. split, cut out) Irse de un lugar, retirarse. *Ej.* "They're not here, they took off a while ago." 2) Experimentar éxito rápido o repentino. *Ej.* "Her business really took off with the new advertising."

TAKE ONE'S SWEET TIME: *exp-vi.* Demorarse más de lo necesario en hacer algo o llegar a alguna parte. *Ej.* "My car's been in the garage for over a month. They're certainly taking their sweet time fixing it." Or "Don't bother me, I'm gonna take my sweet time getting ready."

TAKE OUT: *exp-vi.* Destruir, eliminar. *Ej.* "They took out the safe's door with plastic explosive."

TAKE (SOMEONE) APART: (sin. tear apart) *exp-vi.* Pegarle fuerte a alguien, golpear en forma sostenida a una persona. *Ej.* "He'll take you apart if you fight him."

TAKE SOMEONE FOR A RIDE: (sin. pull one over on someone, pull the wool over someone's eyes) *exp-vi.* Engañar o estafar a alguien. *Ej.* "Did he ever take her for a ride, pretending he loved her when he was only interested in her money."

TAKE (SOMEONE) FOR BAD: *exp-vi.* Derrotar (a alguien) en un deporte o competencia. *Ej.* "You talk a good game, but you know that on the court I will take you for bad."

TAKE SOMEONE OFF SOMEONE'S HIGH HORSE: *exp-vi.* Poner a alguien en su lugar, esp. cuando tal persona tiene una actitud superior a los demás. *Ej.* "They act so stuck up that it's time someone took them off their high horse."

TAKE (SOMEONE) OUT: *exp-vi.* Matar a alguien, esp. cumpliendo una orden de la Mafia. *Ej.* "Yeah, they took him out for squealing to the cops." Ver waste.

TAKE SOMEONE/SOMETHING

TAKE TO THE CLEANERS

APART: (sin. tear apart) *exp-vi.* 1) Dar una paliza, golpear. *Ej.* "Tyson took Foreman apart in one round." VER *beat someone up.* 2) Criticar con mucho rigor. *Ej.* "The professor took his thesis apart in front of the whole class."

TAKE TEN: *exp-vi.* Tomarse un breve descanso, generalmente de unos 10 minutos. *Ej.* "I told them to take ten and they've been gone for over an hour."

TAKE THE BULL BY THE HORNS: (sin. get the bull by the horns) *exp-vi.* Tomar, conseguir, o tener el control total de una persona o situación. *Ej.* "If you want to control the situation, you need to take the bull by the horns and tell them who's boss."

TAKE THE CHAIR OUT FROM UNDERNEATH ONE: *exp-vi.* Quitarle el trabajo a otro en forma artera. *Ej.* "I was all set to get a promotion, but then Jane came and took the chair out from underneath me."

TAKE THE HEAT: *exp-vi.* Soportar una fuerte crítica o censura. *Ej.* "Listen, if you can't take the heat from the press, you'd better get out of the kitchen."

TAKE THE HELM: VER *grab the helm.*

TAKE THE PLUNGE: *exp-vi.* Dar un paso en territorio desconocido, esp. después de un largo período de deliberación o duda. *Ej.* "After dating for three years, they decided to take the plunge and tie the knot."

TAKE THE RAP: *exp-vi.* Ser inocente y aceptar el castigo o la culpa por un delito. *Ej.* "She was always taking the rap for her little brother because she hated to see him get in trouble."

TAKE THE WIND OUT OF ONE'S SAILS: (sin. knock the wind out of someone's sails) *exp-vi.* Sentirse humillado o perder el entusiasmo por algo o alguien. *Ej.* "I thought we had something serious between us, so it took the wind out my sail when I saw him with another girl."

TAKE TO THE CLEANERS: (sin. lose one's shirt) *exp-vi.* Perder todo el dinero o posesiones, esp. producto de las apuestas o divorcio. *Ej.* "I figure I might as well

 **TA**le

go to Vegas, 'cause my ex-wife is going to take me to the cleaners anyway."

TALE: VER *tall tale; tattle tale.*

TALK: VER *all talk, no action; pep talk; small talk; smooth talk; sweet talk.*

TALK SHOP: *v.* Conversar sobre un tema de interés común relacionado con el trabajo. *Ej.* "That was a great dinner darling. If you'll excuse us, Joe and I will go outside and talk shop for a while."

TALK THROUGH ONE'S HAT: *exp-v.* Hablar de algo sobre lo cual no se tiene conocimiento. *Ej.* "He was talking through his hat when he told you how to repair your car."

TALK TURKEY: *exp-v.* Hablar franca y sustantivamente, ir al grano de un asunto. *Ej.* "Enough BS, let's talk turkey."

TALKING HEAD: *s.* Comentarista de televisión que aparece en la pantalla sólo con la cabeza y la parte superior del cuerpo visibles. *Ej.* "He's not very intelligent, but he makes a good talking head."

TALL ORDER: *s.* Pedido o solicitud difícil o imposible de cumplir. *Ej.* "It's a tall order to be both a good father and a successful business man."

TALL TALE: (sin. *fat lie, whopper**) *s.* Mentira o exageración. *Ej.* "You caught a 50-pound salmon? That sounds like a tall tale to me."

TAN SOMEONE'S HIDE: *exp-v.* Zurrar, azotar o golpear a alguien. *Ej.* "My daddy's gonna tan my hide for breaking his favorite record."

TANK: *s.* Prisión, cárcel. VER *clink /the/.*

TANKED: *adj.* Borracho, muy ebrio. *Ej.* "You were so tanked last night that you started hitting on your best friend's girlfriend." VER *plastered.*

TAPPED (OUT): *adj.* Estar sin dinero. *Ej.* "I can't go to the movies, I'm tapped."

TATTLE TALE: *s.* Alguien que revela secretos, gen. usado por o refiriéndose a niños. *Ej.* "Keep it a secret, don't be a tattle tale."

TEAR: *s.* Una borrachera, una juerga, una parranda. *Ej.* "He's a laid-back guy, but when he goes on a tear...watch out!"

TEAR APART: VER *take (someone)*

TEN-FOOT POLE

apart.

TEAR INTO: *exp-vi.* 1) Atacar con entusiasmo, esp. comer con gran ahínco. Ej. "Tear into the chicken, it's delicious!" 2) Criticar dura y severamente. Ej. "She tore into me for flirting with another girl."

TEARJERKER: *s.* Una historia, situación o actuación demasiado sentimental o dramática. Ej. "The movie was such a tearjerker, I was blubbering like an idiot."

TEASE: *s.* Aquel que entusiasma sexualmente a otro para finalmente decir no. Ej. "I thought I was going to get lucky, but she was just a tease."

TEE SOMEONE OFF: *exp-v.* Enojar o irritar. Ej. "You sure know what buttons to push to tee me off." Or "I got teed off when she came home late again."

TEENYBOPPER: *s.* Un adolescente, esp. uno interesado en la última moda. Ej. "To make this hair product a success, we need to exploit the teenybopper market."

TEETH: VER *by the skin of one's teeth; lie through one's teeth; kick in the teeth; cut one's teeth on.*

TELL IT LIKE IT IS: (sin. *not mince words, tell the naked truth*) *exp-vi.* Expresar una opinión en forma muy directa y sin tomar en cuenta los sentimientos de la persona con quien se habla, esp. si se trata de algo difícil o doloroso. Ej. "I like that about her. She doesn't mince words, she just tells it like it is."

TELL ME ABOUT IT: *int.* Expresión que significa que no es necesario explicar o decir nada más sobre algo porque uno lo comprende totalmente. Ej. "Tell me about it, I had the same problem with my insurance company last month."

TELL (SOMEONE) OFF: *exp-vi.* Gritarle a alguien, retar severamente. Ej. "She told me off for insulting her younger brother."

TEMPER: VER *throw (a) temper tantrum(s).*

TEN: *adj.* Nota máxima, puntuación más alta en una evaluación o prueba. Ej. "She's definitely a ten." Or "I'd give that performance a ten." VER TAMBIEN *take ten.*

TEN-FOOT POLE: VER *touch something/someone with a ten-*

TEN SPOT

foot pole.

TEN SPOT: s. Un billete de diez dólares. Ej. "Who's got a ten spot I can borrow?"

TGIF: *abr.* Thank God It's Friday; significando el fin de la semana laboral y hora de fiesta. Ej. "After such a stressful week, all I can say is TGIF."

THAT EMPTY FEELING: *exp.* La sensación que se tiene cuando, luego de hacer planes para hacer algo, no es posible realizarlos debido a algún contratiempo inesperado y, sin embargo, queda el deseo de desarrollar esa actividad. Ej. "I hate that empty feeling. We were all set to go when something came up at the office and I had to work."

THAT'S THAT: *exp.* Punto final, término del asunto en cuestión; expresión para poner término a algo. Ej. "You're not going out tonight and that's that."

THAT'S THE WAY THE BALL BOUNCES: VER *that's the way the cookie crumbles.*

THAT'S THE WAY THE COOKIE CRUMBLES: (sin. that's the way the ball bounces) *exp.* Una afirmación que reconoce lo imprevista que puede ser la vida y la impotencia de uno para cambiar esta situación. Ej. "Sorry you didn't win the contest, but that's the way the cookie crumbles."

THERE: VER *not all there; hang in there; take it there.*

THERE IS NO GETTING AROUND IT: *exp.* Una acción o decisión que hay que tomar. Ej. "I know you don't want to go to your in-laws, but there's no getting around it."

THERE IS TRUTH IN WINE: *exp.* Un poco de alcohol basta para que se diga la verdad, al perderse las inhibiciones. Ej. "Well, if she said it after a few drinks, it probably is how she feels. As they say, there's truth in wine."

THERE STILL BURNS A SPARK: (sin. spark still burns) *exp.* Todavía sentir afecto por alguien, gen. un amante o querido, después de haber terminado la relación o perder contacto. Ej. "Despite the fact that they split up five years ago, there still burns a spark on his part."

THERE YOU GO: *exp.* Estás en lo correcto. Bien, has dado en el clavo; expresión que indica que la otra persona ha comprendido nuestra idea. *Ej.* "There you go, now you understand what I'm talking about."

THICK: *adj.* Duro de mollera, que le cuesta entender. *Ej.* "Are you thick or do you have cotton in your ears?" VER TAMBIEN *lay it on thick*.

THICK HEADED: *adj.* Duro de mollera, que le cuesta entender. *Ej.* "How many times do I have to explain? You're so thick headed it's incredible."

THING: *s.* 1) Una aversión, una obsesión, un fuerte deseo. *Ej.* "He's got this thing about women in pink panty hose." 2) La moda o manía actual. *Ej.* "A talented marketer knows beforehand what the latest thing will be." Ver tamién *one's (own) thing; poor thing*.

THING OR TWO /A/: *exp.* 1) Que se sabe de lo que se está hablando. *Ej.* "Ask my grandma, after raising ten kids she knows a thing or two about parenting." 2) Que se tienen amplios conocimientos al respecto. *Ej.* "Before you decide to get married, I have a thing or two I want to say."

THINGAMAJIG: (sin. *thingy, whatchamacallit*) *s.* Cosa, objeto, artefacto cuyo nombre se ha olvidado o se desconoce. *Ej.* "Pass me that thingamajig on top of the whatchamacallit."

THINGY: VER *thingamajig*.

THIRD BASE: *exp.* Acariciar los genitales de otro. *Ej.* "I was so psyched! We went to third base on the first date!" VER etimología de *first base*.

THIRD TIME'S THE CHARM /THE/: *exp.* La perseverancia en un intento conduce finalmente al éxito. *Ej.* "You should give it another shot. Oftentimes, the third time's the charm."

THIRD WHEEL: (sin. *odd man/woman out*) *exp.* Ser la tercera persona con una pareja o estar sin pareja cuando todos los demás están acompañados. *Ej.* "I hate going out with Bob and Linda, I always feel like the third wheel."

THOU: (sin. *grand, gee**) *s.* Mil dólares. *Ej.* "I'll give you two thou

THREADS

for the car."

THREADS: (sin. rags, rag*) s.pl. Ropas. Ej. "Nice threads you've got there."

THREE SHEETS TO THE WIND: exp. Muy borracho, casi inconsciente. Ej. "He wasn't just drunk, he was three sheets to the wind." Ver *plastered*.

THRONE /THE/: (sin. head, can /THE/*, john /THE/*) s. Excusado. Ej. "My dad does all of his reading on the throne."

THROW /A/: (sin. pop /a/, shot /a/) adv. Cada uno. Ej. "The shirts are only five bucks a throw." VER TAMBIEN *trust someone as far as one can throw someone*.

THROW (A) TEMPER TANTRUM(S): exp-vi. Enojarse gritando y pataleando, gen. porque no se puede tener algo. Gen. se refiere a niños. Ej. "He's 35, but he still throws temper tantrums." Or "My kid throws a temper tantrum every time he wants something."

THROW BACK: 1) exp-vi. Beber mucho alcohol durante una fiesta o una tomatera, cuyo efecto es una resaca al día siguiente. Ej. "I knew she wouldn't feel too swift today the way she was throwing back them beers last night." VER *hit it hard*. 2) s. Persona que tiene los modales de un tiempo pasado. Ej. "George is a throw back. He rushes to open doors for women and rises from his seat whenever they do."

THROW IN THE TOWEL: (sin. say uncle) exp-vi. Desistir, darse por vencido. Ej. "After trying to win her over for five years, he finally threw in the towel."

THROW MONEY OUT THE WINDOW: exp-vi. Se dice de un gasto sin justificación o después de un despilfarro. Ej. "I feel like all the rent I'm paying is like throwing money out the window."

THROW OUT THE BABY WITH THE BATH WATER: exp-vi. Equivocadamente botar el elemento más importante de algo junto con aquellos no deseables. Ej. "Just because the experiment failed, it doesn't mean you should throw out your notes. You might be throwing out the baby with the bath water."

TIGHTEN THE BELT A NOTCH

THROW THE BOOK AT: *exp-vi.* 1) Hacer todas las acusaciones posibles. *Ej.* "The feds threw the book at him, charging him with every crime known to man." 2) Dar el castigo máximo. *Ej.* "They threw the book at him for stealing a police officer's car."

THROW TO THE LIONS: *exp-vi.* Dejar a alguien solo en un medio extraño, esp. una situación difícil. *Ej.* "It's my first day teaching, and I feel like I'm being thrown to the lions."

THUMB A RIDE: *exp-v.* Pedir a la orilla del camino que lo lleven a uno, indicando con el pulgar. *Ej.* "There are no buses, but I think we can thumb a ride."

TICK OFF: *exp-v* 1) Causar rabia o enojo a otro o a uno mismo. *Ej.* "She ticked me off when she told me she still loved her last boyfriend." 2) Retar, regañar. *Ej.* "She got ticked off for arriving late again."

TICKER: *s.* El corazón. *Ej.* "My gramp's ticker is still going strong."

TICKET /THE/: *s.* La cosa o solución apropiada, recomendable o deseable en un momento dado. A menudo *that's the ticket*; exclamación al hacer o decir algo correctamente. *Ej.* "Yeah, I'll buy her some flowers. That's the ticket to get me back in her good graces."

TICKLED TO DEATH: *exp.* Extremadamente complacido, muy feliz. *Ej.* "I'd be tickled to death to deliver the commencement address at my alma mater."

TIE ONE (1) ON: *exp-v.* Beber demasiado alcohol pagando las consecuencias posteriormente. *Ej.* "With all the stress at work, I need to tie one on every once in a while."

TIE THE KNOT: *exp-v.* Casarse. *Ej.* "After dating for five years, they finally decided to tie the knot."

TIGHT FISTED: (sin. cheapskate) *adj.* Avaro, poco generoso. *Ej.* "They guy has a million dollars, but he is so tight fisted he wouldn't give his own mother a dime."

TIGHT WITH: *adj.* Cercano, íntimo, de confianza. *Ej.* "I can get us into the club for free — I'm tight with the owner."

TIGHTEN THE BELT A NOTCH:

TIGhTY WhiTles

exp-v. No comer o comer muy poco. *Ej.* "I don't get paid for another three days, so I'll have to tighten the belt a notch."

TIGHTY WHITIES: *s.* Calzoncillos muy cortos y de color blanco. *Ej.* "You look silly in your tighty whities."

TIME: VER *give someone a hard time; hard time; make time; pay back time; take one's sweet time; sack time; serve time; stitch in time saves nine; third time's the charm; two-time.*

TIME IS MONEY: *exp.* Un dicho que da el mismo valor al tiempo y al dinero y que, por lo tanto, el tiempo debe usarse productivamente. *Ej.* "Time is money, so let's get down to business, shall we?"

TIME OF THE MONTH /THAT/: (sin. *period, on the rag**) *exp.* Estar la mujer en su ciclo menstrual. *Ej.* "She's feeling kind of bitchy today. It's that time of the month, if you get my drift."

TIME OUT: 1) *exp.* Interrupción de una conversación para dar una opinión y/o disminuir el nivel de antagonismo de la situación. *Ej.* "Let's take a time out here and lower the decimals a bit." Or "Time out, I want to get my two cents in." 2) *s.* Un castigo, gen. en la forma de un descanso forzado, que resulta del mal comportamiento de un niño. *Ej.* "Bobby, if you don't start behaving, you're going to have to take a time out."

TIGhTY WhiTles

TIP BACK: *exp-v.* Beber alcohol. *Ej.* "Let's go down to the watering hole and tip back a few brewskies."

TIP ONE'S HAND: *exp-v.* Divulgar los planes, recursos o intenciones de uno, esp. hacerlo sin intención. Ej. "He tipped his hand about buying her a present by asking her dress size."

TIPSY: *adj.* Un poco ebrio. Ej. "I get tipsy after two drinks."

TIT: [Vul.] *s.* 1) Seno de mujer. Ej. "Check out the tits on that babe." 2) Algo muy bueno o extraordinario. Ej. "It's tit that you got hooked up with that film gig."

TIT FOR TAT: *exp.* Un intercambio parejo, esp. un intercambio entre dos hechos negativos. Ej. "He took my car without asking so I took his motorcycle without asking. Hey it's tit for tat."

TIZZY: *s.* 1) Estado de excitación y nervios. Ej. "Take it easy, there's no need to get in a tizzy about the exam." 2) Estado de gran enojo. Ej. "She went into a tizzy after finding out I had t.p.'ed her room."

TLC: *abr.* Tender loving care = Cuidado amoroso y tierno. Ej. "You just need a little TLC and you'll feel much better." Or "It's an old house in need of some TLC."

TO A 'T': *exp.* Hacer algo perfectamente. Ej. "He's difficult to work for because he wants everything done to a 'T.'"

TO BOOT: VER *boot /to/.*

TOAST: *adj.* 1) En muy mala condición, en un gran lío. Ej. "You're toast if you don't get it done." 2) Muerto. Ej. "If we fell off this cliff, we'd be toast."

TOASTY: *adj.* Tibio, de una temperatura agradable. Ej. "It's nice and toasty by the fire."

TOES: VER *on one's toes.*

TOGETHER: *adj.* Emocionalmente estable y saludable. Ej. "He was able to get it together after talking with a shrink."

TOKE: (sin. hit*, drag*) *s.* Una bocanada de un cigarrillo de marihuana o pipa que contiene marihuana, hachís u otra droga ilegal. Ej. "Don't kill the pipe. I want a toke."

TOMATO: *s.* Una mujer muy 'sexy'. Ej. "She's one tomato I'd like to make some sauce with!" VER *babe.*

TOMCAT: *s.* Hombre que persigue o tiene actividad sexual con varias mujeres a la vez. Ej. "Once he got the reputation for being a tomcat, none of the ladies were interested

TONGUE

in him."

TONGUE: VER *loose tongue; on the tip of one's tongue.*

TONGUE IN CHEEK: *exp.* Comentario o acción insincero/a o en broma. *Ej.* "I can't believe he took my advice seriously. I said it tongue in cheek when I suggested he become a priest."

TONS (OF): *adv.* Hartos, muchos, una gran cantidad. *Ej.* "Mary has tons of friends." Or "Money? He's got tons!"

TOOL: 1) *v.* Usar a alguien como instrumento, no tratar a alguien como persona sino como un medio para alcanzar un fin. *Ej.* "Don't let him tool you around. You shouldn't accept his B.S." 2) *s.* Persona que haría cualquier cosa que uno pida. *Ej.* "He's such a tool, he'd rob a bank if you told him to." 3) *v.* Conducir o andar en un auto o camión, esp. a altas velocidades. *Ej.* "Let's take out my Vette and tool down the highway."

TOOTSY: *s.* El pie o dedo del pie. *Ej.* "He stubbed his tootsy on the chair."

TOP BANANA: *s.* La persona más alta de la jerarquía, esp. en el trabajo. *Ej.* "Watch out guys, the top banana is on the warpath. Some clients called to complain about customer service."

TOP OF THE HEAP: *exp.* El máximo, "top", dícese en relación a autoridad o poder, esp. dentro de un nivel altamente competitivo. *Ej.* "You can't take any prisoners if you want to get to the top of the heap in this business."

TORCH: 1) *s.* Un pirómano. *Ej.* "We have to catch the torch before he strikes again." 2) *v.* Quemar, incendiar, esp. causar incendio premeditado. *Ej.* "He torched his car to collect the insurance."

TOSS ONE'S COOKIES: *exp-v.* Forma graciosa de decir "vomitar". *Ej.* "She tossed her cookies after drinking three whiskies." VER *chuck up.*

TOTAL: *v.* Demoler, destruir o arruinar totalmente. *Ej.* "She totaled her car in the accident."

TOTALLY: *adv.* Extremadamente, mucho, muy. *Ej.* "He's totally cool." Or "I'm totally psyched for the party."

TRASH

TOTEM POLE: s. La jerarquía. Ej. "After thirty years at the company, he finally made it to the top of the totem pole."

TOUCH: v. Pedirle dinero a un amigo o conocido. Ej. "Here comes Tim, I'm sure he'll try to touch me for a five or ten spot."

TOUCH BASE: exp-v. Tomar contacto o comunicarse con, esp. para renovar una comunicación o correspondencia. Ej. "I should touch base with my college buddies and see what they're up to."

TOUCH SOMETHING/SOMEONE WITH A TEN-FOOT POLE /NOT/: exp. No querer tener nada que ver con alguien, despreciar incluso el mínimo contacto. Ej. "Kiss him? You must be joking, I wouldn't touch him with a ten foot pole!"

TOUCH UP: (sin. once over) exp-v. Superficialmente mejorar el aspecto de algo o alguien. Ej. "I'll be ready in a sec, I just need to touch up my war paint."

TOUGH COOKIE: s. Alguien duro, de carácter fuerte. Ej. "You don't want to mess with her, she's one tough cookie."

TOUGH GUY: s. Persona que cree que intimida y se impone físicamente a los demás. Ej. "Hey, tough guy, why don't you try picking on someone your own size."

TOUGH SHIT: [Vul.] (sin. tough titty) int. Exclamación para referirse a una realidad o verdad inflexible e inalterable, esp. denota la mala suerte del otro. Ej. "If you don't like the terms, tough shit!"

TOUGH SKINNED: exp. Con el cuero duro, capaz de soportar si-tuaciones muy difíciles. Ej. "You've got to be tough skinned to survive in this cut-throat business."

TOUGH TITTY: VER tough shit.

TOWEL: VER throw in the towel.

TRACKS: s.pl. Huellas de agujas de inyecciones endovenosas en el uso de drogas. Ej. "He says he's clean, but he's got tracks on both arms." VER TAMBIEN make tracks; on the wrong track; on the wrong side of the tracks; inside track.

TRAP: (sin. yap*, kisser) s. La boca humana. Ej. "Shut your trap before I shut it for you!"

TRASH: v. 1) Tirar a la basura,

TRASHED

desechar. Ej. "This chair is so old I'm just gonna trash it." 2) Destrozar o destruir hasta el punto de arruinar algo. Ej. "My house got trashed during the party." 3) Criticar rigurosamente. Ej. "I'm so bummed the judges trashed my performance."

TRASHED: adj. Ebrio, muy borracho; Ej. "I got trashed last night on a pint of gin." VER *plastered*.

TREAD ON THIN ICE: VER *walk on thin ice*.

TREE: VER *bark up the wrong tree; up a tree*.

TRICK: s. El cliente de una prostituta. Ej. "He was the strangest trick she'd ever had. He got off on her walking on his face."

TRIP: 1) s. Efecto o sensación provocada por drogas alucinógenas, especialmente el LSD. Ej. "Hey, that was some trip last weekend." 2) s. Una experiencia emocionante. Ej. "Francis is on a real power trip after getting promoted." 3) Persona interesante o misteriosa. Ej. "That guy at the circus was a real trip, huh?" 4) s. Interés apasionado que a menudo sólo es temporal. Ej. "George is on a health food trip." 5) v. Tomar una droga alucinógena. Ej. "Do you want to trip at the concert? I've got some good acid." 6) s. Algo fantástico, sorprendente y/o emocionante. Ej. "I ran into my first girlfriend after not seeing her for 15 years. It was a trip."

TRIPE: s. Disparate, opinión o consejo sin valor. Ej. "Stop that tripe, you have no idea what you're talking about."

TRIPPING: adj. 1) (sin. *whacked out*) Excéntrico, loco, como si uno estuviera bajo los efectos de una droga alucinógena. Ej. "You're trippin' to ride on the roof of the car!" 2) Pensar cosas ridículas o planificar locuras. Ej. "You're tripping if you think I'm gonna help you rob a bank!"

TROTS /THE/: (sin. *runs /the/*) s.pl. Diarrea. Ej. "She got the trots eating at a greasy spoon."

TRUST SOMEONE AS FAR AS ONE CAN THROW SOMEONE: exp-v. No confiar en absoluto en alguien. Ej.

TURN ONE'S NOSE UP AT OTHERS

"He's such a liar, I trust him about as far as I can throw him."

TRUTH: VER *there is truth in wine; moment of truth.*

TRYING TO HEAR THAT /NOT/: *exp.* No querer oír o escuchar algo, esp. para no tener que decir al que habla que más vale que no diga lo que está diciendo. *Ej.* "I'm not trying to hear that man, who are you to give me advice?"

TUBE: (syn boob tube, idiot box) *s.* Televisión. *Ej.* "Too much tube and you'll end up a boob."

TUBE STEAK: *s.* Cecina. *Ej.* "Tube steaks for dinner- again?"

TUNE IN: *exp-v.* Tomar conciencia de, prestar atención a. *Ej.* "You'd better tune in to the situation pal, or she's going to leave you."

TUNE OUT: *exp-v.* 1) No prestarle atención a, no responder a. *Ej.* "When she starts talking about calculus, I just tune out." 2) Desconectarse del entorno. *Ej.* "My job is so stressful, I'd go crazy if I didn't tune out at times."

TURD: *s.* 1) Un trozo de excremento. *Ej.* "Who left the turd in the toilet bowl?" 2) Una persona desagradable y despreciable. *Ej.* "She's a turd for bad mouthing you to everybody."

TURF: *s.* El dominio de la autoridad o influencia de uno. *Ej.* "If you come onto my turf, you'd better pay your respects." Or "Let's talk politics, that's my turf."

TURKEY: *s.* Una persona callada, reservada, impopular, y considerada inepta. *Ej.* "What kind of turkey would rather play on his computer than go to a football game?" VER TAMBIEN *go cold turkey; talk turkey.*

TURN: VER *good turn; one good turn deserves another.*

TURN INSIDE OUT: *exp-v.* Crear un tremendo desorden, desorganizar totalmente. *Ej.* "I turned my apartment inside out looking for my keys."

TURN ON THE WATERWORKS: *exp-v.* Comenzar a llorar, esp. llorar copiosamente. *Ej.* "My daughter can sure turn on the waterworks when she wants something bad enough."

TURN ONE'S NOSE UP AT OTHERS: *exp-v.* Ignorar a otros esp.

TURN (SOMEONE) OFF

tomando una actitud de superioridad. *Ej.* "The guy wins a million bucks and then turns his nose up at his friends. What a schmuck!"

TURN (SOMEONE) OFF: *exp-v.* 1) Causar desagrado o disgusto; dejar descontento. *Ej.* "My boyfriend really turns me off when he talks about his old girlfriend." Or "What do you get turned off by? Tacky men? jocks? slimeballs?" 2) Causar desinterés. Literalmente, desviar completamente la atención, perdiendo así todo interés en algo o en alguien. *Ej.* "When the teacher starts talking about his dog, he turns the whole class off."

TURN (SOMEONE) ON: *exp-v.* Sentirse estimulado o entusiasmado por. *Ej.* "My wife gets turned on just by the sight of me." Or "Those tight jeans turn me on."

TURN (SOMEONE) ON TO: *exp-v.* Introducir o presentar por primera vez algo muy agradable o grato. Interesarse por, crear entusiasmo o deseos. *Ej.* "My friend turned me on to this cool band called <u>The Figments</u>."

TURNOFF: *s.* Algo o alguien que origina la pérdida de interés o el sentirse asqueado. *Ej.* "Picking your nose in public is a total turnoff."

TURN-ON: *s.* Algo o alguien que excita, estimula o crea interés. *Ej.* "Romantic dinners are such a turn-on."

TUSH: *s.pl.* Las nalgas. *Ej.* "Get off your tush and help me clean up." Ver *bum*.

TWAT: [Vul.] *s.* 1) La vagina. 2) Una

TURN (SOMEONE) ON

UNCOOL

mujer. (Desp.) *Ej.* "Your sister's a twat! I hate her guts!"

TWENTY-FOUR/SEVEN: *exp.* Todo el tiempo: Veinticuatro horas al día, siete días a la semana. *Ej.* "Man, you are on my case twenty-four/seven, give it a rest!"

TWERP: *s.* Una persona irritante, inútil. *Ej.* "My sister is dating a real twerp."

TWIDDLE ONE'S THUMBS: *exp-v.* No hacer absolutamente nada. *Ej.* "Don't just stand there twiddling your thumbs, come help me!"

TWIST SOMEONE'S ARM: *exp-v.* Forzar a alguien que haga algo supuestamente desagradable (en realidad, se ocupa esta expresión cuando uno quiere hacer algo que sabe que no debe hacer). *Ej.* "Go ahead, twist my arm...okay, I'll have another beer."

TWIT: (sin. dweeb) *s.* Una persona despreciada, o al menos no querida, por considerársele rara, poco elegante y/o demasiado diferente a uno. *Ej.* "She's a total twit, how can you be friends with her?"

TWO CENTS IN: *exp.* La opinión de uno, dada esp. para interrumpir o tratar de interrumpir una conversación y expresar el pensamiento de uno. *Ej.* "With that motor mouth, I can never get my two cents in."

TWO-BIT: (sin. rinky-dink) *adj.* Insignificante, de muy bajo valor o mérito. *Ej.* "You call this two-bit present a fiftieth anniversary gift?!!"

TWO-TIME: *v.* Serle infiel el/la esposo/a o amante. *Ej.* "She kicked him out for two-timing with his secretary."

U

UGLY AS SIN: *exp.* Feo, feo, feo. *Ej.* "That dog is ugly as sin. Where did you find it?"

UMPTEENTH: *adj.* Alto número sucesivo no especificado. *Ej.* "This is the umpteenth time I've told you to clean your room. Now get to it!"

UNCOOL: *adj.* 1) Expresa una mala actitud. *Ej.* "That guy's uncool, he's always mooching off of his friends." 2) Cualquier cosa que, según el observador, sea lo contrario de *cool*. *Ej.* "Hey, it's uncool to do your homework." "Oh yeah, well it's

UNDER ONE'S SKIN

uncool to be a loser your whole life."

UNDER ONE'S SKIN /GET/: *exp-vi.* Irritar tremendamente a alguien. *Ej.* "He really gets under my skin with his constant bragging."

UNDER THE GUN: *exp.* Bajo mucho estrés o presión para hacer o completar algo, gen. un trabajo. *Ej.* "Please don't disturb me. I'm really under the gun to get this done by tomorrow."

UNDER THE TABLE: *exp.* Hacer algo ilegal. *Ej.* "He's getting paid under the table to avoid taxes."

UNDER THE WEATHER: *exp.* No sentirse bien, estar enfermo/a. *Ej.* "I've been under the weather since I was out in the snow storm."

UNDIES: *s.pl.* Ropa interior. *Ej.* "It's not a good sign that he only changes his undies once a week."

UNLOAD (ON): *v.* Desahogarse de los problemas, ansiedades o tensiones, revelándoselos a otro. *Ej.* "I asked her what's wrong and she unloaded on me for an hour." Or "I'm all ears, go ahead and unload."

UNREAL: *adj.* Excelente, fantástico, buenísimo. *Ej.* "We had an unreal time on the camping trip." Ver awesome.

UP A CREEK WITHOUT A PADDLE /BE/: *exp-vi.* Encontrarse en una situación muy difícil o con serios problemas. *Ej.* "I'm up a creek without a paddle. The caterer for the wedding canceled at the last minute."

UP A TREE: *exp.* En una situación difícil. *Ej.* "I'll be up a tree if I don't finish this assignment on time."

UP FOR GRABS: *exp.* 1) Regalar mucho de algo deseable (ej. dinero, chocolate, etc.) y la reacción de otros cuando lo toman. *Ej.* "Everyone ready? I'm going to throw the candy up for grabs." 2) Algo al alcance de todos. *Ej.* "No one has the inside track. The job is up for grabs."

UP FOR: *exp.* Listo para participar en una actividad o para hacer algo. *Ej.* "Who's up for a swim?" Or "Who's up for a beer?"

UP FRONT /BE/: *exp-vi.* Ser franco, claro y honesto. *Ej.* "I'll be up front with you; you're a lousy athlete and you'll never make the team."

UP SHIT CREEK WITHOUT A

UPTIGHT

PADDLE /BE/: [Vul.] *exp-vi.* Encontrarse en una situación muy difícil o con serios problemas. *Ej.* "I got hammered and gave my wedding ring to some girl. I'm up shit creek without a paddle."

UP THE WALL: *exp.* En estado de extrema agitación, gen. de irritación, aburrimiento o frustración. *Ej.* "He was going up the wall waiting for the phone call." Or "She drives me up the wall with her whining!"

UP TO ONE'S ASS IN: *exp.* Tener un exceso de o estar demasiado ocupado con. *Ej.* "I'm up to my ass in irate customers and back orders!"

UP YOURS: [Vul.] *int.* Sirve para expresar el gran disgusto que nos provoca alguien. *Ej.* "Up yours idiot, get out of my way!"

UPCHUCK: *v.* Vomitar. *Ej.* "He upchucked all over the bathroom." VER *chuck up.*

UPPER: *s.* 1) Una anfetamina, un estimulante. *Ej.* "She's taking uppers to stay up and study for the big exam." 2) Una experiencia estimulante o alentadora. *Ej.* "It was such an upper being elected class President."

UPPER CRUST: *exp.* Lo más alto de una sociedad. *Ej.* "You go to a real upper crust school, don't you?"

UPPITY: *adj.* Presumido, altivo, esp. al asumir ademanes que no corresponden con la realidad socioeconómica de uno. *Ej.* "Their friend got so uppity after he inherited his uncle's fortune."

UPSIDE: *s.* Sobre, en. *Ej.* "He got smacked upside the head."

UPSTAIRS: *s.* En el cerebro, la capacidad intelectual que uno posee. *Ej.* "She must have a lot upstairs to get a scholarship to Harvard." VER TAMBIEN *kick upstairs.*

UPTIGHT: *adj.* 1) Describe a alguien que observa estrictamente las reglas de comportamiento social, esp. para criticar la conducta ajena. *Ej.* "She's so uptight, she carries a manners book around with her." 2) Tenso/a y nervioso/a. *Ej.* "Relax, you're so uptight you look ready to pop."

UPTOWN

UPTOWN: s. Elegante, muy distinguido, de primera categoría. Ej. "I'm gonna take you to a real uptown joint for our anniversary. We're going to Denny's!"

USE: v. Tomar drogas ilegales. Ej. "Is she using or is she clean?"

U-Y: VER pull a U-y.

V.D.: abr. Venereal disease = Enfermedad venérea. Ej. "Is it true that he got V.D.?"

VAMOOSE: v. Partir, o salir apresuradamente. Ej. "This bar sucks, I say we vamoose!"

VAMP: s. Mujer sexy y agresiva que usa los hombres para sus propios fines y/o que persigue maridos y/o novios de otras mujeres. Ej. "I don't want that vamp at my party, she's always after my boyfriend."

VEGETABLE: s. Persona en estado de coma, o persona que no da grandes señales de vida, ya sea como resultado de su estupidez o de mucho cansancio, gen. Como resultado de mucha fiesta la noche anterior. Ej. "If you crash on a motorcycle, you'll either die or end up a vegetable." Or "After slamming beers last night, I feel like a vegetable today."

VEGG: (sin. vegg out) v. Relajarse totalmente hasta quedar con la mente en blanco. Gen. no hacer absolutamente nada productivo y disfrutar de cada momento de esta inercia. Ej. "My brothers do nothing but vegg in front of the TV on Sunday."

VEGG OUT: VER vegg.

VEGGIE: s. 1) Verduras. Ej. "If you don't eat your veggies, you can't have dessert." 2) Un vegetariano. Ej. "He doesn't eat meat, he's a veggie."

VETTE: abr. Corvette; auto deportivo elegante, duradero, hecho por Chevrolet. Ej. "There's nothing more stylish than an old Vette."

VIBE: s. Vibration, sensación general que se tiene de alguien o algo. Gen. se dice vibes. Ej. "I get good vibes from the new teacher."

WACKO: (sin. psycho) 1) s. Un psicópata o una persona excéntrica, loca. Ej. "Only a wacko would try and climb a fifty story

WALKING PAPERS

building." 2) *adj.* Loco, demente. *Ej.* "He's been acting wacko ever since the operation."

WACKY: *adj.* Excéntrico, loco, excesivo. *Ej.* "Are you feeling a little wacky today, or do you always dress in 18th century clothing?" VER bats.

WAGON: VER *off the wagon; on the wagon; fix someone's wagon.*

WAIL (ON): *v.* 1) Golpear o abusar verbalmente, gen. lo primero. *Ej.* "My older brother always wails on me just for fun. He's such a loser!" 2) Desempeñarse al más alto nivel, actuar con gran entusiasmo y excelencia. *Ej.* "The band was wailing at the concert."

WAKE UP AND SMELL THE COFFEE: *exp-vi.* Finalmente asumir una realidad, esp. una desagradable. *Ej.* "Jane, this is the fifth time your husband has had an affair and promised not to do it again. I think it's time you wake up and smell the coffee!"

WAKE UP ON THE WRONG SIDE OF THE BED: *exp-vi.* Despertar de mal humor. *Ej.* "Don't mind him, he woke up on the wrong side of the bed and has been crabby all day."

WALK: *v.* 1) Escapar del castigo, quedar libre. *Ej.* "He's gonna walk on the murder rap unless we can find some concrete evidence." 2) Dejar o abandonar algo por sentirse insatisfecho con las condiciones. *Ej.* "They were arduous negotiations, with both sides alternately threatening to walk if their conditions were not met." VER TAMBIEN *cake walk; take a walk; take a long walk off a short pier.*

WALK ON EGG SHELLS: *exp-v.* Tratar a alguien con gran cautela para no ofender. *Ej.* "She's so sensitive about criticism, I feel like I'm walking on eggshells around her for fear I'll say the wrong thing."

WALK ON THIN ICE: (sin. *tread on thin ice*) *exp-v.* Hacer algo, consciente o inconsciente, que en cualquier momento podría resultar desastroso. *Ej.* "She's walking on thin ice with her unorthodox methods."

WALKING PAPERS: (sin. *pink slip*) *s.* Notificación de despido. *Ej.* "Word is they're gonna give him his walking papers at the end of the week."

WALL

WALL: VER *climb the walls; drive someone up the wall; nail someone to the wall; off the wall; up the wall.*

WALTZ: (sin. *breeze in*) *v.* Actuar o llegar como una fresca brisa primaveral - sin cuidado y despreocupado. Ej. "What gall! He stands me up and then comes waltzing in to the office as if nothing had happened."

WANK OFF: *exp-v.* 1) [Vul.] Masturbarse. Ej. "His mom caught him wanking off in the bathroom." 2) No hacer nada, esp. no trabajar. Ej. "Why don't you stop wanking off and get a job?"

WANKER: Ver *jerk*.

WANNA: *abr.* Want to = Querer. Ej. "You wanna go to the park?"

WANNABE: *s.* Persona que desea con vehemencia ser distinta a lo que es, esp. ser como otras a quienes envidia. Ej. "He's such a wannabe artist the way he wears black clothes and acts all hip and sophisticated, but he can't even draw!"

WAR PAINT: *s.* Cosméticos, maquillaje, arreglo usado por hombres o mujeres en situaciones especiales. Ej. "It takes over an hour for her to put on her war paint."

WARM AND FUZZY FEELING: *exp.* Sensación contenta y tonta después de unos tragos, o sentirse así sin haber tomado. Ej. "I don't like to get drunk, I just like that warm and fuzzy feeling every once in a while."

WAR PAINT

WAX IT

WARM FUZZY: s. Persona muy cálida y amorosa. Ej. "She'd be better off dating a warm fuzzy than that macho jerk."

WARM THE COCKLES OF ONE'S HEART: exp-v. Algo que enternece, tocando lo íntimo del corazón. Ej. "It warms the cockles of my heart to see my children playing happily together." (Ing.)

WARPATH: VER *on the warpath*.

WASH: VER *even out in the wash; you wash my back, I wash yours*.

WASP: s. Un *White Anglo Saxon Protestant*, o de un abolengo o linaje igualmente distinguido. Ej. "It's a WASP country club, no one else is allowed to be a member."

WASTE: (sin. whack, blow away, bump off, buy it, take (someone) out*, cap, clap someone's ass, do someone*, dust, get*, ice*, knock off*, off*, smoke someone, snuff) v. Matar, asesinar. Ej. "I'll waste the bastard."

WASTE OF SPACE /BE A/: exp-vi. Ser considerado como inútil e improductivo. Ej. "I don't know why we hired Joe. He's just a waste of space."

WASTED: adj. La condición de uno después de consumir mucho alcohol o drogas, o el efecto del alcohol o drogas. Ej. "That joint got me wasted."

WATCH SOMEONE'S BACK: exp-v. Proteger(se) el lado indefenso para prevenir un ataque sorpresivo, ya sea físico o de otro tipo. Ej. "In this business you always need to watch your back." Or "Watch his back, he's new out here."

WATERING HOLE: s. Un establecimiento para el consumo de bebidas alcohólicas, gen. el lugar preferido de alguien para ejercer esta actividad. Ej. "Where's John?" "Oh, he's down at the watering hole."

WATERWORKS: VER *turn on the waterworks*.

WAVELENGTH: VER *on the same wavelength*.

WAX IT: [Vul.] exp-v. 1) Tener una relación sexual. Ej. "I hear they've been waxing it for a long time." 2) Masturbarse. Ej. "You spend so much time waxing it, you must have calluses on your hand."

WAY-OUT

WAY-OUT: *adj.* Sumamente original, raro, muy radical. *Ej.* "She's way-out there with her radical gender views."

WAZOO: *s.* El ano, pero se usa metafóricamente. *Ej.* "Ted has problems up the wazoo."

WEAR ONE'S SUNDAY'S BEST: *exp-vi.* Vestirse dominguero. Vestirse en ropa muy elegante para la normalidad. *Ej.* "It's a very formal gathering, I'll need to wear my Sunday's best."

WEAR OUT ONE'S WELCOME: *exp-vi.* Quedarse en un lugar, gen. la casa de otro, más tiempo de lo conveniente. *Ej.* "After a month staying with us, my in-laws really wore out their welcome."

WEAR THIN: *exp-vi.* Tornarse viejo o pesado. *Ej.* "It is wearing thin your always asking me for money."

WEASEL ONE'S WAY OUT OF SOMETHING: *exp-v.* Zafarse de una situación desagradable de la cual uno es responsable. *Ej.* "You screwed up these reservations, so don't try to weasel your way out of dealing with it."

WEATHER: VER *under the weather.*

WEDGIE: *s.* Calzoncillos puestos muy arriba entre las nalgas y por lo tanto muy incómodos para la persona. Típico de los niños, esp. hombres, subir desde atrás el calzoncillo de otro como burla. *Ej.* "He's gonna be shooting blanks if he continues to get all those wedgies."

WEED: *s.* 1) Cigarillo o tabaco. *Ej.* "In the old days, people used to smoke weed for medicinal purposes." 2) Marihuana. *Ej.* "One day the Feds are going to legalize weed."

WEENIE: *s.* 1) El pene, gen. en lenguaje infantil. *Ej.* "Mommy, my weenie hurts." 2) Un macho débil, cobarde e inútil, gen. en lenguaje infantil. *Ej.* "Don't be such a weenie, come with us to the park." VER *yellow-belly.*

WEIGHT OFF ONE'S SHOULDER: *exp.* Deshacerse de una situación o problema onerosa/o. *Ej.* "I'm so happy I finally sold that damn motorcycle. It feels good to get that weight off my shoulder."

WEIRDO: *s.* Una persona muy rara o excéntrica, a menudo con-

WHACKED-OUT

siderada trastornada y potencialmente peligrosa. *Ej.* "He turned into a real weirdo after experimenting with drugs."

WELCH: VER *welsh*.

WELCOME: VER *wear out one's welcome*.

WELL-SCRUBBED: *adj.* Muy limpio, bien presentado o de buenos modales. *Ej.* "It's important to look well-scrubbed in the fashion business."

WELSH: (sin. welch) *v.* 1) Estafar o engañar al no pagar una deuda. *Ej.* "She welshed on the $100 she owed me." 2) Fallar en el cumplimiento de una responsabilidad o compromiso. *Ej.* "You'd better not welsh on the deal or I'll never speak with you again."

WET BEHIND THE EARS: (sin. babe in the woods) *exp.* Persona inocente o inexperta. *Ej.* "She might be wet behind the ears, but I still think she'll make a good teacher."

WET NOODLE: *s.* Una persona indecisa, tan flexible como un tallarín mojado. *Ej.* "Make a decision for once! You're such a wet noodle about everything."

WET RAG: *s.* Persona aburrida, latosa. *Ej.* "I sat next to this wet rag at the dinner party. All he talked about was the finer elements of hot air ballooning."

WET THE WHISTLE: *exp-vi.* Beber alcohol. *Ej.* "I'll just have a quickie to wet the whistle."

WETBACK: *s.* Descripción despectiva de un inmigrante gen. hispánico. [Derog.] (etim. Al cruzar ilegalmente el Río Grande de México a los EEUU, mojándose.) *Ej.* "It ain't right. Any unsolved crime here and they blame the wetbacks."

WHACK: *exp-v.* Matar a alguien en jerga de la Mafia. *Ej.* "They whacked the rat for talking to the feds." VER *waste*. VER TAMBIEN *out of whack; take a whack at*.

WHACK OFF: [Vul.] *exp-v.* Masturbarse. *Ej.* "He was whacking off in the bushes when his mom found him." VER *beat off*.

WHACKED-OUT: *adj.* 1) Loco, demente. *Ej.* "My uncle's been whacked-out ever since the Vietnam War." 2) Drogado o peli-

WHAt GIVes?

grosamente borracho. *Ej.* "He must've been whacked-out to be driving on the wrong side of the highway."

WHAT GIVES?: *exp.* 1) Pregunta qué pasa o qué sucede. *Ej.* "What gives? Is there a party or something tonight?" 2) Pregunta la razón de algo. *Ej.* "You're in a bad mood. What gives?"

WHAT THE FUCK!: [Vul.] *exp.* Expresión de gran sorpresa y desagrado. *Ej.* "What the fuck happened to my car!"

WHAT THE HECK!: *int.* 1) El equivalente verbal a levantar los brazos y rendirse a la opinión popular. *Ej.* "Okay, what the heck, I'll come along too." 2) Expresión de irritación o enojo. *Ej.* "What the heck are you two doing naked together!"

WHAT THE HELL!: [Vul.] *int.* El equivalente vulgar de *what the heck*. *Ej.* "What the hell is going on here?!"

WHAT'S HAPPENING?: *exp.* Un saludo informal.

WHAT'S SHAKING?: *exp.* Un saludo informal. *Ej.* "What's shaking dude?"

WHAT'S THE GOOD WORD?: *exp.* Un saludo informal. *Ej.* "So what's the good word Tim? Things going all right with the old lady?"

WHAT'S UP?: *exp.* Un saludo informal, también una averiguación en cuanto a lo que está sucediendo. *Ej.* "What's up Ted? What seems to be the problem?" Or "Hey Mike!" "What's up John?"

WHAT'S YOUR PROBLEM?: *int.* Pregunta cuál es el motivo de la mala actitud de otro. *Ej.* "What's your problem? I wasn't bothering you, so why are you bothering me?"

WHAT'S-HIS/HER-FACE: *exp.* El nombre de una persona que se le ha olvidado a uno (momentáneamente). *Ej.* "Tell what's-his-face to come in here."

WHATCHAMACALLIT: VER *thingamajig*.

WHATEVER: *int.* Expresión de irritación y un deseo de interrumpir cierta conversación. *Ej.* "Whatever dude, next time just keep your opinion about my girlfriend to yourself."

WHEEL AND DEAL: *exp-v.* Hablar

WHERE IT'S AT

mucho para vender algo o tomar contactos. Ej. "She believed in her idea and just wheeled and dealed till she found investors."

WHEELER AND DEALER: s. Persona versada en ventas o en tener contactos. Ej. "Oh yeah, Aaron is a real wheeler and dealer. He knows how to get things done."

WHEELMAN: s. Chofer, conductor, esp. quien maneja un vehículo durante un robo o algún otro tipo de delito. Ej. "They shot the wheelman as he was driving away."

WHEELS: (sin. ride, set of wheels) s.pl. Un auto, camión o motocicleta. Ej. "I need to get me some wheels for the weekend." VER TAMBIEN squeaky wheel gets the grease; third wheel.

WHEN IN ROME, DO AS THE ROMANS DO: exp. Una recomendación para hacer lo que hacen los demás, esp. en cuanto a costumbres sociales. (nota de editor: Un refrán universal que debe ser usado en forma prudente.) Ej. "I know they say when in Rome, do as the Romans do, but just because we're here doesn't mean I'm going to eat monkey's brain."

WHEN IT RAINS, IT POURS: exp. 1) Cuando a la mala suerte le sigue más mala suerte. Ej. "Damn it, when it rains it pours. First my dog runs off and now my girlfriend dumps me." 2) Cuando a la buena suerte le sigue más buena suerte. Ej. "Boy when it rains, it pours. First I get a promotion and then my wife tells me we're going to have a baby. I'm one lucky duck!"

WHEN PUSH COMES TO SHOVE: VER if push comes to shove.

WHEN THE SHIT HITS THE FAN: [Vul.] exp. Una situación desagradable que se produce repentinamente, afectando a varias personas. Ej. "When the shit hits the fan, you find out real quick who you can trust and who you can't."

WHERE IT'S AT: exp. 1) Donde está el espectáculo, lo entretenido y/o el lugar de moda. Ej. "You've got to be where it's at if you want to hook up with a hot chick." 2) El área o actividad rentable o apropiada. Ej. "The computer industry is where it's at."

WHErE ONe'S HEaD IS aT

WHERE ONE'S HEAD IS AT: *exp.* El proceso de reflexión o la actitud que uno tiene en un momento determinado. *Ej.* "I want to understand where your head is at, but you've got to open up to me." Or "Man, where's your head at to be doing something so stupid?"

WHERE THE SUN DOESN'T/DON'T SHINE: *exp.* Manera humorística de referirse al trasero. *Ej.* "I got a tatoo where the sun don't shine!"

WHIPPED: *adj.* Bajo el mando del compañero romántico de uno. *Ej.* "Don't even bother asking Bob to go fishing. He's so whipped he never goes out without his wife."

WHISTLE: VER *wet the whistle; whistle blower; bells and whistles; blow the whistle on; clean as a whistle.*

WHISTLE BLOWER: *s.* Persona que informa sobre actividades ilegales en negocios u otras actividades. *Ej.* "The whistle blower was rewarded by the government for reporting the company's illegal dumping of chemicals."

WHITE TRASH: *s.* Persona caucasiana de clase baja, que se caracteriza por malos modales, poca educación y mal gusto. *Ej.* "Those guys are bad news. They're a bunch of white trash."

WHITEY: (sin. honky) *s.* Una persona blanca. (Desp.) *Ej.* "Whitey's been keepin' us down long enough. It's time we fought for our rights!"

WHIZ: 1) *s.* Persona con habilidad o talento sobresaliente en un campo dado. *Ej.* "My brother-in-law is a whiz with computers." 2) *v.* Orinar. *Ej.* "Pull over, I have to whiz." VER *pee.* 3) *s.* Orina. VER *pee.*

WHOLE ENCHILADA /THE/: *exp.* El todo, la totalidad de algo. *Ej.* "I'm gonna bet the whole enchilada on this horse."

WHOLE KIT AND CABOODLE /THE/: VER *whole shebang /the/.*

WHOLE SCHMEAR /THE/: *exp.* Varias cosas relacionadas entre ellas, el todo de algo. *Ej.* "I'm not interested in bits and pieces, I want the whole schmear."

WHOLE SHEBANG /THE/: (sin. the whole kit and caboodle) *exp.* El todo de algo, enteramente, todo incluido. *Ej.* "She got the whole

WIN BONUS POINTS

shebang in the divorce: kids, car, house and a fat alimony payment."

WHOOP: *v.* Golpear o pegar severamente. *Ej.* "I could whoop you with one hand tied behind my back!" VER *beat someone up*.

WHOOPEE: *int.* Expresión de alegría, júbilo. No obstante, a menudo se usa en forma sarcástica. *Ej.* "Yeah whoopee, I got third place. I wanted to win damn it."

WHOPPER: *s.* 1) Una gran mentira. *Ej.* "She's got quite an imagination judging from the amount of whoppers she comes up with." 2) Algo enorme o extraordinario. *Ej.* "That was a whopper writing a biography of Shakespeare."

WICKED: *adj.* Excelente, fantástico, buenísimo. *Ej.* "He's got a wicked cool car." Ver *awesome*.

WIENER: *s.* Pene. *Ej.* "She laughed when she saw the size of his wiener!" VER *jimmy*.

WIG OUT: *exp-v.* 1) Entusiasmarse o emocionarse locamente por algo. *Ej.* "Liz wigged out when she won the grand prize." 2) Enloquecer, o perder el control emocional. *Ej.* "My mom'll wig out when I tell her I joined the Marines."

WILD: *adj.* Alegre, entretenido, emocionante. *Ej.* "We had a wild time at the dance."

WILD GOOSE CHASE: *s.* El hecho de esforzarse y cansarse sin llegar a la meta propuesta. *Ej.* "We went on a wild goose chase trying to find some Barbie outfit for our daughter's birthday present."

WILLIES /THE/: *s.* Nerviosismo, miedo, julepe. *Ej.* "I get the willies every time I hear talk of murder."

WIMP: *s.* Persona cobarde, débil y/o inútil, esp. se usa en referencia a una persona miedosa de hacer algo. *Ej.* "Don't be a wimp. It'll be fun to go rafting." Or "That wimp is still afraid of the dark." VER *yellow-belly*.

WIMP OUT: *exp-v.* Detenerse o retirarse de una línea de acción (planificada) por sentirse atemorizado. *Ej.* "I won't be your friend any more if you wimp out again."

WIN BONUS POINTS: *exp-vi.* Hacer algo que aumenta el prestigio de

WINd

uno frente a los demás. *Ej.* "After being in the doghouse, I won major bonus points by making a delicious dinner for my wife."

WIND: VER *blow with the wind; break wind; fly like the wind; knock the wind out of someone's sails; take the wind out of one's sail; three sheets to the wind.*

WINdbAG

WINDBAG: s. Una persona aburrida que habla demasiado a quien nadie quiere escuchar al pronunciar el *windbag* un monólogo vacío más. ¿Qué sucedió con esta gente en el momento de nacer? *Ej.* "Who's the rocket scientist who invited that windbag to speak at the conference?"

WING AND A PRAYER: *exp.* Situación muy precaria. *Ej.* "I'm getting by on a wing and a prayer. I've got no money in the bank and my salary just covers my living expenses."

WINNER: s. Lo contrario de *loser*. Persona de gran personalidad y vida aparentemente protegida por arte de magia. *Ej.* "You are a winner Charlie, don't listen to what the other kids say."

WINO: s. Un alcohólico indigente que toma vino barato y que tiene muy mal aliento y mal olor. *Ej.* "There are ever more winos on the streets these days."

WIPE OUT: *v.* 1) Caer(se) y lastimarse en un accidente. *Ej.* "If he wipes out at that speed, he's a goner." 2) Estar demasiado cansado para hacer algo, gen. una actividad física. *Ej.* "No, I'm wiped out, there's no way I can go running." 3) Quedar sin nada, esp. dinero. *Ej.* "I got wiped

WISeASS

out at the casino last night. I didn't even have money to take a bus home."

WIRE: s. Un micrófono escondido, llevado en el cuerpo de alguien o colocado en una residencia u oficina. *Ej.* "Search him to see if he's wearing a wire."

WIRED: *adj.* 1) Equipado con dispositivos escondidos para escuchar secretamente. *Ej.* "He went wired to talk to the mob boss." 2) Bien relacionado, bien conectado con personas importantes y poderosas. *Ej.* "She's a good friend to have as she is wired in with the right people." 3) Nervioso, alterado, gen. como resultado de algún estimulante (ej. café, té, bebida) o un flujo de adrenalina. *Ej.* "I was wired after drinking coffee all day." Or "The news of my promotion got me wired." 4) Tomando drogas, esp. cocaína, y sintiéndose inquieto, nervioso o agitado. *Ej.* "Either he's wired or he has a serious problem with his nervous system." 5) Muy informado o conectado a la tecnología del futuro, esp. en cuanto a computadores y el internet. *Ej.* "You need to be wired if you want to know what's happening now and in the future."

WISE: *adj.* Atrevido, irritantemente presumido. Creído, farsante. *Ej.* "Don't be wise with me little girl, or you'll regret it." Or "You're awfully wise for someone who's flunking all of his classes."

WISE GUY: s. 1) (sin. smartaleck) Una persona arrogante, irritantemente presumida. Creído, farsante. *Ej.* "If you act like a wise guy, you've got to expect that people aren't going to like you." 2) Persona que pertenece a la Mafia. *Ej.* "A wise guy never carries his money in his wallet and never pays for a drink."

WISE TO: *adj.* Al tanto de, informado acerca de. *Ej.* "If the teacher gets wise to our pranks, we're gonna be in big trouble."

WISE UP: *exp-v.* Tomar conciencia o informarse de algo. Se usa esp. como un aviso o advertencia. *Ej.* "You'd better wise up pal and go straight, or you'll be booking a trip to the big house!"

WISEASS: VER smart-ass.

WISECRACK

WISECRACK: s. Un comentario o réplica impertinente o sarcástico/a. Ej. "She was expelled for making too many wisecracks to the school's principal."

WISHY-WASHY: adj. Muy indeciso; se dice de una persona que decide algo y luego cambia de parecer varias veces. Ej. "Stop being so damn wishy-washy and decide which movie you want to see."

WITH ONE'S TAIL BETWEEN ONE'S LEGS: exp. Sentirse muy humilde frente a alguien o sentir vergüenza por una acción previa. Ej. "After being away for three nights, he came home with his tail between his legs, begging to be forgiven."

WITH-IT: (sin. hip*) adj. Bien informado de la última moda y/o de las nuevas tendencias. Ej. "Get with-it George, bell bottom pants are cool now!"

WOLF: VER cry wolf; keep the wolf from the door.

WOLF DOWN: (sin. scarf up/down) v. Devorar, comer o tomar vorazmente. Ej. "Susan was so hungry, she wolfed down her diner in no time flat."

WOOD: VER sporting wood; neck of the woods; babe in the woods.

WOODY: (sin. hard-on, boner*, sporting wood) s. Erección. Ej. "It was so cute when my infant son got a woody in the bath."

WOOL: VER pull the wool over someone's eyes.

WOP: s. Italiano, un ítaloamericano. (Desp.) Ej. "You hear what that wop said about you? What you gonna do about it?"

WORD IN EDGEWISE /A/: exp. Oportunidad de decir algo, esp. expresar una opinión acerca de algo que está siendo debatido. Ej. "The guy doesn't shut up. It's almost impossible to get a word in edgewise."

WORD UP: (sin. straight up) exp. La verdad. Ej. "Word up, I ain't gonna take it no more from that chump!"

WORK A CROWD: exp-v. Conversar con mucha gente, hacer muchos negocios y/o contactos en una fiesta o reunión social, esp. caer simpático a todos. Ej. "There's no one who works a crowd like Susan.

WRAPPED UP IN SOMETHING

She'll be sure to get five new contacts at this party."

WORK LIKE A DOG: *exp-v.* Trabajar duro para sobrevivir. *Ej.* "I'm working like a dog out there and you're spending money like it grows on trees."

WORK ONE'S ASS OFF: [Vul.] *exp-v.* Trabajar arduamente; trabajar tanto hasta llegar a bajar de peso en el trasero, lo que ciertamente, y como muchos podrán afirmar, no es algo fácil de lograr. *Ej.* "I work my ass off while you just sit around watching the boob tube!"

WORK SOMEONE OVER: *exp-v.* Golpear o dañar físicamente a alguien. *Ej.* "You either pay us the money or we're going to work you over so bad not even your mother will recognize you!" VER *beat someone up.*

WORKING GIRL: (sin. *hoe, hooker*) *s.* Prostituta. *Ej.* "She's a working girl if you know what I mean."

WORKS /THE/: *s.pl.* Con todo incluido, totalmente equipado. *Ej.* "Give me a pizza with the works." Or "Her Jag is equipped with the works." VER TAMBIEN *shoot the works.*

WORRY ABOUT IT /DON'T/: *exp.* Una respuesta a 'gracias' después de hacer algo bueno, esp. un favor. *Ej.* "Don't worry about it, it was no problem fixing your sink."

WORTH A DIME /NOT/: (sin. *worth a wooden nickle*) *exp.* De poco o ningún valor, se dice de una cosa o persona. *Ej.* "Your advice is not worth a dime."

WORTH A RAT'S ASS: [Vul.] *exp.* Absolutamente sin ningún valor. A menudo estructurado con una connotación negativa, pero siempre con el mismo significado. *Ej.* "Your opinion isn't worth a rat's ass!" Or "As a mechanic, he ain't worth a rat's ass."

WORTH A WOODEN NICKEL: (sin. *not worth a dime*) *exp.* De poco o ningún valor, se dice de una cosa o persona. *Ej.* "Your opinion is worth a wooden nickel."

WRAPPED UP IN SOMETHING /BE/: *exp-vi.* Estar muy entusiasmado o involucrado en un proyecto. *Ej.* "Don't even bother asking him to go this weekend, he's so wrapped up in his building project he'll never leave."

WRINKLE

WRINKLE: s. Dificultad, barrera, un impedimento esp. uno inesperado. Ej. "There's always some wrinkle that comes up at the last minute to mess up our plans."

WRITE SOMEONE OFF: exp-vi. No querer saber nunca más de otra persona. Ej. "After she stole my boyfriend, I wrote her off for good."

WRONG SIDE OF THE TRACKS /THE/: exp. 1) Vivir en el sector pobre de un pueblo o ciudad. Ej. "You can't date him, he lives on the wrong side of the tracks." 2) Estar en una situación conflictiva con las autoridades. Ej. "You get on the wrong side of the tracks and you're gonna spend some time in the clink."

Y'ALL: exp. Modo de dirigirse a un grupo de gente ya sean hombres o mujeres o ambos. Ej. "Y'all want to go to the movies?"

YAK: v. Conversar ociosamente, esp. de asuntos relativamente insignificantes o triviales. Ej. "My teenage daughter can yak for hours on the phone."

YANK: v. Sacar, remover. Ej. "He's playing terribly, it's time we yanked him."

YAP: 1) v. Hablar de modo irritante, necio y muy fuerte. Ej. "I can't get any work done while you're yapping in my ear." 2) (sin. trap, kisser) La boca. Ej. "Would you please shut your yap. I really don't want to hear about your hairdresser"

YARN: VER spin a yarn.

YEAH, RIGHT!: int. No, de ninguna manera. Ej. "Yeah, right! And I'm the president of the US."

YELLOW: (sin. gutless, yellow-bellied) adj. Cobarde. Ej. "You're yellow for not coming on the kayak trip with us."

YELLOW-BELLIED: VER yellow.

YELLOW-BELLY: (sin. chicken*, pussy*, weenie*, wimp) s. Persona cobarde, débil y/o inútil, esp. se usa en referencia a una persona miedosa de hacer algo. Ej. "They branded him a yellow-belly because he didn't believe in fighting."

YING-YANG /UP THE/: [Vul.] exp-vi. Algo en abundancia, frecuentemente tener más de lo que uno quisiera o de lo que es saludable. Ej. "He's got problems up the ying-yang; what with five

YUPPIE

kids, two jobs and an anorexic wife, it's no wonder he's stressed-out."

YO: *int.* Se usa como saludo, bienvenida o para llamar la atención de alguien. *Ej.* "Yo, how's it going brother?" Or "Yo, we're over here."

YOU CAN'T TEACH AN OLD DOG NEW TRICKS: *exp.* Un proverbio que significa que ni a los viejos ni a los perros viejos se les puede enseñar algo nuevo. *Ej.* "I've been doing it this way my whole life. You can't teach an old dog new tricks."

YOU SCRATCH MY BACK, I SCRATCH YOURS: VER *you wash my back, I wash yours.*

YOU WASH MY BACK, I WASH YOURS: (scratch my back, I scratch yours) *exp.* La afirmación que implica que si alguien ofrece ayuda o hace algo por alguien, esa persona hará lo mismo. *Ej.* "You got me those playoff tickets and now I'm gonna do you a good turn. You wash my back, I wash yours, right?"

YO-YO: *s.* Una persona estúpida o tonta. *Ej.* "You're a yo-yo whose opinion means zilch to me."

YUCK: *int.* Expresión de rechazo o disgusto. *Ej.* "Yuck, that food looks gross!"

YUCKY: *adj.* Repugnante, asqueroso. *Ej.* "He's such a yucky guy I don't even want to shake his hand."

YUK: *s.* Risa. *Ej.* "I always get a yuk watching the <u>Three Stooges</u>."

YUK IT UP: *exp-v.* Reír en forma histérica y/o bromear constantemente. *Ej.* "You can yuk it up now, but one day you're going to have to get serious."

YUKE: *v.* Vomitar. *Ej.* "Who yuked in the john?" VER *chuck up.*"

YUMMY: *adj.* Apetecible, delicioso; agradable a los sentidos. *Ej.* "That pie smells yummy!"

YUPPIE: *s.* Una persona joven de educación universitaria que vive en un área urbana y tiene un trabajo bien pagado,

YUPPIE

ZAP

gen. profesional. El *yuppie* no tiene ningún escrúpulo en hacer alarde de sus posesiones materiales, ya que se ha fijado como meta el bienestar económico. Los máximos representantes del yupismo son Martha Stewart y Michael Milken, por su sabiduría estética y monetaria respectivamente. *Ej.* "I don't know what I'll do if my child grows up to be a yuppie!"

ZAP: *v.* 1) Lastimar, destruir o matar por contacto de corriente eléctrica. *Ej.* "If you touch that wire, you'll get zapped." 2) Calentar en el horno microondas. *Ej.* "I'm gonna zap these leftovers and have it for dinner."

ZERO: VER *loser*.

ZILCH: *s.* 1) (sin. zip, diddly*, jack) "You'll get zilch from me and like it!" 2) Una nulidad, una persona sin importancia y despreciable. *Ej.* "She can't pull any strings here, she's a zilch in the office. She has no power."

ZINGER: *s.* 1) Un comentario o crítica que es divertido/a, cáustico/a o probatorio/a. *Ej.* "It should be a fun debate as they're both excellent at delivering zingers." 2) Un evento desagradable y chocante. *Ej.* "My children love to hit me with these zingers like 'Dad, I want to go on the pill'. They're gonna give me a heart attack one day."

ZIP: *s.* Nada, absolutamente nada, cero. *Ej.* "I got zip from them when I retired."

ZIPPY: *s.* Pagano(a) profesional inspirado(a) en el Zen. *Ej.* "First the hippies and now the zippies. Well, I guess we're in the nineties."

ZIT: *s.* Espinilla, acné. *Ej.* "Is that a zit on your nose?"

ZOMBIE: *s.* Persona que está tan cansada que él/ella tiene aspecto de estar medio muerto(a). *Ej.* "After working all night, I felt like a zombie the next day."

ZONK: *v.* Agotar, cansar, hacer que se canse. *Ej.* "I was zonked after the football game."

ZONK OUT: *exp-v.* Quedarse dormido, a menudo de manera inesperada y repentina. *Ej.* "Bob zonked out while watching TV."

Zoom in On

zoo: s. Situación o lugar muy confuso o desorganizado. *Ej.* "How can anyone get any work done in this zoo?"

ZOOM IN ON: *exp-v.* Fijar la atención resueltamente, ser o convertirse en el centro de atención para uno. *Ej.* "When I heard someone mention my name, I zoomed in on the conversation." Or "She's successful because she zooms in on the essential details."